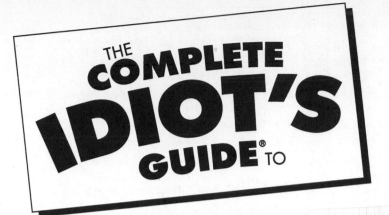

THE COMPLETE IDIOT'S GUIDE® TO

Buying Foreclosures

by Bobbi Dempsey and Todd Beitler

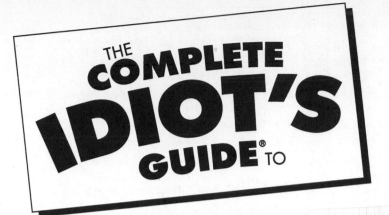

ALPHA

A member of Penguin Group (USA) Inc.

ALPHA BOOKS

Published by the Penguin Group

Penguin Group (USA) Inc., 375 Hudson Street, New York, New York 10014, U.S.A.

Penguin Group (Canada), 10 Alcorn Avenue, Toronto, Ontario, Canada M4V 3B2 (a division of Pearson Penguin Canada Inc.)

Penguin Books Ltd, 80 Strand, London WC2R 0RL, England

Penguin Ireland, 25 St Stephen's Green, Dublin 2, Ireland (a division of Penguin Books Ltd)

Penguin Group (Australia), 250 Camberwell Road, Camberwell, Victoria 3124, Australia (a division of Pearson Australia Group Pty Ltd)

Penguin Books India Pvt Ltd, 11 Community Centre, Panchsheel Park, New Delhi—110 017, India

Penguin Group (NZ), cnr Airborne and Rosedale Roads, Albany, Auckland, New Zealand 1310 (a division of Pearson New Zealand Ltd)

Penguin Books (South Africa) (Pty) Ltd, 24 Sturdee Avenue, Rosebank, Johannesburg 2196, South Africa

Penguin Books Ltd, Registered Offices: 80 Strand, London WC2R 0RL, England

International Standard Book Number: 1-59257-395-9

Library of Congress Catalog Card Number: 2005925422

07 06 05   8 7 6 5 4 3 2 1

Interpretation of the printing code: The rightmost number of the first series of numbers is the year of the book's printing; the rightmost number of the second series of numbers is the number of the book's printing. For example, a printing code of 05-1 shows that the first printing occurred in 2005.

Printed in the United States of America

Note: This publication contains the opinions and ideas of its author. It is intended to provide helpful and informative material on the subject matter covered. It is sold with the understanding that the author and publisher are not engaged in rendering professional services in the book. If the reader requires personal assistance or advice, a competent professional should be consulted.

The author and publisher specifically disclaim any responsibility for any liability, loss, or risk, personal or otherwise, which is incurred as a consequence, directly or indirectly, of the use and application of any of the contents of this book.

Most Alpha books are available at special quantity discounts for bulk purchases for sales promotions, premiums, fundraising, or educational use. Special books, or book excerpts, can also be created to fit specific needs.

For details, write: Special Markets, Alpha Books, 375 Hudson Street, New York, NY 10014.

Publisher: *Marie Butler-Knight*
Product Manager: *Phil Kitchel*
Senior Managing Editor: *Jennifer Bowles*
Acquisitions Editor: *Mike Sanders*
Development Editor: *Ginny Bess Munroe*
Production Editor: *Megan Douglass*

Copy Editor: *Keith Cline*
Cartoonist: *Richard King*
Cover/Book Designer: *Trina Wurst*
Indexer: *Heather McNeil*
Layout: *Angela Calvert*
Proofreading: *Mary Hunt*

Contents at a Glance

Contents

Foreword

I considered it an honor to write the foreword for this book because Todd Beitler has been a friend and colleague of mine for many years. I know that Todd is immensely qualified to write this book, as he has made a name for himself as one of the leading experts on the topic of foreclosure investing.

Foreclosure investing is hotter than ever right now. Interest rates have begun the inevitable climb, which unfortunately means many borrowers will find it increasingly tough to afford their mortgage payments. That's a bad thing for borrowers, of course, but it has a big silver lining for investors who can take advantage of the many foreclosure properties available right now.

You can make a nice living through foreclosure investing. In fact, I know many people who do just that. First you need to learn the ropes, and that's where a great teacher like Todd (with some help from his excellent coauthor Bobbi) can be such a valuable asset. Todd walks you through the entire process, sharing some advice and insight that will save you many headaches along the way.

Like any type of investing, foreclosures involve their share of risks. In this book, Todd makes sure that you fully understand all the risks before you attempt your first foreclosure buy. More important, he arms you with the knowledge—gained from years of experience—that will help you avoid or minimize many of these risks.

This book is packed with tons of information, advice, and resources. Even if you've already done a few foreclosure deals, you can still learn many new things after reading this book. This is one book that should be on the shelves of all foreclosure investors, both novices and veterans alike.

Study this book carefully. Read it several times until you fully understand the concepts involved in foreclosure investing. And then, get out there and pursue your piece of the foreclosure fortune!

—Dr. Albert Lowry

Dr. Lowry has written and published more than 20 books. His first, *How You Can Become Financially Independent by Investing in Real Estate*, earned the distinguished Best Sellers List of the *The New York Times* for three consecutive years. In addition to attaining many professional real estate designations, Al Lowry has a doctorate in Business Administra-tion and was recruited to teach the very first Masters Degree Program in Real Estate. Al Lowry was added to the Academy of American Exchangers "Hall of Fame," perhaps the highest single honor accorded any individual engaged in real estate.

Introduction

To most people, a foreclosure is a bad thing. To a real estate investor, it can be a goldmine. Sure, nobody wants to see anyone lose their home. And unfortunately you or I aren't in the position to forgive the loans of defaulting homeowners. However, with some practice and lots of know-how, you can learn how to help the homeowner make the best of a bad situation—while earning yourself a nice reward in the process.

Maybe you're a total novice when it comes to investing. In fact, you have trouble even envisioning yourself as an "investor." Perhaps the only home you've ever bought is the one you're currently occupying. Don't despair. We'll walk your though the entire process. If you have good people skills, a knack for negotiations, a head for numbers, and lots of determination, you've already won half the battle.

If you take your time, do your research and—of course—read this book carefully (several times, if necessary), we think you'll find foreclosure investing to be much easier than you'd expected. Before long, you might find yourself addicted to the search for your next great foreclosure deal.

We'll start with the basics: what foreclosures are, why they happen, how often, and to whom. We'll go over important issues—like the difference between judicial and non-judicial foreclosures—and explain why these are important to aspiring investors like yourself.

In many cases, you can take the words right out of our mouths—we'll provide actual sample dialogue to show you what to say in specific situations. We've also included handy extras like worksheets that will be a big help in calculating potential profits of a particular deal.

In the end, we're confident we'll provide you with all the tips and tricks of the trade to make you a successful foreclosure investor. In fact, we'll be eager to hear your success story—maybe we'll include it in the updated version of this book!

What You'll Find in This Book

This book is designed to be easily understood by the average person—a beginning investor who wants to learn everything he needs to know in order to become successful at buying foreclosure property. With that in mind, we start at the very beginning. The chapters follow a logical order, starting with the most basic information and working up to the more advanced strategies.

Readers with some investment experience may find they can skim the early chapters and dive right into the meatier stuff. Then again, we think the first few chapters contain lots of tips, tidbits, and helpful info that would prove useful even to veteran investors.

If you lose your place or forget where a particular topic was covered, there's a wonderfully comprehensive and detailed group of contents pages, so you can easily locate everything in a snap. The 22 chapters have also been organized into 6 separate parts, to further simplify your research. They are:

In **Part 1, "Foreclosure Basics,"** you'll learn what a foreclosure is, why it happens, and how the process varies from state to state. We'll tell you how banks feel about foreclosures, and why this is important to you. You'll get the basic building blocks on which we'll help you build a profitable foreclosure investing future.

In **Part 2, "How You Can Profit From Foreclosures,"** we'll show you exactly how foreclosure investors make money. We'll describe—in great detail—the benefits and pitfalls you need to know about. We'll also cover important issues you need to address before taking your first step.

In **Part 3, "Making Your First Foreclosure Purchase,"** we'll explain the three different phases of foreclosures, and show you how to find the best deals at each stage. We'll walk you through the process of negotiating with homeowners, landing an excellent auction buy and finding a great REO property. You'll learn how to find out about property you can buy from Uncle Sam. Last but certainly not least, we'll give you lots of helpful information on financing your foreclosure purchase.

In **Part 4, "After the Sale,"** we'll show you what your next steps should be, and guide you through some common post-purchase pitfalls. You'll learn what it's like to be a landlord, and how to make the most of that rental property. Not landlord material? No problem—we'll show you how to sell that property quickly for a nice profit.

In **Part 5, "Beyond Basics—Advanced Strategies for Experienced Investors,"** we'll tell you about some strategies that will prove more challenging, but also potentially more rewarding. You'll learn all about subject to financing and lease option deals. We'll also throw in a few other creative financing techniques, just to keep things interesting.

In **Part 6, "Real-Life Lessons,"** we'll share tips and advice from numerous successful investors. By sharing the good and bad, they'll help you avoid making the same mistakes they made, while allowing you to copy their winning ways.

We're not done yet, though. Following these chapters, you'll find several helpful appendixes. Appendix A is a glossary of common real estate and foreclosures terms. Appendix B features a ton of helpful resources. Appendix C contains many forms and worksheets that will make your life as an investor a lot easier. Appendix D offers some special tips for buying property out of probate. Finally, Appendix E lists the top financing mistakes you need to avoid.

Extras

In addition to the main narrative of *The Complete Idiot's Guide to Buying Foreclosures*, you'll find other useful types of information. Here's how to recognize these features:

Land Lingo

Real estate investing has a language all its own. These sidebars will provide helpful definitions of many terms related to real estate and foreclosures.

Promissory Note

These sidebars contain tips and other nuggets of information that should prove helpful to an aspiring investor.

Watch Out!

These sidebars will warn you about common pitfalls or problems that can spell trouble for the unknowing investor.

Foreclosure Fact

Learn interesting facts and trivia about foreclosures.

Acknowledgments

Bobbi Dempsey would like to thank her co-author, Todd, for all his input and guidance. In addition, a big thank you to all the investors, real estate pros, and other experts who provided advice, anecdotes, and other helpful info for this book. Also, to my agent, Marilyn, and editors, Mike and Ginny, along with technical editor Jennie Phipps, for helping to make this book possible. And, as always, I want to recognize Brandon, Nick, and John for motivating me to achieve my goals.

Todd Beitler wishes to thank all the bankers, attorneys, publishers, asset managers, court clerks, real estate brokers, investors, foreclosure specialists, and industry experts I've known for providing valuable and timely information through the years.

A very special thanks to my co-author Bobbi. I thank you for asking me to write this with you. Your exceptional efforts have made this entire project much easier. Your attention to detail and dedication to providing the most accurate information is more than appreciated. Outstanding work, partner.

Special thanks to J.B. for helping me make all this information coherent. Thanks also to all my friends in the industry for their unwavering support. For almost a dozen years, they've made a challenging environment fun to work in. They continue to inspire me and make all the good work worthwhile. In no particular order, they are: D.P., K.L., J.V., B.C., A.L., W.H., and B.H. Thanks too, to L.M., G.R., E.C., D.B., E.F., and B.B. I am fortunate to have you in my life.

Special Thanks to the Technical Reviewer

The Complete Idiot's Guide to Buying Foreclosures was reviewed by an expert who double-checked the accuracy of what you'll learn here, to help us ensure that this book gives you everything you need to know about buying foreclosures. Special thanks are extended to Jennie Phipps.

Trademarks

All terms mentioned in this book that are known to be or are suspected of being trademarks or service marks have been appropriately capitalized. Alpha Books and Penguin Group (USA) Inc. cannot attest to the accuracy of this information. Use of a term in this book should not be regarded as affecting the validity of any trademark or service mark.

Part 1

Foreclosure Basics

Before you think about attempting your first foreclosure purchase, you need to know the basics. By understanding the foreclosure process, you'll have a better understanding of a homeowner's situation, which will be a huge advantage when trying to negotiate with distressed property owners.

In these first few chapters, we explain the foreclosure process step by step and outline the important differences between judicial and nonjudicial foreclosure processes.

Foreclosures 101

In This Chapter

- ◆ Foreclosures defined
- ◆ Why you should avoid acceleration
- ◆ Judicial vs. nonjudicial foreclosures
- ◆ Redemptions and reinstatements
- ◆ Types of foreclosure properties

Chances are, you understand the basic idea of a foreclosure. But do you know the difference between a mortgage and a trust deed? A judicial foreclosure and nonjudicial foreclosure? If not, don't even think about taking the first step toward foreclosure investing until you do your research. A simple mistake or easily overlooked detail can spell trouble—not to mention financial loss and lots of headaches—for the novice investor. In this chapter, we explain the basic principles and terms involved in the foreclosure process, and hopefully help you avoid many pitfalls along the way.

What Is a Foreclosure?

Most people have a basic idea of what a foreclosure is. At the very least, they know it's something they want to avoid. In simple terms, a foreclosure is generally viewed as what happens when the bank takes control of your house. As in, if you don't pay, you no longer have a house.

In reality, of course, it's more complicated than that. So how does a foreclosure work? Basically, a foreclosure is the action taken by a lender or *mortgage* holder when the terms of the contract aren't met and the borrower is in *default*. The contract (mortgage or trust deed) says that the borrower must adhere to the contract terms—mainly, keeping payments current—or the lender can gain possession of the property in order to recoup the loan.

Land Lingo

A **mortgage** is a contract allowing a borrower to buy a property while using it as security for a loan. The bank or other lender puts a lien on the property. When the loan is paid off, the bank removes its lien on the property. **Default** is defined as the nonperformance of a contractual or other kind of obligation, such as not making payments on a note.

Sample Mortgage Deed

A typical mortgage deed document looks something like the following:

Mortgage Deed

This Indenture, made this ____ day of ____ between _____, hereafter called the Mortgagor, and _____, hereafter called the Mortgagee, witnesseth that the said Mortgagor, for and in consideration of the sum of One Dollar to __ in hand paid by the said Mortgagee, the receipt whereof is hereby acknowledged, granted, bargained and sold to the said Mortgagee, heirs and assigns forever the following described land, situate and being in the County of _____, State of _____, to wit:

Mortgagee and said Mortgagor do hereby fully warrant the title to said land, and will defend the same against the lawful claims of all persons whomsoever.

Provided always that if said Mortgagor, heirs, legal representatives or assigns, shall pay unto the said Mortgagee, legal representatives or assigns, a certain Promissory Note dated the ____ day of ____ for the sum of ____ dollars, payable ____ with interest at ____ percent, and shall pay all sums payable, and perform, comply with an abide by each and every stipulation, agreement, condition and covenant of said Promissory Note and of this Mortgage, and shall duly pay all taxes and insurance premiums reasonably required and all costs and expenses including a reasonable attorney's fee, which said Mortgagee may incur in collecting money secured by this Mortgage, and also in enforcing this Mortgage by suit or otherwise, then this Mortgage and the estate hereby created shall cease and be null and void.

In Witness Whereof, the said Mortgagor, set hand and seal, the day and year first above written.

Signed, sealed and delivered in the presence of:

_____

(Witness Signature)

_____

(Grantor Signature)

I hereby certify that on this day, before me, an officer duly authorized in the State Aforesaid and in the County aforesaid to take acknowledgements, personally appeared _____ who executed the foregoing Mortgage Deed and acknowledged before me that __ executed the same.

_____

Notary Signature

This sample mortgage document is a very simple, basic one, but it contains the basic points: amount due, term, interest, etc. Many mortgage documents would include additional terms and conditions, and would probably also outline the possibility of acceleration.

Acceleration

Let's say a borrower violates the terms of their mortgage contract. Generally, this means they haven't made timely payments. However, a borrower can usually also violate the contract if they aren't current on their property tax payments, or if they don't maintain adequate homeowner insurance on the property.

However it happened, they've violated the contract. What happens now? Well, with most contracts or agreements of this nature, the lender has the right to make the full amount of the principal due immediately—not just the portion that is past due. This is known as accelerating the loan.

CAUTION

Watch Out! _____

To avoid having the lender accelerate a loan, it's important for a borrower to notify the lender immediately if the payment will be late or if there will be some other type of problem. The more forthcoming and honest the borrower is, the more cooperative the lender is likely to be.

Acceleration, commonly known as "calling in the loan," is done so the lender can avoid having to chase a borrower through cycles of being behind in payments and playing catch-up. Most lenders will make an attempt to work with the borrower, especially if they've encountered some kind of emergency or unforeseeable hardship that caused them to fall behind. However, if the borrower can't show their ability to make timely payments from now on, or if they're uncooperative with the lender, the odds of the lender accelerating the loan will greatly increase.

The Repossession Analogy

To get a clearer picture of how a foreclosure works, take the similar process of repossession. When you buy a new car, you often need a loan—which you usually get from a bank, credit union, or other financial institution. Generally, after your loan is approved, you happily drive off the lot in your shiny new car, which is registered in your name as well as that of the lender. When you pay off the loan, you get the title all to yourself, free of liens. Now, suppose Bill Borrower "forgets" to make his car payments for a few months. His lender will not be happy, and will send Bill some letters in the mail. Make no mistake, these aren't love letters, and they'll get increasingly more demanding. Eventually, if Bill still hasn't coughed up any money or made suitable payment arrangements, the lender may decide to cut its losses and exert its legal right to claim the property that secured the loan—meaning, Bill's shiny new car.

Let's say Bill bought a $12,000 car. He put $2,000 down and borrowed the remaining $10,000 at 9.5 percent interest for 36 months. His monthly payments would be around $320. If he made no payments at all, here's what would happen:

After 30 days, he owes ... $320.

After 60 days, he owes ... $640, plus late fees for one month.

After 90 days, he owes ... $960, plus late fees for two months.

After 91 days, he owes ... $10,000 (because the lender has most likely accelerated the loan), plus late fees for three months, interest charges for three months, and collection fees (yikes!).

At this point, unless Bill makes satisfactory arrangements with the lender—or he has an extra ten grand lying around—he'd better make sure to remove his treasured CD collection, fuzzy dice, and any other personal belongings from the car. Because, chances are, he's about to get a visit from a guy we call "the repo man."

Why This Info Is Important to You

Right now, you may be thinking, "Hey, I wanna be an investor. Why should I care about how the borrower gets into this mess?" Well, for one thing, most investors are also borrowers at some point, so it's helpful for you to know how to avoid finding yourself on the other side of foreclosure misfortune. More important, savvy in-vestors must be very familiar with the entire process leading up to foreclosure. This insight is crucial for you to understand the borrower's position (as well as that of the lender). This is also important in helping you decide at which point in the process you can best capitalize from foreclosure investment opportunities.

Types of Foreclosures

Banks and other lenders are not in the business to sell used cars or four-bedroom bilevels. They make money from the interest they charge. If the loan is not perform-ing, the bank isn't making a profit. In that case, the bank often believes its only option is to foreclose and take control of the property, which it can then sell to make some kind of profit from its investment.

All banks are regulated, which means they have to operate within very strict, specific guidelines. Foreclosure laws differ from state to state. A common trait is that fore-closure is generally a lengthy process, with additional fees, interests, and other costs levied against the delinquent borrower with each step along the way.

Mortgage Foreclosures

When a borrower gets a home loan from a bank, they will sign two very important documents. First is the promissory note. This outlines the terms and conditions of the loan, and details the borrower's obligation to make the required monthly payments. This document basically acknowledges the debt and—as the name implies—the "promise" to repay it.

The second document is the mortgage contract. This establishes the security for the loan—*collateral*

> **Land Lingo**
>
> **Collateral** is something of value—usually a high-value item such as property or a car—that is provided by a borrower as a guarantee that will repay a loan.

for the debt. This contract gives the lender (also known as the mortgagee) certain rights to the property, in the event the borrower doesn't live up to his end of the deal. By agreeing to a mortgage contract, a borrower allows a lien to be placed on the property. The lien is removed when the loan has been paid in full.

Foreclosure Fact

With trust deeds, banks and lawyers use impressive-sounding names to refer to the people involved in the deal. The borrower is called a "trustor," the lender becomes the "beneficiary," and an independent outside party who holds the title is called a "trustee."

Trust Deed Foreclosures

About half the states in the country use the "mortgage method" of foreclosing on real estate. The other most popular method is the trust deed. A trust deed is a legal contract used in the same manner as a mortgage is used. The deed of the property is placed "in trust" with a third party, generally a title or trust company.

A trust deed is a type of mortgage contract that pre-authorizes the lender to foreclose and claim the property title in the event the borrower defaults on the loan.

Strict Foreclosures

In some states, there is the legal view that the lender is the rightful owner of the property, and may simply order the borrower to vacate the premises, when the borrower's right to redemption has ended. This is known as a strict foreclosure.

Table of Types by State

The types of contracts used to secure a home loan—and foreclose on the home, if necessary—vary by state. Most states use a mortgage, a trust deed, or both. The following table shows what type is used in each state.

Types of Home Loan Contracts by State

State	Type
Alabama	Mortgage
Alaska	Trust deed
Arizona	Trust deed
Arkansas	Mortgage & trust deed

State	Type
California	Trust deed
Colorado	Trust deed
Connecticut	Mortgage
D.C.	Mortgage & trust deed
Florida	Mortgage
Georgia	Mortgage
Hawaii	Mortgage
Idaho	Trust deed
Illinois	Trust deed
Indiana	Mortgage
Iowa	Mortgage
Kansas	Mortgage
Kentucky	Mortgage & trust deed
Louisiana	Mortgage
Maine	Mortgage
Maryland	Mortgage & trust deed
Massachusetts	Mortgage
Michigan	Mortgage
Minnesota	Mortgage
Mississippi	Trust deed
Missouri	Trust deed
Montana	Trust deed
Nebraska	Trust deed
Nevada	Trust deed
New Hampshire	Mortgage
New Jersey	Mortgage
New Mexico	Trust deed
New York	Mortgage
North Carolina	Mortgage
North Dakota	Trust deed
Ohio	Mortgage
Oklahoma	Mortgage

continues

Types of Home Loan Contracts by State   (continued)

State	Type
Oregon	Trust deed
Pennsylvania	Mortgage
Rhode Island	Mortgage
South Carolina	Mortgage
South Dakota	Mortgage
Tennessee	Trust deed
Texas	Trust deed
Utah	Trust deed
Vermont	Mortgage
Virginia	Trust deed
Washington	Trust deed
West Virginia	Trust deed
Wisconsin	Mortgage
Wyoming	Mortgage

Judicial vs. Nonjudicial Foreclosures

All trust deeds contain a power-of-sale clause. This clause allows the trustee to adver-tise and sell the property if the trustor (borrower) defaults. The trustee doesn't need the authorization or approval of the courts to sell the property. This is known as the nonjudicial foreclosure method.

Promissory Note

If a bidder at the foreclo-sure auction successfully buys the property for more than the lender is owed (including principal, interest on late payments, and other legally allowed expenses), the excess amount is given to the borrower.

Obviously, lenders prefer the nonjudicial route, because it allows them to foreclose more quickly and take control of the property without lengthy court proceedings and additional legal costs. Unfortunately for the borrower, the nonjudicial process gives them less time to try to salvage their interest in the prop-erty and prevent the foreclosure. A nonjudicial fore-closure is also known as a "power-of-sale" foreclosure.

In states that use the mortgage/lien system, a judicial foreclosure process is required. In this case, the lender petitions the court to begin foreclosure proceedings, which usually end with an auction of the property. By law, the lien holder isn't allowed to profit from the auction—they can only recoup their losses.

Table of Processes by State

As an investor, it's important to know the type of foreclosure process used by the state in which you want to invest. The following table lists the type by state.

Foreclosure Process by State

State	Type
Alabama	Power of sale
Alaska	Power of sale
Arizona	Power of sale
Arkansas	Power of sale
California	Power of sale
Colorado	Power of sale
Connecticut	Power of sale
Delaware	Judicial
D.C.	Power of sale
Florida	Judicial
Georgia	Power of sale
Hawaii	Power of sale
Idaho	Power of sale
Illinois	Judicial
Indiana	Judicial
Iowa	Judicial
Kansas	Judicial
Kentucky	Judicial
Louisiana	Judicial
Maine	Entry & possession
Maryland	Power of sale
Massachusetts	Power of sale

continues

Foreclosure Process by State (continued)

State	Type
Michigan	Power of sale
Minnesota	Power of sale
Mississippi	Power of sale
Missouri	Power of sale
Montana	Judicial
Nebraska	Judicial
Nevada	Power of sale
New Hampshire	Power of sale
New Jersey	Judicial
New Mexico	Judicial
New York	Judicial
North Carolina	Power of sale
North Dakota	Judicial
Ohio	Judicial
Oklahoma	Judicial
Oregon	Power of sale
Pennsylvania	Judicial
Rhode Island	Power of sale
South Carolina	Judicial
South Dakota	Power of sale
Tennessee	Power of sale
Texas	Power of sale
Utah	Judicial
Vermont	Strict foreclosure
Virginia	Power of sale
Washington	Judicial
West Virginia	Power of sale
Wisconsin	Power of sale
Wyoming	Power of sale

Deficiency Judgments

We've already discussed what happens if a buyer bids more than the amount owed to the bank for the property. However, what happens if the successful bid is less than what is owed, which is often the case? Unfortunately for the defaulting borrower, his troubles may not be over yet. The lender can seek a deficiency judgment, which is a court order requiring the borrower to pay the remaining amount not collected at the time of the sale.

Reinstatement

After a foreclosure has technically begun, there is still a period during which time the actual sale of the property can be avoided by paying the past due amount and any added fees. This is called the *reinstatement* period. In some states, the clerk of courts or other administrator must verify the sale was conducted appropriately before deed or title to the property can be transferred to the successful bidder. This process can take anywhere from a few days to a month. Meanwhile, if the borrower can pay all of the arrears and other expenses, they may still be able to keep the property, even though it has technically already been sold at auction.

Land Lingo

Reinstatement is the period after the foreclosure begins when the borrower still has the opportunity to avoid losing his home by paying overdue balances and other fees.

Right of Redemption

In certain states, after a foreclosure auction, the borrower still has a limited period of time during which he can reclaim his home. If the borrower can come up with all the past due payments—plus any additional fees and foreclosure costs—they can get their property back. The person or company that bought the property at auction is then given a refund.

Watch Out!

If you plan to invest in foreclosure properties, it's vital that you familiarize yourself with the reinstatement and redemption laws in the specific state where you plan to buy property. Otherwise, you might be blissfully unaware that the lovely townhouse you just acquired can still be reclaimed by its previous owner. And, unfortunately, you may be in for a rude awakening.

Deed in Lieu of Foreclosure

In some situations where a pending foreclosure is looming, the property owner may be certain that he will be unable to pay his overdue payments and prevent foreclosure. As a result, he may want to just get the situation over with. Instead of waiting for the actual foreclosure, the owner may simply agree to give the lender the deed to the property. This is known as deed in lieu of foreclosure. However, nothing in the mortgage or trust deed contract gives the borrower this right. It is entirely up to the lender to decide whether to agree to this arrangement. The terms of this kind of arrangement can vary widely. It's generally a negotiated agreement which, ideally, offers some benefit to both parties.

In states using the judicial process, foreclosure can be a very expensive and time-consuming process for the lender. Accepting a deed in lieu allows the lender to sell the property quickly. This can benefit the lender if there's enough equity in the property.

> **Foreclosure Fact**
>
> Years ago, a down-on-his-luck property owner may have simply mailed the deed and the house keys right to the lender. This was the early version of the deed in lieu of foreclosure process. Needless to say, with all the laws and regulations currently in place, that's no longer an option.

How Many Foreclosures Are There?

If you think there aren't many foreclosure opportunities available in your area, think again. People who are facing foreclosure generally don't blab this fact to the world. Odds are, a homeowner near you—perhaps one of your friends or neighbors—is in danger of losing their home to foreclosure at this very moment.

> **Foreclosure Fact**
>
> Borrowers with less-than-perfect credit, spotty employment histories, or other risk factors are often called "subprime" borrowers. Lenders usually offer these borrowers higher interest rates and less-attractive terms than they'd be willing to give "prime" borrowers. Not surprisingly, foreclosure rates among subprime loans tend to be higher than the figures for prime borrowers.

National Statistics

According to the second-quarter 2004 National Delinquency Survey (NDS) conducted by the Mortgage Bankers Association (MBA), the delinquency rate for mortgage loans on one-to-four-unit residential properties stood at 4.43 percent. The inventory of loans in foreclosure was 1.16 percent. Although the exact number of foreclosures constantly changes, most experts generally estimate that anywhere between 1 and 2 percent of all residential properties in the United States are in foreclosure at any given time. Translation? Millions of foreclosure investment opportunities are out there.

The following table—illustrated by statistics from the Mortgage Bankers Association—shows foreclosure rates across the country.

Total Number of Loans in Arrears or Foreclosure

State, Area, and Census Region	Number of Loans Serviced	Percent of Loans with Installments Past Due			Percent of Loans in Foreclosure		
		Total Past Due	30 Days	60 Days	90 Days or More	Inventory at End of Quarter	Started During Quarter
Connecticut	458,252	3.22	2.27	0.52	0.43	0.76	0.23
Maine	106,164	3.43	2.40	0.57	0.47	0.92	0.26
Massachusetts	658,658	2.83	2.06	0.45	0.32	0.44	0.19
New Hampshire	158,219	2.71	1.97	0.42	0.32	0.42	0.17
Rhode Island	107,623	2.93	2.16	0.44	0.32	0.46	0.20
Vermont	51,839	2.43	1.81	0.35	0.27	0.64	0.19
New England	1,540,755	2.97	2.14	0.47	0.36	0.57	0.20
New Jersey	1,073,267	3.88	2.56	0.61	0.70	1.09	0.30
New York	1,824,837	3.77	2.56	0.59	0.61	1.12	0.30
Pennsylvania	1,245,758	5.28	3.19	0.93	1.16	1.94	0.42
Mid Atlantic	4,143,862	4.25	2.75	0.70	0.80	1.36	0.34
Illinois	1,482,503	4.28	2.78	0.72	0.77	1.46	0.41
Indiana	708,415	6.24	3.88	1.08	1.28	2.78	0.76
Michigan	1,355,684	5.45	3.45	0.98	1.03	1.65	0.50
Ohio	1,238,520	5.78	3.59	0.99	1.19	3.33	0.86
Wisconsin	547,271	2.71	1.83	0.43	0.44	0.96	0.28
East North Central	5,332,393	5.02	3.19	0.87	0.97	2.06	0.57
Iowa	280,726	3.57	2.40	0.66	0.51	1.34	0.37
Kansas	284,377	4.22	2.76	0.72	0.73	1.28	0.43
Minnesota	800,241	2.63	1.81	0.47	0.35	0.56	0.23

continues

Total Number of Loans in Arrears or Foreclosure   (continued)

State, Area, and Census Region	Number of Loans Serviced	Percent of Loans with Installments Past Due			Percent of Loans in Foreclosure	
		Total Past Due	30 Days	60 Days	90 Days or More	Inventory at End of Quarter	Started During Quarter
Missouri	734,512	4.56	3.00	0.81	0.75	1.01	0.37
Nebraska	220,653	6.44	2.70	0.84	2.91	0.86	0.30
North Dakota	44,142	2.26	1.59	0.35	0.32	0.51	0.19
South Dakota	61,157	2.22	1.53	0.37	0.33	0.82	0.25
West North Central	2,425,808	3.84	2.42	0.65	0.77	0.90	0.32
Delaware	134,988	3.81	2.43	0.66	0.71	1.33	0.32
District of Columbia	81,145	3.85	2.58	0.65	0.61	0.82	0.27
Florida	2,768,012	4.02	2.77	0.69	0.56	0.84	0.29
Georgia	1,342,975	5.94	3.72	1.04	1.17	1.33	0.50
Maryland	961,371	4.24	2.67	0.72	0.86	0.96	0.27
North Carolina	1,119,948	5.37	3.43	0.95	1.00	1.56	0.47
South Carolina	499,543	5.56	3.59	0.99	0.98	2.46	0.55
Virginia	1,215,784	3.22	2.19	0.56	0.47	0.46	0.18
West Virginia	102,533	6.05	3.93	0.98	1.13	1.50	0.45
South Atlantic	8,226,299	4.54	2.97	0.79	0.78	1.09	0.35
Alabama	470,189	6.03	3.86	1.05	1.13	1.16	0.42
Kentucky	343,778	4.69	3.08	0.81	0.80	2.00	0.52
Mississippi	201,400	8.35	5.26	1.44	1.65	2.27	0.63
Tennessee	722,923	6.27	3.74	0.97	1.56	1.44	0.47
East South Central	1,738,290	6.13	3.82	1.01	1.30	1.57	0.49
Arkansas	255,446	5.08	3.27	0.84	0.97	1.24	0.51
Louisiana	418,410	6.69	4.37	1.12	1.20	1.73	0.61
Oklahoma	345,213	5.29	3.42	0.91	0.97	1.83	0.59
Texas	2,391,798	6.19	3.95	1.10	1.14	1.24	0.50

| State, Area, and Census Region | Number of Loans Serviced | Percent of Loans with Installments Past Due | | | Percent of Loans in Foreclosure | |
		Total Past Due	30 Days	60 Days	90 Days or More	Inventory at End of Quarter	Started During Quarter
West South Central	3,410,867	6.08	3.90	1.07	1.11	1.36	0.53
Arizona	955,053	3.74	2.51	0.64	0.58	0.67	0.33
Colorado	872,587	3.26	2.07	0.57	0.61	1.03	0.43
Idaho	195,841	3.50	2.35	0.59	0.55	1.08	0.38
Montana	109,977	2.77	1.84	0.48	0.44	0.67	0.28
Nevada	420,060	3.56	2.33	0.58	0.64	0.64	0.23
New Mexico	210,853	4.25	2.77	0.71	0.77	1.46	0.46
Utah	350,980	4.65	2.81	0.78	1.06	1.56	0.61
Wyoming	58,544	2.60	1.83	0.42	0.35	0.56	0.22
Mountain	3,173,895	3.65	2.37	0.62	0.65	0.94	0.38
Alaska	79,195	3.16	2.18	0.58	0.40	0 40	0.20
California	5,001,709	2.19	1.58	0.35	0.26	0.27	0.14
Hawaii	146,599	1.99	1.37	0.32	0.30	0.36	0.11
Oregon	535,520	2.72	1.81	0.46	0.46	0.86	0.31
Washington	1,036,441	2.82	1.84	0.49	0.48	0.78	0.30
Pacific	6,799,464	2.34	1.64	0.38	0.32	0.39	0.18
Puerto Rico	40,421	10.89	7.20	1.61	2.08	2.35	0.43
Northeast	5,684,617	3.90	2.58	0.64	0.68	1.15	0.30
North Central	7,758,201	4.65	2.95	0.80	0.91	1.70	0.49
South	13,375,456	5.14	3.32	0.89	0.93	1.22	0.41
West	9,973,359	2.75	1.87	1.87	0.42	0.57	0.24
United States	37,843,779	4.36	2.83	0.74	0.79	1.16	0.38

Trends

Foreclosure rates have dipped slightly recently, with some areas experiencing record-low figures for the number of homes in delinquency and foreclosure. Fear not, aspiring investor. There are still plenty of foreclosures out there, especially in certain areas.

The Delayed Reaction

It's important to note that foreclosure rates generally lag behind the economy. A borrower who loses his job today may still be able to keep up with his payments for a short time. Likewise, someone who bought more homes than needed—or could afford—because of the lure of low-interest rates may be okay for a while as interest rates creep up. But eventually both these people will find it increasingly tough to keep their heads above water.

The Least You Need to Know

♦ Foreclosure occurs when a borrower cannot live up to the obligations of his home loan contract.

♦ The nonjudicial foreclosure process used in trust deed states is quicker, easier, and less expensive for the lender than the judicial process.

♦ Rights of the lender and homeowner vary from state to state, as do the rights of redemption and the foreclosure process itself.

2

Why Foreclosures Occur

In This Chapter

- ◆ The major causes of foreclosure
- ◆ How a divorce can lead to foreclosure
- ◆ Why investors need to understand the causes
- ◆ Buying distressed properties

If you want to be a successful foreclosure investor, it's vital that you understand the various reasons why people end up in this situation. This is especially important when pursuing pre-foreclosures because understanding the owner's situation is vital to formulating an arrangement that will help the owner and address their concerns, while at the same time allowing you to get a good deal on the property.

Divorce

Divorce is one of the main reasons for foreclosure. Typically, the divorce-related foreclosure falls under one of two scenarios.

One-Income Households

When there is only one income earner in the family (traditionally that was the man, but these days more and more women are the family's breadwinner), a divorce can be a huge financial strain. The same money that previously supported one household must now support two. One spouse may remain in the home, but might find it difficult to keep up with the mortgage payments and other expenses. Often the wife gets the house—especially if she isn't employed—but she might find it difficult or impossible to keep up with the mortgage payments and other expenses. The husband may be paying alimony, but his resources are also strained because he's most likely paying expenses on his new house or apartment.

Of course, not all single-income households are the result of a divorce. More and more people are remaining single once they leave the family home and become independent. In these cases, a foreclosure may occur as a result of unemployment or other situations we discuss later in this chapter.

> **CAUTION**
>
> **Watch Out!**
>
> Another complicating factor in the divorce situation is the frequent presence of strong feelings of anger, hurt, and other negative emotions. In highly charged times such as these, people may act out on anger or simply behave irrationally. As a result, they may allow foreclosure to proceed even if they are not having financial difficulties.

Two-Income Households

These days, many families have two income earners. The problem is, the more money you have, the more you tend to spend. A dual-income couple often becomes accustomed to a certain standard of living. When they try to maintain two households after a divorce, they may not be able to adjust to their new lower-budget lifestyle.

> **Foreclosure Fact**
>
> Even if a borrower finds another job within, say, a few months, odds are good that he has now fallen behind on his bills, perhaps to a serious extent. By the time he starts earning money from his new job, the foreclosure process may already be underway.

Other Reasons Foreclosures Occur

In addition to divorce, there are many other reasons why foreclosures occur. We discuss the most common scenarios here.

Unemployment

Unfortunately, many Americans live one or two paychecks away from financial trouble, including bankruptcy and possibly foreclosure. An unexpected and sudden job loss can send an individual or family into a serious crisis. Often people are shocked at how quickly their savings—if they have any—can be depleted once they must rely on it for basic household expenses.

Health Problems

As many of us are unfortunately all too aware, the country is experiencing a health-care crisis. Just as a sudden job loss can disrupt your finances, a health crisis—or even a fairly short hospital stay—can often completely wipe out your bank account.

A large percentage of Americans are underinsured, or not insured at all. It's amazing how expensive even a five-minute doctor visit can be. A medical problem that requires numerous doctor visits or medical tests can easily pile up the bills until they soon reach overwhelming dollar figures. Extended medical problems can obliterate a family's finances practically overnight. To make matters worse, if the illness or injury affects an employed person, the family might also lose some or all of the household income.

The Economy

Just as the economy experiences frequent highs and lows, so does the real estate market, which is heavily influenced by the unemployment rate, interest rates, and other factors that influence the general economic outlook.

When the economy takes a downturn and businesses downsize or close completely, layoffs and unemployment may occur. Real estate may take a nosedive in communities in which this occurs.

California is a perfect example of how changes in the economy can affect the number of residential foreclosures. Downsizing in the high-tech, aerospace, and defense industries has taken a tough toll on California and its residents. As a result, many high-tech employees—who just a few years ago were making big bucks—are now losing their homes to foreclosure.

Relocation

A homeowner may be happily making his payments, and everything seems to be smooth sailing. Then suddenly his boss informs the happy homeowner that he's being transferred to another company location on the other side of the country. In times when good jobs can be scarce, an employee often has no choice but to accept relocation without complaint.

Now the homeowner is faced with supporting two homes and juggling two sets of expenses. He must try to pay for and maintain a home from hundreds or thousands of miles away. Often this proves impossible, and he faces foreclosure on his former residence.

Overwhelmed Landlords/Investors

Many people—especially those who may have come into a sudden windfall, or those lured by tales of a real estate boom—start buying properties before they are fully informed or educated about what's involved. They may not be prepared or able to maintain or resell their investment properties. In the case of rental properties, the owner may have gotten a crash course on the harsh realities of life as a landlord, especially if he has had a few problem tenants.

> **Foreclosure Fact**
>
> Expenses on investment or rental properties can quickly add up, especially in the case of rental properties with vacant units. Add to that the cost of evicting problem tenants or making repairs caused by irresponsible occupants and the owner can unknowingly be setting himself up for foreclosure.

Other Reasons

Many factors may lead to foreclosure, including death or disability, business failure, overspending and mismanagement of family finances, loss of income due to military service, and more. It is important to remember that each homeowner and each situation you encounter will be different.

Why Knowing Is Important

You may be wondering why you need to know—or care—about the reason a homeowner is facing foreclosure. Here's why: in negotiating with the homeowner, you'll try to come up with a solution that makes everyone happy. By knowing the homeowner's situation, you'll best be able to figure out exactly what they hope to gain—and what you can offer them to help with that goal. For example, someone who is relocating would mainly be concerned with eliminating the financial obligation of this soon-to-be former house, which they will no longer need.

When You Can Buy Distressed Properties

Finally, we talk about when you can buy a distressed property. Bank-foreclosed properties can be purchased anytime throughout the foreclosure process. We explain the specific types of foreclosure properties in more detail in later chapters, but right now we wanted to give you a quick introduction into the types of foreclosed properties.

You can buy a property before the auction, when the homeowner is in default but still controls the property. This is called buying a pre-foreclosure. The process involves working closely with the homeowner, and possibly the lender.

You can also buy a property at an auction or sheriff's sale. This requires you to bid on the property, usually competing with the lender and any other bidders interested in the property.

Lastly, you can buy a property after the auction process. This is called an REO, or real estate owned, property. Typically, when buying an REO property, you will deal with someone who works in the REO department or special assets division of the bank.

The Least You Need to Know

- Divorce and unemployment are the most common factors that lead to foreclosure.

- An unexpected and costly medical crisis can easily lead a homeowner into a foreclosure situation.

- Although there are several common causes of foreclosure, every homeowner and situation is different.

Chapter 3

How It Works

In This Chapter

◆ When is the loan officially late?

◆ How timelines differ by state

◆ Judicial versus nonjudicial process

◆ Foreclosure sales aren't always final

Now that you have some basic information about foreclosures, we explain exactly how the process works. In this chapter, we walk you through the foreclosure process step by step, from when the payment is a day overdue until the foreclosure sale—and beyond.

When Is a Late Payment Really Late?

It's the first day of the billing cycle, and the mortgage payment is due. If the payment isn't made by the end of this day, technically the payment is late. This is the very beginning point of the road that eventually leads to the foreclosure process. However, many people find themselves at this point without traveling any further. People often make their mortgage payment a few days late without ever finding themselves anywhere near the danger point of foreclosure. In fact, many *lenders* give borrowers a customary "grace period" during which they can make a payment without incurring late charges or other fees.

Missed Payments

By Day 15, the mortgage payment is usually considered officially late. At this point, Harvey Homeowner will probably start getting calls or letters from the bank—basically saying "Hey, what's up? Where's our money?" If Harvey is having some kind of problem—and he can convince the bank it's a temporary thing he'll be rectifying very soon—most lenders will usually be pretty agreeable to working with him at this point. It's early in the game, and they haven't yet begun to get too nervous that the borrower will default on the loan. They may be offering options like changing the due date, which can give the borrower a short window to catch up on his payment.

Generally, the first thing a bank would be willing to do is accept the payment on a specific date in the very near future. They may or may not be willing to waive late fees. Generally, this would be a one-time event.

Late Charges

After the borrower has passed his due date (or the grace period, if the bank offers one), he will start incurring late charges. These vary from bank to bank, but have one common theme—they seem to add up at an amazing speed, causing the amount due to soar pretty quickly. At this point, if the borrower pays only the regular payment (without taking care of the extra charges), the account is still considered past due.

Breach of Contract

Usually somewhere between Day 45 and Day 60, the lender will send a "demand" letter by certified mail. This letter states that the borrower has officially breached the mortgage contract. Generally, the term "foreclosure" will be mentioned—frequently and in urgent terms. The demand letter will specifically spell out what the borrower needs to do to stop the process at this point. It also will provide details of any other options or sources of assistance that may be available.

Foreclosure Proceedings Begin

Somewhere around Day 90, the foreclosure process will really pick up steam. The lender will generally refer the case to its foreclosure department at this point. This is when legal proceedings usually begin.

Depending on the state, the lender's lawyers or foreclosure representative may start filing court papers and recording a legal notice of the foreclosure status. This may be published in the newspaper. Hearings may be scheduled during this period.

Watch Out!

Even if a primary mortgage is current, a homeowner can still face foreclosure if they fall behind on a secondary mortgage or home-equity loan. Bottom line: Homeowners need to pay close attention to the status of any loan secured by a home or property.

Judicial Process

In the judicial foreclosure process, the lender must file a complaint that declares its intent to take legal action against the borrower. The court will require the lender to produce evidence that the borrower has defaulted on their loan agreement. Because the mortgage contract allows foreclosure if the agreement terms aren't met, the process can begin—unless, of course, the borrower can prove the lender wrong and show they have abided by the contract terms.

This judicial process is the common method in "lien theory" states. The lien theory means the mortgage contract itself promises the title of the property in question to the lender. Although the lender doesn't actually hold the title, it is assumed to be the rightful owner by virtue of the mortgage contract until the terms of the deal have been fulfilled.

However, the lender must ask the court for permission to foreclose on the property. Although a jury trial is possible, it's very rare. In some judicial states, a summary judgment hearing is held. At this hearing, a judge will almost always rule in favor of the lender, unless the defendant (borrower) presents compelling evidence showing they've upheld their end of the deal.

In other judicial states, the lender pleads with the court to summon the borrower to court to explain their case. If the borrower doesn't provide sufficient evidence, or fails to appear, the judge will usually rule in favor of the lender.

State laws vary greatly, as do the timeframes involved. That's why it is difficult to provide a specific timeline for the foreclosure process that would be accurate nationwide. Court timelines can vary, as do redemption periods when a borrower can still reclaim his home. Even within one state, the process can vary widely. One lender may be slightly more patient than another, so each bank's "cutoff" point as to how far they'll let a borrower go into default can be different.

However, here's the basic route a judicial foreclosure will take.

Notice of Intent

The foreclosure process starts when the loan is in default. Technically, this is when it becomes even a day late, but in reality a borrower generally isn't viewed as in default until their payment is 30 or 60 days late.

The lender sends the borrower a Notice of Intent to Foreclose, usually by certified or registered mail. This makes it clear that the loan is in default and that the lender may foreclose if the situation isn't resolved. The notice outlines the ways to resolve the problem—mainly, curing the default by paying the amount due (past payments plus interest and fees), which is clearly stated in the notice. The notice generally also includes information on any state-allowed alternative remedies, such as consulting an assistance agency or enlisting the help of a credit counselor.

> **Watch Out!**
>
> At this point, many homeowners are still in denial, so they may be reluctant to discuss a sale, because they haven't yet faced the possibility of losing their home. It is also tougher to learn about homeowners at this stage, because the Notice of Intent is sent privately and the default hasn't been posted publicly yet.

Complaint of Foreclosure

Next, the lender files a Complaint of Foreclosure or Motion to Foreclose at the local county courthouse. This is when investors may first become aware of the foreclosure—usually by researching the courthouses or subscribing to reporting services. This document includes information such as the property address, homeowners' names, loan amount, lender, and other pertinent details.

Lis Pendens

Obviously, anyone who has a claim or lien on the property will want to know that it's at risk of being foreclosed. The lender's attorney does a title search to identify any interested parties, and then sends them a warning notice, which is legally recorded as the *Lis Pendens*.

The *Lis Pendens* is served as a summons by the court. This is often viewed as the first official court-related step in foreclosure proceedings. At this point, the homeowner can no longer deny there's a problem. They can, if they are able, pay off the amount in arrears (including late fees and other charges).

Land Lingo

The *Lis Pendens* (Latin for "suit pending") is a written notice that a lawsuit has been filed concerning the title to the property.

The *Lis Pendens* states that a suit has been initiated by the plaintiff (lender) against the defendant (borrower) involving a particular contract (loan, deed, or mortgage) and that relief is sought in the form of foreclosure against the property that has been pledged as security for the debt.

In addition, the *Lis Pendens* usually states the following:

♦ That a default has occurred

♦ A declaration by the plaintiff of the full amount due and payable

♦ The principal amount due, plus expenses

♦ Any expenses paid by the plaintiff to pursue the debt

♦ That other plaintiffs may have a claim to the property (It will also list any other interested parties identified through the title search.)

♦ That the plaintiff seeks a judgment to foreclose the mortgage

A copy of the original mortgage or loan contract is usually attached to the *Lis Pendens*.

The *Lis Pendens* is an official court document and a matter of public record. This is often when the general public—including interested investors—first takes notice of the impending foreclosure.

Summary Judgment

The lender now petitions the court, as entitled by law, to enter a Summary Judgment of Foreclosure. A Notice of Hearing is sent to all interested parties. Foreclosure hearings are generally quick and simple, because it's usually an open-and-shut kind of thing.

After the court hearing(s) conclude, the court will issue a judgment, which is virtually guaranteed to be in the lender's favor. This judgment gives the lender legal permission to auction or take possession of the property to recoup the losses incurred as a result of the default of the loan.

This judgment basically says the court acknowledges the plaintiff's rights under the law and gives a final judgment amount, includes the property's legal description, and sets a date and time for a sale of the property to be held. That's the important stuff. This document can sometimes be long and wordy, spelling out all the specific details about the property and loan, citing lots of state laws that may apply in this situation. It also specifies instructions for distribution of proceeds of the sale, if the sale actually takes place.

The Summary Judgment or Final Judgment is the green light signaling the beginning of the end. The clock is really ticking at this point, and the property owner is quickly running out of time to cure the default. The property will be sold, typically by the sheriff, if the debt isn't satisfied.

Notice of Sale

The court will send a Notice of Sale to all interested parties. The Notice of Sale informs everyone that the property will be sold at a given time and place. A copy of the judgment is usually attached.

If the homeowner doesn't pay up at the last minute, the property is then sold to the highest bidder. If the homeowner doesn't live in a state granting him rights of redemption, he has just lost all control and ownership of that property.

Vacating the Property

Depending on their situation—and whether they intend to try and cure the default and keep the property—the homeowners' actions concerning vacating the property vary widely. Some just pick up and leave whenever it's convenient for them. Some go into hiding, especially if they have many debts they're trying to avoid. Legally, they don't have to leave until forced to by the court. This typically occurs after the sale, when the sheriff or other court representative will arrive to evict them.

Nonjudicial Process

We've explained how the foreclosure process works in lien theory states. In *title theory* states, however, the nonjudicial foreclosure process is used.

The security instrument used in this case is the Deed of Trust. This deed differs from the mortgage in that the borrower (trustor) conveys their title to the property to the neutral third party (trustee), who becomes the legal titleholder until the trustor has completed the terms and obligations of the note with the lender (beneficiary).

We think the biggest difference between the judicial and nonjudicial methods of foreclosure is obvious. As the name implies, the judicial method involves the courts. The nonjudicial method doesn't. Court approval to foreclose on the property isn't required, because the method of foreclosure is stipulated and agreed upon when the original loan is made.

This agreement, a trust deed, pre-authorizes the sale of the property if a default should occur. The Power of Sale clause found in all trust deeds authorizes the trustee to sell the property if the beneficiary informs them the loan is in default.

The following section discusses how a typical nonjudicial foreclosure works.

> **Land Lingo** _____
>
> Some states follow the **title theory**—meaning, the state interprets a mortgage to mean that the lender is the owner of mortgaged land. Upon full payment of the mortgage debt the borrower becomes the landowner.

Notice of Default

The lender notifies the trustee of the default and instructs the trustee to start the foreclosure process. The point at which this happens will vary from one lender to another. Each lender has their own individual threshold as to the number of days late—or dollar amount owed—it will tolerate before getting the trustee involved. Local and state laws also affect the timeframe associated with this process.

The trustee prepares a Notice of Default and files it with the county courthouse. Typically, this notice identifies the trustor, trustee, and beneficiary, and it includes information on the amount of the loan, the amount in default, and other relevant details. A copy of the notice is mailed or delivered to the property owner. The notice may be posted in a public place and on the property itself. The notice will most likely be very clear and to the point. It's short, but not very sweet—at least, not to the home-owner. It will usually say something like this:

> IMPORTANT NOTICE:
>
> IF YOUR PROPERTY IS IN FORECLOSURE BECAUSE YOU ARE BEHIND IN YOUR PAYMENTS, IT MAY BE SOLD WITHOUT ANY COURT ACTION.

And, yes, it is often written in all capital letters. That'll get your attention, huh? This will generally serve as a wake-up call to the homeowner and quickly snap them out of denial.

This will also get the attention of interested investors (not to mention nosy neighbors).

The homeowner is given time to cure the default. This is called the reinstatement period or redemption period, and varies from state to state. The reinstatement period is indicated in the Notice of Default. It could be as little as 15 days and usually starts from the day the notice was recorded.

Notice of Sale

If the default isn't cured within the allotted time period, a Notice of Sale or Notice of Trustee's Sale is recorded just like the Notice of Default was. This notice is distributed and advertised according to local policies.

The notice states that the trustor is in default and that the property will be sold at a public sale to the highest bidder. It lists the date and time of the scheduled sale. If the problem isn't resolved before that point, the property is sold at auction.

Stopping the Process Along the Way

In both foreclosure methods, there are lots of opportunities along the way to halt the process. We've already explained why a lender wants to avoid the hassles of fore-closure. It goes without saying that the unfortunate homeowner also really wants to avoid losing his home. So there are generally attempts by both sides at various points in the process to reach a mutually agreeable solution that avoids foreclosure. This can be very frustrating for the investor, because the property you've been eagerly eyeing up can easily slip through your fingers right up to—and sometimes after—the moment of the auction.

Comparing the Processes

The judicial process as we've outlined it is a very simplified version. Things can get a lot more complicated, as they have a tendency to do when courts are involved. Still, even in a simple case, you can clearly see that the judicial method is more complex and time-consuming. That's good news for defaulting borrowers—it means more time to scramble for cash and cure the default—but bad news for investors, who really must have patience.

The nonjudicial example is also simplified, but you can probably clearly see why lenders strongly prefer the nonjudicial system. They don't have to get lawyers involved, and there are no lengthy court proceedings to bother with.

Another major difference affects the homeowner's rights, and the impact these rights have on the lender and an interested investor. Specifically, we're talking about the right of redemption. In several states, the homeowner has the legal right to reclaim their property after it has been sold at auction. This redemption period can be anywhere from a few weeks to a year or more.

Public Posting

After the borrower has reached the demand letter stage, the lender may post the notice of default in the newspaper, or even tack a notice of the upcoming sale on the property itself. To many people, this is one of the worst parts of the whole process. Even if they manage to save their property, they still had to face the embarrassment of the neighbors—and possibly the entire town—knowing they had fallen behind on their mortgage payments.

> **Foreclosure Fact**
>
> Unfortunately for borrowers in nonjudicial states, their clock is ticking much more quickly than those in judicial states. Unlike the slow pace of the judicial foreclosure process, the nonjudicial process can be swift. The road from demand letter to foreclosure sale can be as short as a few months.

Foreclosure Sale

After the foreclosure process has run its course—if the borrower hasn't managed to stop it yet—the property will be sold at a foreclosure sale, which often takes place in the form of an auction at the county courthouse. We cover auctions in greater detail in Chapter 10.

Watch Out!

Although redemption periods can be a lifesaver for defaulting borrowers, they can be a thorn in the side of investors. Be sure to investigate the redemption period (if any) in the state where you plan to invest. Only then will you know whether the property is irrevocably yours after you hear "Sold!"

In some states, the owner/occupant of the property can be evicted immediately following a foreclosure sale. However amazingly, in many states, a foreclosure sale doesn't necessarily mean the borrower has definitely lost their home. Many states offer a redemption period, during which the borrower can reclaim his home. However, given the late fees, interest, and court costs that have accumulated up to this point, the borrower would need to cough up considerable cash. Not surprisingly, many borrowers are unable to take advantage of this redemption option.

The Least You Need to Know

◆ How quickly—or slowly—the foreclosure process moves can vary greatly from state to state.

◆ At many points along the way, a borrower can save his property if he can come up with the cash.

◆ The judicial process is more complicated—and moves much more slowly—than the nonjudicial version.

◆ If a state has a redemption period, the borrower can still occupy the home—and possibly reclaim it—long after the foreclosure sale.

Chapter 4

How Lenders and Agencies View Foreclosures

In This Chapter

- ◆ How bank regulations affect foreclosures
- ◆ Mortgage corporations, and why they matter
- ◆ Who are Fannie Mae and Freddie Mac, anyway?
- ◆ Government agencies get involved, too

Just as it's important for you—as an aspiring investor—to understand the homeowner's position, you should also understand the *lender*'s point of view. There are reasons why banks must proceed the way they do with regard to foreclosure—although this is often at a much slower pace than eager investors would like. In this chapter, we give you some insight into the bank's motivation—and explain why it might be very eager to unload foreclosed properties.

The Bank's Legal Obligations

The federal government regulates all banks and lending institutions. When you think of people losing their homes to foreclosure, you may conjure up images of those mustache-twirling type villains from old TV shows, who would prey on poor widows, waving a piece of paper allowing him to throw them out onto the street. Fortunately, modern laws don't allow this type of behavior.

All banks are chartered. A charter is basically a written document authorizing the formation of a corporation or institution that will be regulated by the authority granting the charter—usually a government or legislative body. The charter also outlines the rights and responsibilities of the organization. Violating these guidelines can be grounds for removal of the charter. To a bank or other institution, losing your charter is akin to losing your license to do business.

Banks are regulated by federal agencies. They can be held highly accountable for their performance—and any problems within their institution—by numerous agencies, including the Department of Housing and Urban Development, the Internal Revenue Service, the Federal Deposit Insurance Corporation, the Federal Reserve, and many others.

Not long ago, we witnessed a rash of bank failures. Lawmakers are now turning up the heat through various agencies to keep a watchful eye on banks, because there was a lot of taxpayer outrage about the use of tax dollars to bail out the failing banks.

From the bank's point of view, a foreclosed home is a *nonperforming asset*. The loan is no longer earning interest, and therefore it is no longer profitable for the bank. Banks that have a large number of nonperforming assets make governing federal agencies very nervous, because it's often a sign that the lender has been careless in its lending decisions and needs to tighten up its lending practices.

> **Foreclosure Fact**
>
> The Federal Reserve Board is a group of economists who dictate the nation's monetary policy through its ability to control interest rates. The Federal Home Loan Bank Board is a federal agency that monitors federal savings and loan associations. These are just two of the agencies that monitor and/or regulate lending institutions.

> **Land Lingo**
>
> A **nonperforming asset** is an asset that is not producing any income, such as a loan in default or a home that has been foreclosed.

Other Influences

In addition to the agencies already mentioned, other agencies influence how the lender will treat a nonperforming asset.

Often a lender or mortgage company will sell the mortgages it holds to a larger mortgage company. The original lender's role is then basically just to "service" the loan—taking payments and keeping track of the account. It is the larger company, though, that actually has control over the loan.

Unfortunately, this isn't a good thing for borrowers, especially those who may run into hard times. In past times, a homeowner in default could pay a visit to his friendly neighborhood banker, explaining their hardship and promising to make good on their loan. Over a handshake, the banker might agree to be patient or make other arrangements to help the borrower through this rough patch.

These days the loan is unfortunately more likely to be under the control of a big, not-too-friendly corporation. The borrower may be dismayed to discover that Big Mortgage Corporation doesn't care about sob stories, and makes no exceptions to its hard-and-fast rule of initiating foreclosure proceedings after payments are 60 days late.

These corporations (sometimes also known as investing pools) can set strict policies for actions that must be taken regarding nonperforming assets. The local lender servicing those loans must adhere to these rules and regulations.

Introducing Fannie Mae and Freddie Mac

The most popular investing groups local lenders tend to work with are Fannie Mae and Freddie Mac.

There's a lot of confusion and misconceptions—especially among new homeowners—about these large mortgage corporations. For example, Fannie Mae used to be a part of the U.S. Department of Housing and Urban Development, but is no longer a branch of that government entity.

Also Fannie Mae used to handle management, liquidation, and financing of the government's low-rent housing. These tasks have since been taken over by the Government National Mortgage Association (nickname: Ginnie Mae).

Promissory Note

Fannie Mae and Freddie Mac are actually nicknames. The real corporate names are the Federal National Mortgage Association (FNMA) and the Federal Home Loan Mortgage Corporation (FHLMC). However, most people would have no idea what you were talking about if you mentioned these formal names, as the two institutions have become so well-known by their frequently used nicknames.

Although Fannie Mae is no longer part of a federal agency, it is still closely regulated by the federal government.

Today Fannie Mae's main purpose is buying mortgages from banks, insurance companies, smaller mortgage companies, trust companies, and other lending institutions. This helps the lenders by allowing them to free up more available dollars to use for new home loans.

The Bank's Exposure

Banks are more than happy to lend money for sound, secure investments such as real estate. Yet even these relatively safe investments must meet guidelines established to ensure profitable loans for the bank.

Thus, the ultimate bank loan Catch-22: those who need a loan from a bank but don't have many assets or savings often can't get approved, whereas rich people with lots of assets and available cash can easily get approved for a loan.

Banks are businesses—corporations driven to make profits. In addition, as we've explained, they must adhere to strict guidelines, both from federal agencies and larger mortgage companies. As a result, banks are very careful about making high-risk loans.

When bad investment decisions are made, it's a negative reflection on that lender's ability to make wise investment decisions. In addition, this affects the bank's balance sheet, because these nonperforming loans are costly to banks, in the form of additional expenses related to collections and management of this problem account.

> **Foreclosure Fact**
>
> Banks can help lessen the risk of foreclosure-related losses by requiring borrowers to obtain private mortgage insurance (PMI). Subprime loans, and those involving low down payments, often require PMI coverage.

In real estate foreclosure, the lender can incur lots of expense in the repair, collection, and eventual sale of the property.

How Much Does It Cost the Bank?

After the bank gains possession of a property, it is faced with a lose-lose situation. It's like a double loss—not only does the bank lose income from the loan, it also has incurred extra expenses related to handling the property. Property taxes must be paid. The property must be maintained and any local or state code violations must be addressed. Maintenance and upkeep can be costly to the banker, especially if the property is located outside the bank's normal business area.

Bankers don't want to be bothered taking prospective buyers on tours of the home, so they generally enlist the services of a local real estate agent—meaning, they must pay this agent a commission when and if the property is sold. That means more lost dollars for the bank. Banks with large inventories of *REO properties* sometimes have entire departments devoted to the management and sale of these properties. Needless to say, this can be expensive for the bank.

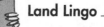

Land Lingo

An **REO**—or "real estate owned"—property is one that has been purchased by a bank or other corporation, usually the lender who foreclosed on the loan.

The Bank's Motivation

Why should you care about the bank's problems? As a potential investor, it's important for you to understand the bank's point of view and motivation in trying to get rid of REO properties quickly.

We've already explained why it is in the bank's best interest to turn nonperforming assets into performing ones as quickly and inexpensively as possible. It all boils down to the banks' desire to eliminate or reduce losses. The banks want to remove these negative figures from their records. By selling a foreclosed property, the bank can either work with the new owner and let him take over the existing loan or create a new and profitable loan. Either way, it removes the red ink from the bank's balance sheet.

Now you can see why a bank really tries to avoid foreclosing in the first place, and—if it must foreclose—then it tries to get rid of the property as quickly and inexpensively as possible.

FHA

The Federal Housing Administration (FHA) was created to help aspiring homebuyers. This agency mainly assists families with low to moderate incomes, and most of the families are first-time homebuyers.

Land Lingo

If a mortgage is **assumable**, it means a buyer may simply take over a seller's existing loan. This is very attractive to buyers because it eliminates a lot of time, hassle, and expense.

Basically, the FHA promises to pay the lender for the loan in the event the borrower defaults. This is like a security blanket for the lender. A lender that may not have granted the loan otherwise is now reassured by the fact that the loan is secured by the FHA. All FHA loans used to be *assumable*, which made them very attractive to buyers interested in taking over a mortgage for little or no money down. Today you may have to qualify to assume an FHA mortgage.

HUD

The Department of Housing and Urban Development (HUD) is a federal agency that sells properties when an FHA-insured mortgage has gone into default and been foreclosed. HUD pays the original lender the amount due on the loan plus additional expenses. HUD then resells the property, usually through a private contractor.

VA

The Department of Veterans Affairs (VA) guarantees loans made by lenders to qualified veterans and military personnel.

If a veteran with a VA loan defaults, the original lender begins the foreclosure process. Then the VA, which guaranteed the loan, steps in and buys the property from the lender. The VA then sells these properties through real estate brokers.

SBA

The Small Business Administration (SBA) handles low-interest loans—either granting loans directly or guaranteeing loans from lenders. As with a VA loan, when a lender forecloses on a mortgage loan guaranteed by the SBA, the SBA will buy the property from the lender. The SBA then usually enlists an auctioneer to sell the property. The majority of SBA properties consist of commercial buildings or plots of undeveloped land.

IRS Foreclosures

The Internal Revenue Service (IRS) also sometimes auctions off homes and other personal property. Obviously, the IRS isn't a lending institution. The agency does, however, foreclose on homes after placing a lien against the owner for unpaid taxes.

We discuss HUD, VA, and other government foreclosure properties in more detail in Chapter 12.

The Least You Need to Know

- ◆ Banks must follow many regulations and must answer to numerous federal agencies.

- ◆ Mortgages are generally sold to large corporations, with the local bank serving only as a servicing agent.

- ◆ A foreclosed home is a nonperforming asset, which looks bad on a lender's books.

- ◆ Several government agencies also often get involved in the foreclosure process.

Part 2

How You Can Profit from Foreclosures

Now that you know how and why foreclosures happen, you may be wondering how you can profit from this type of investment opportunity. In the next few chapters, we explain how foreclosure investors make their money. We describe the benefits of foreclosure investing and we explain the pitfalls you need to avoid. We also review some important issues you need to address before preparing to make a purchase.

Chapter 5

Benefits and Opportunities

In This Chapter

- ◆ Why distressed properties are desirable
- ◆ What kind of bargains to expect
- ◆ Aspiring landlords can benefit from foreclosures

Properties that are in foreclosure—or at risk of being in foreclosure— are said to be distressed. In reality, of course, it's actually the homeowner who is usually in distress. Often the term "distressed" is also used to refer to a property that is dilapidated or needs repair. For our purposes, though, we use the term to mean a property with some kind of financial burden attached to it.

So why exactly should you be so interested in trying to buy these distressed properties? Lots of reasons, actually. We examine these reasons in this chapter.

Bargain Buys

The first and most obvious reason for buying a *distressed* property is that you generally can obtain the property for less than its market value.

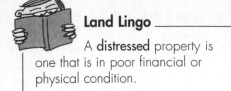

Land Lingo

A **distressed** property is one that is in poor financial or physical condition.

If you're the type of person who spends a few hours each week clipping coupons and scanning grocery store ads, or waiting for a 20 percent off sale to buy that new outfit, then surely you'd be interested in saving a nice chunk of change on the price of a home—which most likely will be one of the biggest purchases you'll ever make.

Purchase price reductions of 20 percent or 30 percent are fairly common. Savings of 50 percent or more are tougher to find, but they do happen. The average foreclosure investor would probably be happy buying property at a 20 percent to 40 percent discount off market price.

Some experts will tell you not to bother with any properties that aren't a specific percentage below market value. We don't believe in those types of hard-and-fast rules. In real estate, each situation is different. There are endless kinds of situations involving many different properties—and there are many different types of investors seeking these properties. Each property must be viewed as an individual situation and opportunity.

For a first-time investor, getting a home for even just 10 percent or 20 percent below market value can be a great deal—not to mention a big thrill.

Still, there are those bargain buys out there. With some patience and detective work, you just may be able to snag a great property for an amazingly low price.

Less Competition

An added advantage, many of the bigger, more experienced investors may not even bother with properties in this discount range, meaning you'll have less competition. Yet these types of properties can often yield higher than average returns for the shrewd investor—meaning that the deal may actually wind up being a pretty smart move after all.

Many prospective homebuyers are unfamiliar with the process of locating or buying a foreclosure property. They also may be intimidated by what they fear will be a complicated or time-consuming process. That's good news for you! You will automatically have less competition when you narrow your home-buying search to focus on foreclosures. In the case of pre-foreclosures, you'll have even less competition, because many investors don't know how to locate these properties—or don't want to invest the energy to try and make a deal with the owner.

Also, the term "distressed" can have a negative connotation that may scare away prospective buyers. As we've said previously, this term often refers to the financial situation of the property and its owner rather than the physical condition of the house. However, even if the home does need repairs (a fairly common situation in foreclosed properties), it may be merely cosmetic problems that can be fixed fairly easily and inexpensively.

Owner Occupancy

What if you're not planning to become an investor—at least, not for the time being—but simply want to buy a new home where you will live? Perhaps you've outgrown your current home, or want to move to a nice neighborhood. Well, a foreclosure can be a godsend for you, because you can save some of your hard-earned money.

If you're not yet at the investor level, chances are you're watching your budget carefully and don't have a lot of cash just lying around. So it's important to get the very best deal on a house as possible. If you have a specific neighborhood in mind, you've probably already checked out the price range and market values of homes in that area. You know what you must be willing to spend if you have your heart set on moving to that area. Getting a foreclosure that's even 10 percent less than that price level is like a little gift. Finding an even bigger bargain may allow you to get a bigger home, or use some of the savings on home improvements or other indulgences.

Or perhaps you've been wistfully driving by homes in your dream neighborhood, wishing you could afford a home there. By patiently watching and researching foreclosures in that neighborhood, you just may be able to buy that dream home you thought you'd never be able to afford.

Investments

In contrast, many people who buy (or consider buying) foreclosures are seeking investment properties. In other words, these are properties that the investor will either resell at some point for a profit or keep and fill with tenants who will provide rental income.

A smart investor will be able to see into the future, in a way, by spotting towns and neighborhoods on

Promissory Note

Foreclosures can be great investment properties. Often they have fallen into recent disrepair or neglect, but in many cases some relatively easy and inexpensive cosmetic repairs may greatly increase the home's "curb appeal" and market value.

the verge of becoming in-demand hotspots. By snapping up a foreclosure in this soon-to-be hot area, you will often see a huge profit when you sell the property after the area has seen growth and improvement. This frequently occurs in urban or suburban areas going through redevelopment or rehabilitation.

Rental Income

People who buy numerous foreclosures are often seeking properties they can rent. Rental properties can be a great source of steady monthly income. However, it's not something you should rush into without careful thought and planning. Being a *landlord* isn't for everyone, especially the faint of heart. At any given time, you need to be a handyman, collections officer, bookkeeper, rule-enforcement agent, and any number of other things. For lots of helpful tips and advice on this topic, consult *The Complete Idiot's Guide to Being a Smart Landlord*.

> **Land Lingo**
>
> A **landlord** is a person or company that owns property that is rented out to tenants.

Being a landlord is almost like having a child who may require your immediate attention at any time of the day or night. Be prepared to get a call at 2 A.M. when the furnace dies, or to chase elusive tenants who are two weeks late with their rent. However, if you are up to the challenge, rental property can be very profitable. It helps if you have home-repair skills or know a trustworthy contractor/repairman who works for a reasonable rate.

Again, it helps if you have that ability to see the future a bit, and can spot neighborhoods on the cusp of exploding. Buying a few buildings at bargain foreclosure rates in that neighborhood may bring you a small monthly windfall in the near future when neighborhood rents skyrocket.

> **Promissory Note**
>
> If you own or are buying numerous rental properties, it may be worthwhile to hire a property manager or management service to oversee the daily maintenance and any tenant issues.

If you plan to rent out the property, it's important to do some research and number crunching beforehand to determine whether this will be a profitable investment. To do this, you need to try to find out the rent range for comparable properties in that area. You can do this informally by checking the classified ads for rental properties, noting the rents mentioned. You can also check with local realtors to determine whether any rent surveys have been compiled recently.

Analyze all income/expenses for the building for the previous year, watching for any areas where you can cut costs or raise income. Would a few minor weatherproofing improvements cut down on your heating costs? Perhaps you can get a discount on the insurance rates by adding a security system or fire alarms. This takes some extra work, but it can save you big bucks—and may make the difference between a so-so deal and one that could be pretty profitable.

Other Benefits to Investors

Foreclosed and distressed properties offer many other attractive benefits, from an investor's point of view. We'll discuss a few of them here.

Lower Purchase Price

As already mentioned, perhaps the biggest lure of buying foreclosures is the opportunity to save money—possibly lots of money—when you obtain a home for lower than its market value. If you were already planning to buy a comparable home anyway, getting this big discount can be like finding a huge windfall.

Lower Down Payments

A lower purchase price means a lower required down payment. Assume you needed a 10 percent down payment for your new $150,000 home. That means you have to come up with $15,000. However, if you can snatch up that home for only $112,500, you only need to come up with an $11,250 down payment—meaning you've saved $3,750 in out-of-pocket, upfront costs right off the bat.

Motivated Sellers

One of the biggest advantages of buying a foreclosure home is that the owner is generally very motivated to sell. Even if they are very unhappy about losing the property, they will generally be eager to resolve the situation as quickly and painlessly as possible. Basically, they often just want to "make it go away."

Motivated Lenders

Lenders are in the business of making interest on loans, not touting the praises of a three-bedroom bilevel with an inground pool. In other words, they aren't in the realty business and don't want to be. They handle properties very reluctantly, and are often eager to unload a property quickly. As a result, they may be very agreeable to sweetening the deal by offering a lower interest rate or better financing terms than they would generally in a typical mortgage deal.

Helping the Homeowner

Buying foreclosures is one of those situations where one person's loss is another person's gain. Obviously, the owner of the property is experiencing a hardship or misfortune that led to the default on the loan.

You may feel guilty about buying this person's property at all—rather than feeling the thrill of getting it for a bargain price.

We may be able to put your mind at ease by pointing out that many times you'll be doing the homeowner a favor. Especially if you buy the home before an auction, you can often help the homeowner make the best of a bad situation—by saving his credit rating from the black mark of a foreclosure. Or you may be providing him with some much-needed cash to find a new house or pay other bills he may be facing.

While each situation is different, in some cases you'll be giving the soon-to-be ex-homeowner cash in hand—usually a relatively small amount, and often just to sweeten the deal and as an incentive to vacate the property quickly and leave it in good condition.

You also may be making the neighbors happy, especially if you fix up a home in need of repairs, thereby making the whole neighborhood look better, which contributes to a rise in overall market values in the neighborhood.

Promissory Note _____

What you can offer homeowners in foreclosure:

◆ A way to at least somewhat salvage their credit, by preventing a completed foreclosure, which is a big strike against them

◆ Possibly some cash in hand, which they can use toward another home or other expenses

◆ A quick end to a stressful and embarrassing situation

Lastly, if you rescue the property—and pay off the loan, or at least bring it to good standing—you'll also likely make the lender very happy.

Bottom line: In the ideal foreclosure transaction, everyone benefits, and you get yourself a great bargain in the process.

Favorable Financing

We've already mentioned the possibility of finding a motivated lender built in with your foreclosure situation. You may actually discover several favorable financing options related to foreclosures. If you buy an REO property, for example, the title-holding lender is eager to get rid of the property, and would therefore probably be more flexible with interest rates and other lending terms. Buying a home owned by HUD or another government agency may also make you eligible for some of their financing programs. In some cases, you can assume the current/previous loan or financing, which would translate to considerable savings in closing costs and other fees.

The Least You Need to Know

- ◆ Distressed doesn't always mean dilapidated.
- ◆ Foreclosures can often sell for 20 percent to 40 percent below market value, but sometimes you can find even bigger bargains.
- ◆ In a foreclosure situation, the seller and lender are frequently much more motivated than in normal sales.

Chapter 6

Pitfalls and Disadvantages

In This Chapter

- ◆ The types of involuntary liens
- ◆ Why cloudy titles are cause for concern
- ◆ Eviction, postponement, and other hassles

Foreclosures can offer many benefits and advantages for a smart buyer, but they can also present some problems and pitfalls they you need to watch out for. In this chapter, we'll describe some of the most common problems and pitfalls associated with foreclosure investing and tell you how to avoid them.

Involuntary Liens

It's extremely important to know whether the property has any *liens* or judgments against it and—if so—the type and amount. Many uneducated novices have their initial euphoria at getting a "steal" at auction interrupted by the rude awakening of huge liens attached to the property. In some cases, these investors may end up actually taking a loss on the property.

As the name implies, an involuntary lien is one placed against the property without the owner's consent. (In contrast, a voluntary lien is one that happens with a mortgage, when the owner willingly allows a lien to be enacted.) This is perhaps the biggest pitfall you need to watch out for. The down-and-out homeowner may not even be aware of which—if any—liens currently exist against the property. Even if they know about the liens, they may not willingly reveal that information to you.

Land Lingo _____

A **lien** is a legal financial claim against a property that must be paid off when the property is sold.

The following sections discuss several common types of involuntary liens, including:

◆ Judgments

◆ Second Liens

◆ Mechanic's Liens

Judgments

If a creditor or other party successfully won a court judgment against the homeowner, they may place a lien against the property as a way to recoup money owed to them.

Second Liens

Second liens—also known as junior liens—are basically any additional liens that have been filed against the property after the initial mortgage. They're called second liens because they take a backseat to the primary lien, which is usually held by the mortgage lender. In the court's eyes, the primary lien holder has first "dibs" on the property and gets to claim proceeds from a foreclosure sale.

Watch Out! _____

To protect against liens, judgments, and other unpleasant surprises, be sure to have a thorough title search performed on the property before making an offer or submitting a bid.

Common types of second liens are second mortgages and home equity loans. A second mortgage—as the name implies—is a secondary loan secured by property that already has a primary mortgage loan against it. A home-equity loan is based on the equity a homeowner has in their property. A home-equity loan is often in the form of a line of credit, where a borrower is approved for up to a certain amount, and only pays interest on whatever amount he actually uses. The two terms are sometimes used interchangeably.

Mechanic's Liens

If a contractor, repairman, or other professional performed work on the property and didn't get paid, they can file a mechanic's lien against the homeowner. This is recorded with the county recorder's office by the unpaid contractor, subcontractor, or supplier.

> **Promissory Note** _____
>
> Second liens and judgments are mainly of concern if you're buying in the pre-foreclosure stage, because at this point you basically assume all the debts/obligations related to the property from its current owner. If a property is auctioned to satisfy the primary lien, all other liens and claims are usually wiped out, although you should confirm that, just to make sure.

Cloud on the Title

If the property has a lien, judgment, or other negative problem against it, it is said to have a *cloud* on the title. There are several common causes of cloudy titles.

> **Land Lingo** _____
>
> A **cloud** is any condition revealed by a title search that negatively affects the property's value or salability.

Liens and Judgments

As already discussed, creditors and contractors can place liens against the property for money owed.

Taxes

If the county or municipal taxes are delinquent on the property, the municipality may place a tax lien against the property, and could even try to sell the property at a tax sale.

Death

If the homeowner passes away and hasn't specified instructions regarding the property in a will or other legal document, heirs may have tried to claim the property. In this case, it's possible the home is embroiled in a legal battle.

Marriage/Divorce

If you've been dealing with one owner of the property, yet the title lists two names, you need to locate this second person and get that person to agree to any deals or transactions involving the property. Should the owner(s) be in the midst of a divorce, the soon-to-be ex-spouse may have filed a claim against the property. In some states, the spouse is entitled to half the value of the property, even if he or she doesn't file suit.

"As Is" Condition

One major foreclosure-related pitfall is the property's condition, which is often less than perfect. If the owner is upset or angry about losing the property, he may even deliberately trash the place before vacating it. Generally, foreclosure properties are almost always sold in "as is" condition, so it really is a case of buyer beware.

If you're buying directly from the owner, you should clearly specify the condition of the home in writing. It is important to spell out in the contract that the home must remain in its present condition until you take possession of it. When buying a home at auction, you may have limited access to the property and may not be able to get a good idea of its condition. If buying an REO property (property owned by a bank or other lender), ask for a walkthrough before making a formal offer. In this case, damage and disrepair can work to your advantage, because you can use it as leverage to negotiate the price down, assuming you're willing to do the repairs.

Additional Problems You Could Encounter

While liens and other title problems are often the most serious and costly foreclosure investment pitfalls, there are some other common problems you need to know about. In this section, we'll describe several more complications that could occur in these situations.

Cured Default

A defaulting homeowner generally has a fairly long period when he can bring his payments current and "cure" the default (usually right up until the foreclosure auction, and sometimes even longer). Although this is good news for the homeowner and lender, it can be very frustrating to you, the investor, who has spent time, energy, and possibly money in the hopes of purchasing this property.

Postponement of Sale

If the owner pays some of his past due money, or comes to some kind of payment arrangement that satisfies the lender, the foreclosure sale may be postponed, perhaps indefinitely. Again, this can be frustrating to the investor who is eagerly awaiting a chance to buy the property.

Financing

A big consideration when buying foreclosures is how you will pay for them. While you may be able to obtain a traditional loan or mortgage in some cases, that may not always be the case. Generally, you need at least some cash in hand to swing the deal. When buying foreclosures, sometimes you can't go the straightforward mortgage route that you would use when financing a home purchase. This could happen for several reasons. Perhaps the home's condition is such that a banker won't issue a loan for it. Or maybe you've had some credit problems in the past, or for some other reason would have problems getting approved for a loan. Or, in the case of buying a foreclosure at auction or sheriff's sale, you simply need to come up with money right away and don't have time to go through a loan approval process.

Bidding Frenzies

One of the biggest risks when buying foreclosures at a sale is the tendency to get carried away and bid more than you'd planned. As with any type of auction, the bidding can sometimes move at a pretty fast pace, with rising intensity. It's easy to get swept up in the momentum and bid more than you intended.

Getting Up to Speed

Any new endeavor requires research and preparation. This is especially important when it comes to buying foreclosures. Making one simple mistake can cost you. It's also easy for novice investors to miss out on

Watch Out!

Don't think your education stops after you've made your first deal. You must constantly keep abreast of various changes in the real estate market, local conditions in your area, foreclosure trends, etc.

great deals, or be taken advantage of by competitors or sellers. Co-author Todd generally recommends that aspiring investors plan to spend at least 10 hours a week for 5 weeks to do their initial "basic training." This means studying foreclosure books such as this one, doing research, seeking out trustworthy advisors, etc.

Evicting Homeowners

Even if you do successfully purchase the property, your problems may be far from over. The owner/occupant may not be too eager to leave the property. In this case, you may have to initiate the lengthy and sometimes costly process of evicting them from the home. During this period, there is also a pretty good chance the disgruntled owners may damage or "strip" the property.

Bankruptcy

Sometimes a defaulting homeowner may declare bankruptcy at some point during the foreclosure process. Although this doesn't necessarily stop the foreclosure completely, it will often delay the process for at least a month or two while court papers are filed and legal issues are sorted out. This is another example of a delay that may put a crimp in the plans of the eager investor.

Too Much Too Soon

Buying foreclosures can be exciting. There's an undeniable thrill you get from finding, pursuing, and (hopefully) acquiring that great "catch." The adrenaline rush can be addictive and tough to resist. It's important, especially for new investors who are still getting their feet wet, to learn to control your urge to buy every foreclosure you see. Don't fall in love with every home, or every deal. Yes, the thrill of the chase can be exciting, but many properties won't be right for you—for one reason or another—and it's vital to know when to walk away. Trying to buy too much too soon can leave you overwhelmed and stretched to your financial limit.

Making Yourself Legally Vulnerable

As with any business transaction, foreclosure investing has inherent risks. Emergencies can arise; things can go wrong. Unfortunately, we live in a time where people seem to be lawsuit-happy. Frivolous lawsuits are commonplace—even if you've done nothing wrong, someone can take you to court, putting you through a time-consuming and costly ordeal, even if you prevail in the end. You should take all possible precautions to protect yourself and your own personal assets in the event of a business loss. Otherwise, you may find that it's *your own* house that's in jeopardy.

> **Watch Out!**
>
> Don't leave your personal assets vulnerable in the event you might take a business loss or face a lawsuit. Many real estate experts recommend forming a LLC (limited liability corporation) or limited partnership. Anthony F. Cutaia, owner of Cutaia Realty Advisors LLC and CEO of Cutaia Mortgage Group Inc. of Florida, echoes this advice. "You should never take title to a foreclosure property in your own name," Cutaia warns. "The fact that you are not the owner individually insulates you from any liability, the LLC gives you the benefit of a corporate veil." This is actually good advice for any kind of investment or business dealings, according to experts. As always, though, you should consult your own attorney before making any kind of legal decisions.

Common Mistakes

Real estate experts and veteran investors often see novice investors making several common—and costly—mistakes. In the following sections, we'll describe some of these common slip-ups and hopefully help you avoid making them.

Do Your Research

Jackie Lange, president of Texas Home Solutions, Inc. and founder of SellYourHousein7Days.com, says many people dive into foreclosure investing without doing the proper research. "You really need to research the laws in your state. Plus, for each specific property, you need to do extensive research—mainly in the form of a thorough title search. Overlooking an IRS lien, for example—which can stay in place even after the property is sold at auction—can be a critical mistake."

Handing Over Money Too Soon

For a desperate homeowner, the money offered by an investor can be a lifesaver. Hand over the lifesaver too soon, though, and you may never get these people out of the pool. This money is your only insurance that the homeowners will follow through with the deal and vacate the house. Don't write any checks until the deal is official and the homeowners vacate the property.

Get the Real Scoop

Sure, a title search can give you vital information about a property, but sometimes you really need to go the extra mile to get the real scoop. Nelson Zide is senior vice president of ERA Key Realty Services in Framingham, Massachusetts, which has offices throughout central Massachusetts and MetroWest and is one of the top 10 ERA franchises in the country. "With an auction property, one of the biggest problems is evicting homeowners or tenants. Drive by the house at several different times of day to see if anyone's there. Also, try to spot any problems that may come with the property. For example, if you spot a recent addition to the home, but there's no record of recent building permits, that's a red flag. Whoever buys that house may be facing problems and/or fines from the local municipality."

Foreclosure Fact

Although plenty of investors are brave enough to buy homes in which homeowners or tenants are in no hurry to leave, Nelson Zide thinks that's asking for trouble. "I don't think I'd touch a property if someone was living there." In fact, Zide once offered some advice to an acquaintance who was in foreclosure and about to lose his home in an auction. "I told him, 'The morning of the auction, make sure your curtains are open, and all your kids are waving. Borrow a few extra kids if you have to.' Sure enough, everyone saw all these kids and nobody bid. They didn't want to be the ones to have to throw that family out."

Being Overly Optimistic About the Resale Value

Zide sees many new investors miscalculate the profit potential in their first few deals. He says, "You need to be totally realistic and practical about exactly how much you can expect to sell the property for, especially if there are negative factors such as damage or a bad neighborhood."

Getting Too Emotionally Involved

It's important to be understanding and sympathetic to the problems of homeowners in crisis, but be careful not to take that emotional connection too far. You won't be able to help every homeowner, and you need to stay objective enough to realize which situations simply won't be financially profitable for you.

Overlooking Closing Costs and Other Fees

When it comes to buying property, there's more to the bottom line than just your buying price. Lawyer fees, taxes, and other closing costs can cause the total figure to skyrocket. Transfer tax, for example, can run as high as 2 percent or 3 percent of the sale price. "You definitely need to find out if there's a transfer tax and, if so, how much," says Jackie Lange of Texas Home Solutions, Inc. "Make sure you figure out all the closing costs and other fees upfront, so you can include those number in your calculations."

The Least You Need to Know

- ◆ Be sure to fully investigate titles of foreclosure properties. You'll often find liens, judgments, and other unpleasant surprises.

- ◆ Ask your attorney about the possibility of forming an LLC or limited partnership to protect your personal assets.

- ◆ Be prepared for last-minute cancellations or postponements of foreclosure sales.

- ◆ Learn self-control. It's neither smart nor practical to buy every foreclosure property you find.

Important Pre-Purchase Issues

In This Chapter

- ◆ Some foreclosure buying basics
- ◆ Titles, realtors, and other pre-purchase issues
- ◆ Figuring out your financing
- ◆ Identifying your target area

You may be chomping at the bit to dive right in and pursue your first foreclosure deal, but you need to consider some important things before you take that first step. Preparation and education are vital to becoming a successful investor, so don't underestimate the importance of this advance legwork. In this chapter, we'll cover the important things you need to consider before making your first purchase—things like whether you need a real estate agent, and how to make sure the property has a clear title. Armed with this information, you may be able to avoid some of the most common—and costly—mistakes made by new investors.

Introduction to Buying

The biggest lure of buying foreclosures is the possibility of a great deal. As any savvy shopper knows, if you're getting a discount, there's usually a reason why. Be prepared for just about anything when it comes to the property's history and condition, and the owner's individual situation.

Because each situation will be different, you should be flexible and creative enough to come up with the perfect arrangement that will suit everyone involved. However, try to stick as closely as possible to the guidelines we explain in the following chapters. This is especially important when you first get your foreclosure-buying feet wet, as you want to keep your risk taking to a minimum until you become more experienced.

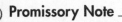

Promissory Note

We suggest reading this book—or at least several chapters—repeatedly until you can actually picture yourself doing the tasks described. Envision yourself working with homeowners and lenders, going to the courthouse to search records, participating in an auction, and doing all of the other steps involved in buying foreclosures. After you've become comfortable with the terminology and techniques involved, you will be much more relaxed—and therefore much more efficient.

The Three Basic Methods

Each of the three phases of the foreclosure process provides unique opportunities for investors:

♦ The early pre-foreclosure phase allows you to buy directly from the homeowner, without having to bid against other investors at an auction.

♦ The sale phase involves bidding at auction, but eliminates the task of negotiating with the homeowner.

♦ The post-auction REO phase involves working with lenders (or realtors on their behalf) who may be eager enough to unload the property that they'll give you a great deal.

Each phase has good points and bad points. Your individual needs, goals, and personal style will probably dictate which phase you prefer. In the chapters that follow, we explain and discuss each phase in great detail, which may help you decide what part of the foreclosure process would be most desirable for you.

How Much Will I Have to Pay?

Lots of books and infomercials claim to have tricks for buying foreclosures and other real estate for no money down. Some of these methods do actually work, but most of them are not something for the novice investor to try. It's much better to get a few more simple foreclosure deals under your belt before you try tackling these advanced techniques.

You'll probably have the best chance of success with little initial cash in hand if you're negotiating directly with the homeowner for a pre-foreclosure. Depending on the homeowner's needs and situation, he might not be expecting much money. Often these homeowners simply want to be rid of the financial burden the house has become, and just want the foreclosure—and its accompanying stress—to go away.

With auctions, you need to have at least a portion of the sale price with you at the sale. The exact amount required will be specified in the auction announcement. Generally, buyers are required to have a specified deposit amount, with the remaining balance due within a few weeks.

When buying an REO property, you will probably need to obtain financing. However, the lender holding the property may be so eager to get rid of it that they'll offer you very attractive terms—perhaps even accepting little or no deposit, especially if you have good credit and a steady income.

> **Foreclosure Fact**
>
> Don't be discouraged if you want to buy foreclosures but fear you don't have the cash to swing the deal. The amount of money you will need will depend on the type of foreclosure property (pre-foreclosure, auction, REO, government property, etc.) and can vary greatly even within those categories.

> **Promissory Note**
>
> Generally, at least for your first few deals, you should have access to at least a couple of thousand dollars—be it cash, credit, pre-approved financing, equity in your own home, and so on.

Do I Need a Real Estate Agent?

Whether you decide to enlist the help of a real estate agent is up to you. It can be useful to have a real estate broker in your corner, especially when you first start out. They can provide valuable insight and advice as to the local market, property values, etc.

Even if you don't use a broker of your own, chances are good you'll have to deal with one at some point. Many REO and government-owned properties are sold by real estate agents.

Clear Titles

It's vitally important—before you even think about buying a foreclosure—that you really learn as much as possible about title-related issues. Even better, you should find a local lawyer or title search expert who is very familiar with these issues and who can handle title-related matters and questions for you. Trust us, this person will be worth his weight in gold to you. Imagine if he saves you from buying that pre-foreclosure that—oops!—has a $75,000 lien that the owners "forgot" to mention. You definitely will consider this person to be one of your best friends in the foreclosure world.

Perhaps the biggest foreclosure-buying pitfall is the possibility of inadvertently buying a property with a "bad" title. Rather than getting a nice new home, buyers may find that they've actually just gotten a heap of new debts and financial obligations that may cost them more than the home is even worth.

CAUTION

Watch Out! _____

Because many people are involved with the processing/recording of real estate transactions—and people do occasionally make mistakes—you should always have a "checks and balances" system to spot any errors that might fall through the cracks. Cross-reference the homeowner's information with that from the attorney; double-check the lender's file against courthouse records, and so on. It also helps to chat with the neighbors. A gossipy neighbor often knows the "inside scoop" that you may not discover anywhere else. You'd be amazed at what you can find out by simply getting out of your car and approaching neighbors in a friendly, casual-yet-curious tone. For example, if it's an abandoned property, they may be able to tell you where the owner went.

Financing

We discuss financing in greater detail in Chapter 13, but we did want to cover it briefly here because this is one of the major pre-purchase points you need to consider. There are many sources to help you come up with the money you need to buy a foreclosure.

Traditional Lenders

The most obvious source of financing is a traditional lender, such as your neighborhood bank. If you have good credit and a steady income, you can generally get money from a bank fairly easily. The lender holding the defaulting mortgage will probably be especially happy to see you. Standing there looking like a solid citizen who pays bills on time can really help expedite the process, especially with smaller lenders.

If you already own a property and can get a mortgage or home-equity loan on that home, it might be your best bet. If you're like most investors, you plan to resell the foreclosure fairly quickly—hopefully at a nice profit—so you'll be able to pay off this loan in the near future. After you've successfully completed a few profitable real estate deals, you may find that banks are much more willing to offer you financing for subsequent deals.

Partners

Partnerships are like marriages. Some have a happy ending, whereas others go down in flames. In a good partnership arrangement, one person typically finds, researches, and prepares to buy the property. The other one is the money partner—the person who has available cash, but doesn't want to do all the legwork. If you can find yourself a good money partner, your investment future can instantly become much brighter and easier.

For your first few deals, you might try enlisting several partners, thus limiting the risk and investment required by each. If you need $20,000 to purchase a property that would return another $20,000 (a 100 percent profit) in 120 days, it would probably be much easier to find three other people who are each willing to match your investment of $5,000. Everyone involved would take a risk, but a much lower risk. Likewise, everyone would profit—by one fourth the dollar amount, but still at a 100 percent profit of their investment.

Lines of Credit

One of the most popular ways to come up with financing is to open a line of credit, usually at your regular bank or another lending institution. Although you still need decent credit and sufficient income (the exact criteria varies by lender), a line of credit offers many advantages as opposed to a "regular" loan. For one thing, you can usually get as little or as much money as you want at any given time, up to your pre-approved limit, quickly and easily and without explaining exactly what you'll be using the money for each time. Also you only incur fees when and if you actually get money from the lender. If you open a credit line and never actually need to access any money, it hasn't cost you anything.

The Team Concept

The buying and selling of real estate—foreclosures or otherwise—can be a pretty complicated process, often involving many different parties (each with their own agendas). So it makes perfect sense for you to get to know some of these people. Lenders, lawyers, title companies, real estate brokers, court clerks, and others are all connected and intertwined in this business. Not only should you get to know these people, but you should also realize how much you can benefit from enlisting their help. Why not recruit some of these people to be on your team?

A wise investor or aspiring investor will assemble a team of industry professionals to serve as aides and advisors. In exchange for their help, you will provide them with as much business as possible, and perhaps help connect them with others in your networking circle who might need their services.

Watch Out!

Pick the people on your team carefully. Not all people affiliated with the real estate industry are interested in—or supportive of—the idea of investing in foreclosures. Make sure your chosen team members have a positive attitude about foreclosures. Also be sure they have the knowledge and skills necessary to assist you.

You will often need to research courthouse records. If you can makes friends with the court clerk, this task will become much easier. You'll also often need to do title searches. Having people on your team who can handle this quickly and inexpensively will be a huge help.

You may also—especially if you'll be a landlord—need a handyman. Try to include a qualified trustworthy contractor among your circle of helpers.

A good real estate lawyer is an absolute necessity. Laws are complicated and constantly changing, so it's vital to have an advisor who can keep up with all the real estate legalities.

It's also very helpful to enlist the help of a real estate broker. They can help you sell any foreclosure properties you don't want to keep. In exchange for the business you throw their way, they can give you valuable insight about the local market and neighborhood comparison values.

Seller's Motivation

A great team of helpers is a wonderful asset, but the bottom line is that one person holds the key to your successful foreclosure-buying future: the seller.

The seller—be it a lender or homeowner—is motivated to fix a bad situation. In the case of a homeowner, they want to avoid (or at least minimize) financial ruin, embarrassment, a bad credit rating, and other foreclosure-related headaches. The lender wants to remove this nonperforming loan from their books.

Either way, the seller is motivated, which is crucial. This motivation is what creates lots of different and potentially profitable opportunities for investors. The more motivated the seller is, the better your chances for bigger profits, less upfront expenses and fewer delays in obtaining the property.

A homeowner who just received a default notice may still be in denial, or may think he has all the time in the world to straighten things out. On the other hand, a stressed-out homeowner who has been worrying about this for months and is days away from losing his home on the auction block is likely to be very motivated to hear any solutions you can offer.

Similarly, the longer a lender has had this distressed property on their books, the more eager they will be to make a deal.

Every foreclosure has a story. With some detective work and good people skills, you can often learn the story behind the foreclosure. This will give you precious insight as to the seller's motivation.

Researching Properties

We believe most good foreclosure investors have a strong investigative gene. Research is vital in this business. We've already explained the importance of checking the title, but there are lots of other investigative tasks involved with foreclosures.

First of all, you often need good research skills just to find the properties. Unlike normal properties for sale, you generally won't find foreclosures in your local classified section. In the case of pre-foreclosures, you need to really be able to sniff out an opportunity early in the process, before other investors have caught the scent.

Then there are those tiny but important details that the paperwork won't tell you— but chatty neighbors will. Perhaps the property has been a neighborhood eyesore for so long that your new neighbors would willingly pitch in to help you clean up the place, just to make the whole street look better. Or maybe the vacant property was recently vandalized—nothing major, but enough to provide leverage in getting the seller to lower the price. Especially in cases where you can't inspect the property personally, neighbors can provide valuable nuggets of important information.

If you did a title search on every foreclosure property that caught your eye, it could get pretty expensive. Doing some basic detective work beforehand can help you weed out properties that would be too much hassle or aren't worth your time.

> **Promissory Note**
>
> A full title search may cost you about $150, and perhaps much more. You might prefer to start off with an Ownership & Encumbrances Report, also known as a Pencil or Simple Search. This will reveal any ownership problems or issues related to the property. It shouldn't be used in place of a full title search, as an O&E report won't disclose important tax or municipal information. Still, at less than $100, an O&E report can uncover some major problems that would serve as huge red flags warning you to stay far away from this property.

Identify Your Target Area

Even the most experienced real estate investor can't keep up with market changes and relevant legal developments in every part of the country—or even every part of their state, for that matter.

Instead, savvy investors zero in on one particular region, and then carefully study every important issue related to real estate and foreclosures in that area.

> **Watch Out!**
>
> When researching your potential target area, don't get too excited or discouraged by things you hear. The person who warns you the area is declining could just be another investor trying to scare you off, or simply someone with no real estate knowledge. Instead of relying on hearsay, ask questions and do your homework. Then—after getting the opinions of a few trustworthy, objective advisors—judge for yourself.

Now that you've studied as much as possible about foreclosures in general (we, ahem, assume you followed our advice from earlier in this chapter), it should be easier for you to determine what regions in your area might fit your particular needs. For example, if you want to buy and sell properties for quick profits, you want a target area with mass appeal, where properties are likely to sell quickly. On the other hand, if you plan to hold on to a property for a while as a future investment, look for areas that show promise for strong and steady growth.

After you've selected your target area, it's your mission to become an expert on that area and its real estate market. Study the classifieds and local real estate publications. Visit area attractions and businesses, taking note of the advantages and disadvantages of obtaining properties close to those locations. Keep abreast of any news or changes that might affect the local real estate market—a planned highway exit nearby, for example, or a large corporation relocating to the area (meaning, employees who'll be seeking new homes).

Promissory Note

These days, thanks to the Internet, it's easy to find out just about anything you'd want to know about a specific community. Most Chambers of Commerce are online, and the town itself may even have its own website. Most likely, a quick search will turn up many real estate sites for that area. You should also be able to get lots of information about the local schools, attractions, and other important details.

Familiar Territory

We already explained the importance of selecting a target area. Many new or aspiring foreclosure investors pick an obvious target area—their own community.

This makes sense, especially if you plan to occupy your foreclosure purchase, or want to buy rental property that you intend to personally oversee.

There are many advantages to shopping for foreclosures in your own backyard. You're probably already at least somewhat familiar with the local housing and real estate scene. You may also have friends or neighbors who work in the industry and can serve as valuable advisors for you.

Even if you're not really familiar with the local market and don't have any industry connections, it's much easier to research and become familiar with your local market. You can start simply by reading your local paper, paying careful attention to the real estate section. Also keep an eye on legal notices that can inform you of upcoming foreclosure auctions.

Land Lingo

Demographic information gives a profile or picture of what the area looks like in terms of population characteristics.

A Distant Area

If you're targeting a distant area, subscribe to the local paper and have it mailed to you. Call the Chamber of Commerce and request any available publications or information about the area. You're especially interested in any kind of *demographic information* on your target locale.

The Least You Need to Know

◆ It's important to learn as much as possible about the foreclosure-buying process before you even consider seeking your first deal.

◆ Good research and detective skills are priceless to an aspiring foreclosure investor.

◆ Select a target area, and then learn everything you possibly can about that area.

◆ Financing is usually a would-be investor's biggest concern, but there are many options available to help with that aspect of the deal.

◆ Good research skills can turn an okay investor into a real estate success story.

◆ A team of trustworthy and qualified advisors can be a priceless asset to an aspiring investor.

Part 3

Making Your
Foreclosure Purchase

Now that you are ready to begin investing in foreclosures, where do you start? These chapters guide you through the process. We tell you how to find properties in foreclosure before everyone else knows about them. We also explain the three methods for buying foreclosed properties, detailing the pros and cons of each.

We walk you through the process—from finding elusive homeowners to finding the money to pay for the property. We also tell you how to find out about great deals on government property.

Chapter 8

Finding Foreclosed Properties

In This Chapter

- ◆ Why the special assets officer is important
- ◆ Get comfortable in the courthouse
- ◆ Watch out for reporting service rip-offs

As mentioned previously, the foreclosure process involves three basic phases: the default (pre-foreclosure) phase, the sale or auction phase, and the REO (bank-owned) phase. In other words: before, during, and after the auction. Your method of locating properties will vary depending on which phase(s) of foreclosure you target. In general, though, you can find lots of info on foreclosures at the local courthouse and in the newspaper classified sections. The staff of local lenders and mortgage companies can also be a big help. We'll discuss these and other ways to find foreclosures in this chapter.

Traditional Lenders

Many new foreclosure investors focus on buying REO properties. This is often seen as the safest route, as well as one of the easiest for an inexperienced investor. When seeking these types of properties, you start by contacting lending institutions.

Banks

Where would you seek bank-owned properties? Why, at the bank, of course. You can start by simply calling your local banks. Odds are in your favor that they have some REO properties in their possession.

Many banks have an REO officer or special assets officer. Larger banks may have an entire division or department that handles foreclosed properties. This department goes by various names—asset liquidation, REO management, or some other variation. These are the people you need to contact for information on REO properties.

> **Foreclosure Fact**
>
> Sometimes, especially with larger banks, you may be able to get information about their REO policies or available properties by searching their website.

Call this person or department and explain that you're interested in learning about available REO properties. Don't be discouraged if you're told there are no available properties in your target area. Ask to be added to their mailing list so you can be notified when properties do become available. Meanwhile, if you reach a friendly bank employee, he may be willing to chat with you for a few minutes, filling you in on the way the bank handles REOs, financing options, etc.

Mortgage Companies

You should also contact mortgage companies. Basically, these companies are lenders that focus exclusively on lending money for home purchases. Check the phone book to locate mortgage companies and related finance companies in your area.

There is additional information on several of the largest mortgage companies in Appendix B.

Insurance Companies

Occasionally, insurance companies have REO properties in their inventory. Your best bet is to call the national or regional headquarters of large insurance companies. They're more likely to have information on these properties than a local agent.

Credit Unions

Like other lenders, credit unions also sometimes must foreclose on properties. Try calling your local credit union for information. They may direct you to the appropriate person or department at the company's headquarters.

Asset Management Groups

Sometimes banks or mortgage companies enlist the help of asset management companies to handle their foreclosed properties. As the name implies, these are companies that specialize in the management and sale of assets such as residential property. A quick online search turns up many websites for large asset management groups. Send them a quick e-mail requesting information on any properties they may have available in your target area.

Real Estate Agents

There are many reasons to work with a real estate agent in your search for good foreclosure deals. For one thing, helping people buy and sell property is their area of expertise. Also real estate agents have valuable information and insight regarding the local housing market.

Ideally, you'll find some real estate agents with foreclosure-related experience and expertise. On the other hand, you may encounter some agents who dislike the whole concept of people, especially "everyday people" like us, investing in foreclosures.

Every area usually has a few brokers who handle the bulk of the government foreclosures in that community. You should be able to locate these brokers pretty easily by asking around in the local realty community.

When contacting real estate agents, make it clear right off the bat that you're specifically interested in foreclosures. It should become immediately obvious if the agent has a negative attitude toward foreclosure investing. If so, politely move on. However, if you get a favorable response, you're off to a good start. This person may prove to be a valuable asset to you.

> **Promissory Note**
>
> Many banks and mortgage companies enlist the help of real estate agents to handle all of their REO properties. When speaking with bank employees, be sure to ask about any real estate agents the lender uses. Should you find a promising property from that agent, there's a good chance the lender would offer you some attractive financing terms.

Good real estate agents are professionals. They adhere to certain codes of ethics regarding real estate transactions and general conduct. However, they're also salespeople who rely on sales commissions for income. Therefore, even the most honest and ethical agent may find it difficult to be totally objective when giving you a sales pitch about an available foreclosed property. Always be firm (but polite) and don't let yourself be talked into any property you don't want to buy.

Newspapers

Newspapers can be a wealth of information on local foreclosures. Foreclosed properties may be advertised by the banks, real estate agents, or a homeowner in default. You can also find legal notices announcing upcoming foreclosure sales in the paper. These may be posted by the local municipality or a federal agency such as the IRS or HUD.

Sample Lender Ad

Here's an example of a typical foreclosure ad from a lender:

> BANK FORECLOSURE LIST
>
> Residential and Commercial Foreclosure List Available
>
> Properties Available in NY, NJ, and PA
>
> Call 1-800-000-0000
>
> ABC Bank & Trust
>
> Special Assets Division
>
> 123 Main Street
>
> Anytown, NY 10000
>
> Equal Housing Lender
>
> Member FDIC

Other Newspaper Tips

Obviously, the real estate section can be a valuable tool to an investor. However, don't just scan the paper for the word "foreclosure." As mentioned previously, you should also study the local real estate market in general. Pay attention to the prices of non-foreclosure properties in your target area. This will help you spot a good bargain when researching foreclosure listings.

VA and FHA foreclosure sale ads often run on a regular schedule. Calling the classified manager at the paper and asking for the schedule can help you organize your search.

Legal Notices

Legal notices can be found in most large daily newspapers. The names or headings of these notices vary, depending upon the type of notice and local lingo.

State laws vary as to the publication requirements for foreclosure sales. Generally, though, the notice must appear in a general circulation newspaper, or the local paper with the largest circulation.

A legal notice announcing a foreclosure will look something like this:

LEGAL NOTICE

Foreclosure Sale

Notice of Judicial Sale by the Court

In the Circuit Court of the First District of Smith County, California, under jurisdiction of Civil Action No 11-222:

Acme Mortgage Company (Plaintiff/Petitioner)

vs.

John and Mary Brown (Defendants/Respondents)

Notice if hereby given that pursuant to an Order of Final Judgment now pending in said court, I will sell to the highest bidder at Smith County Courthouse on January 1 at 11 a.m. the following property:

Lot 15, of Breezy Acres Development, as described in Book 5, Page 20 of the Public Records of Smith County.

By: Martha Jones, County Clerk

Public Records

If you want to be a foreclosure investor, you've got to become comfortable researching and deciphering public records and other official documents. That's an absolute must, and there's no getting around it. You will be dealing with lots of public records, and the more comfortable you become with these materials, the more efficient and successful you will be.

County Courthouse

In our opinion, the best source for foreclosure information is the county courthouse. Real estate transactions are recorded in the county in which the property is located. This information is public record, meaning "regular people" can simply go and look at it. However, courthouses, unfortunately, are not all connected in one big network—meaning, you can't go to a courthouse in California and search for records on a property in New York City.

Watch Out!

Many courthouse offices charge if you make copies. Be sure to ask about this in advance. Legal documents are notoriously long-winded, so copying fees for a huge stack of records can quickly add up.

Most county courthouses are big imposing buildings filled with lots of official departments and offices. The first trip to the courthouse can be intimidating to the nervous visitor. Make the process easier by getting some information in advance. Call and ask which office or department handles real estate transactions. Generally, it's the county clerk or county recorder's office. Call this department and get some basic information such as where in the courthouse they're located, what hours they're open to the public, etc.

Courthouse records are treasure troves of valuable information for foreclosure investors. What exactly are you looking for? That depends on what phase of foreclosure you're dealing with, and the state in which you're located. In trust deed states, for example, you'll look for Notices of Default. In states that use the mortgage system, look for a *Lis Pendens*.

Promissory Note

The county clerk (or whatever staff member is in charge of foreclosure records in your county) can be one of your best allies and can prove to be a priceless resource in your search for records and information. Smart investors treat this person as the treasured resource he or she is. You'd be wise to befriend this individual. We're not advocating "kissing up" in a phony way, and we're not saying you need to ply the clerk with expensive gifts. However, chances are good that this person is overworked and stressed out, and a little kindness can go a long way.

Another tip: Title companies hire freelance searchers, who will often also work for individuals. These people really know their way around the records and, although you'll have to pay them, they can save you a world of grief.

Other Public Records

Other public records of interest can be found at the tax collector's office. People who are seriously behind on their property taxes are often also in default on their home loan. In addition, keep an eye out for notices (either in the newspaper or at the courthouse) of current lawsuits. You may spot information on a legal battle involving a home in foreclosure.

Regional Real Estate Publications

In addition to the daily newspaper, you might have a local daily or weekly real estate publication that specializes in reporting Notices of Default, upcoming foreclosure sales, etc. These publications can be valuable resources, as they cater specifically to real estate investors, bankers, etc.

Foreclosure Fact

Many real estate publications have begun offering extra services geared toward foreclosure investors. For example, some provide special areas of their website where subscribers can access up-to-the-minute foreclosure listing updates. Others provide a mailing label service, providing ready made address labels of delinquent borrowers, lenders, and attorneys.

Don't skip over the ads in these publications. They can provide valuable leads on important people in the local real estate scene, and businesses you should add to your contact list.

Promissory Note _____

Two of the largest publishers of real estate publications are *Homes & Land* and *The Real Estate Book*. Both of these publishers offer full-color monthly magazines covering more than 400 regions of the country. For a free copy of *Homes & Land*, call 1-800-277-7800. For a free copy of *The Real Estate Book*, call 1-800-841-3401.

Using the Internet

Seems like you can do anything faster and easier via the Internet these days, and foreclosure investing is no exception. In fact, you'll find a goldmine of information and resources on the Internet related to buying foreclosures.

Public Records Online

These days, you can find and view many public records online. Some courthouses and other public offices provided (often limited) access to their records through their website. Try using a search engine such as Google.com to find the website for your county courthouse.

> **Promissory Note**
>
> When searching for information online, don't limit yourself to just seeking Notices of Default or foreclosure-specific records. Also keep an eye out for estate announcements, bankruptcy notices, etc. These can all provide clues leading you to properties that may be up for grabs.

However, many courthouses still haven't gotten to that point. In that case, you may need to use the services of a company specializing in allowing online access to court records and other official documents. Although you'll pay for these services, it may be worth it—especially if you're researching properties that aren't in your county. The fee for this online service may be much cheaper than the cost involved in traveling to the courthouse in person.

We've used KnowX.com and SearchSystems.net, and provide information on these and other sites in Appendix B.

Foreclosure Listing Services

You can find some of the best—and most current—foreclosure information via a foreclosure listing service. Some reporting services were created by people originally offering courthouse research for lawyers and title companies. Noticing the growing interest in foreclosures among the general public, these people wisely capitalized on their talents and expanded their target audience to include consumers.

> **Watch Out!**
>
> The quality, type, price, and timeliness of the information offered by listing services can vary greatly. Some top-notch organizations understand the needs and goals of foreclosure investors and strive to deliver timely, accurate information that meets these needs. On the other hand, lots of outfits publish foreclosure directories after a minimum amount of research, with skimpy or inaccurate details, outdated listings, often accompanied by hard-sell pitches for overpriced additional services.

The type of listing service you need depends on your personal method of foreclosure investing. If you like pursuing pre-foreclosures, you want daily updates on loans going into default, which are complaints recently filed, signaling the foreclosure process has just begun. If you're a fan of buying properties at auction, you need a service that provides an accurate listing of sheriff sales and foreclosure auctions.

Listings on REOs are probably the most prevalent—and the most widely abused—type of reporting service. Some publishers claim to work with thousands of banks nationwide. This is a fairytale. There is no national network of bank REO departments. Some banks aren't even networked within their own branches. The downtown branch of Hometown Bank may not even be aware that their uptown branch recently acquired an REO property.

Therefore, the only way a reporting service could obtain a nationwide listing is directly from the banks. Meaning, they'd have to contact each and every bank—including each individual branch—and request a list of their REO properties. Do you really think the reporting service has the time or motivation to even attempt that feat? Not very likely.

Promissory Note

With the fast-paced nature of real estate transactions, subscribing to a monthly foreclosure listing publication is virtually useless. By the time you get the information, most of the best properties will have either been sold or will no longer be in default.

Reporting services are notorious for making exaggerated claims, or for telling flat-out lies. We recently visited the sites of several reporting services, each of which claimed to have "all" the current listings for a specific area. Yet one had about 200 listings, another had about 750, and the third had more than a 1,000! Obviously, at least two of these reporting services were making false or inflated claims.

Watch Out!

Co-author Todd relates this story from his personal experience: "I recently ordered a list of foreclosures from a national reporting service after spotting their ad in a national daily paper. I received 75 pages containing over 5,000 properties. Sounds impressive, right? Not once you took a closer look. I found one property listed 11 times. Also the majority of listings were for commercial property or unimproved land, not residential homes. Plus the information was inconsistent. Some had addresses, some didn't. Some had assessed values, whereas others didn't."

Before subscribing to a listing publication or reporting service, make sure they offer the type of information you need. Request a sample copy, or a trial membership. Do some research on the organization, check the Better Business Bureau for any negative reports, or do an online search for complaints from unhappy former subscribers.

Shameless self-promotion: We'd be remiss if we didn't mention co-author Todd's listing service, which contains a huge selection of listings from all over the country. You can find this listing at www.ForeclosureNet.net.

In Appendix B, there is information for some of the foreclosure listing services we've found most helpful.

Promissory Note

Be sure to tell everyone you know that you're interested in hearing about properties that are in foreclosure, or may soon be. This way, you'll have a whole network of friends and family acting as your "lookouts" and passing along possible leads.

Word of Mouth

Don't underestimate the power of good old-fashioned word of mouth. When it comes to finding foreclosures—especially those in the pre-foreclosure stage—gossip can be your friend. Unfortunately, bad news tend to travel fast; so if someone in your neighborhood or social circle has been threatened with foreclosure, there's a good chance the word will spread fast. Keep your ears open for news—or even just rumors—of someone who may be in financial trouble and facing foreclosure.

The Least You Need to Know

- ◆ Become familiar with the county courthouse, and be nice to the people who work there.

- ◆ Thanks to the Internet, you can find a wealth of foreclosure information without ever leaving home.

- ◆ Be leery of reporting services that make unrealistic promises or exaggerated claims.

- ◆ By contacting lending institutions, you can often get lots of leads on available properties.

- ◆ Local newspapers can be a wealth of information when it comes to distressed properties and foreclosures.

9

Buying Pre-Foreclosures

In This Chapter

- ◆ Pros and cons of pre-foreclosures
- ◆ Why negotiating skills are vital
- ◆ Understanding the purchase agreement and other important documents
- ◆ How to contact homeowners in pre-foreclosure
- ◆ Calculating potential profits and making an offer

Many authors and "experts" disagree about the advantages and disadvantages of the pre-foreclosure investing method. Some feel it's too risky, and others dislike the required contact with homeowners. On the other hand, some investors prefer this method and will only pursue properties in the pre-foreclosure stage.

It's true that an unavoidable factor in pre-foreclosure buying is contact with the homeowner. You need to be the kind of person who can communicate well with people and be sympathetic to their problems. You need to keep in mind, though, that you can't help everyone and will have to walk away from quite a few pre-foreclosure situations.

As for the risk, all foreclosure deals—like any other form of investing—carry some risk, however small. We would never claim that any strategy was guaranteed or would never fail. However, you can greatly minimize the risks by learning as much as possible and being well prepared before you even make the first move toward buying a pre-foreclosure. Buying this book was a good step toward that goal, because in this chapter we explain how to pursue these properties with minimum risk.

The Basic Process

When buying pre-foreclosures, it all comes down to a basic formula:

1. Locate loans in default, research property, evaluate choices, and narrow selections to pursue.

2. Contact the homeowner, inspect the property, and evaluate the homeowner's needs.

3. Calculate possible sale price and potential profits.

4. Negotiate with the homeowner and lender.

5. Close on the property, make the necessary repairs, and sell for a profit.

We address each step in detail later in this chapter.

Investing Overview

When a loan goes into default and the foreclosure process begins, both the lender and homeowner are in a bad situation. Neither may relish the thought of an auction: The homeowner will lose their home (and possibly still be sued for the remaining amount owed the lender), and the lender will have to deal with the cost and hassle of maintaining and eventually selling the property. It's a lose-lose situation for both parties involved.

So both the lender and the homeowner may be eagerly seeking the least painful and least costly way out of the situation. This is a key thing to remember: The lender and homeowner are motivated to cure the problem. Thus, this becomes a great window of opportunity for the informed investor. Your job as a good foreclosure investor is to make this lose/lose situation into a win-win, by helping both the homeowner and the lender. How do you make this happen? By coming up with a solution that makes both parties happy. Obviously, what would make them happiest of all is if the loan had never been a day late and they'd never gotten in this situation. However, you can't go back in time and undo the default. What you can do, however, is make the very best of an unpleasant situation.

If a homeowner is in serious default on their home loan, they've most likely also fallen behind on other financial obligations. For most people, their house payment is the first priority, so they'll let everything else fall behind—perhaps even suffer repossession of their car—before letting their home default. So after they've gotten to this point, they're most likely in serious financial trouble. They're desperate, probably depressed, and seeking someone to rescue them. That's where you come in.

The loan needs to be brought current or cured in some other fashion, or the homeowner's credit will be destroyed. If there's sufficient equity in the property, there's the potential to come up with a solution that satisfies everyone involved while allowing you, the investor, to profit nicely.

It boils down to this: buying the equity in the property, working out arrangements with the lender and borrower, maintaining or repairing the property, and then, usually, selling it for a profit.

Exactly how much profit are we talking about? That depends on many factors: equity in the property, amount owed the lender, liens and other debts that must be paid, costs associated with repairing or maintaining the property, etc.

Investors in pre-foreclosures often acquire property with little or no money down, making this an attractive investing method. After you've gotten some experience under your belt, you'll probably develop the ability to "flip" properties quickly, thus reducing your costs and increasing profits.

Promissory Note

In states that follow the nonjudicial foreclosure process, the clock is ticking pretty quickly and the homeowner has less time to react or solve the problem. Pressure builds quickly, and they may become frantic to find a solution. This short time span is to your advantage, as the homeowner can't afford to stall or deny the problem for very long.

The disadvantages of buying pre-foreclosures? For one thing, desperate homeowners tend to be reluctant to disclose any negative information. They probably won't be very forthcoming with details about liens, structural problems, or anything else they fear might scare you away. Also people in these kinds of dire situations sometimes act irrationally. Then there's the expense of researching the property. Lastly, there's always the possibility that the homeowner will somehow find a way to cure the default at the last minute on their own, thus allowing them to keep their home.

Locating Properties in Default

How do you find properties in the default (pre-foreclosure) stage? Check the courthouse for the *Lis Pendens* or Notice of Default notices we described earlier; these are the first signs of default. You can also use some of the methods we described in Chapter 8 (record searches, legal notices, and word of mouth), but don't bother asking real estate agents—they usually don't handle properties until the post-auction phase.

> **Promissory Note**
>
> After a *Lis Pendens* or Notice of Default is filed, other investors may also begin swarming around the property. You can get a head start by looking for divorce or bankruptcy filings or similar documents signaling a financial crisis. These can often alert you to an impending foreclosure before it actually happens.

The Notice of Default contains the legal description of the property. This is not the address; it's a method of identifying the property's exact location—typically described in a Lot/Block/Subdivision manner, as recorded in municipal map books. However, you need the property's actual address to determine whether it falls within your target area. Your helpful county courthouse clerk can probably help you determine the property address. One of your advisors—a lawyer or real estate agent, perhaps—can also help you figure this out.

Evaluating the Selections

After you've found a promising foreclosure property and verified it's in your target area, you need to evaluate whether it's worth pursuing.

When you first start out, it's easy to get caught up in the thrill of the chase. You can get so caught up in the pursuit that you may lose sight of the fact that a particular property isn't a profitable choice.

Resist the temptation to fall in love with every house you see. Also it's important to be objective. If the numbers don't add up, ignore the fact that you love the yard or that it reminds you of your childhood home.

The exception to this is if you're pursuing a property with the intent of occupying it yourself, in which case you can be more subjective. Obviously, you want to be pretty fond of a house you'll be living in. At the same time, though, you still need to take an honest look at the property—and the figures involved—and make sure it's a profitable situation.

Begin with the Property Evaluation Worksheet. Fill in as much information as you can from the *Lis Pendens* or Notice of Default. This will help you get the basic information—homeowner's name, address, amount owed, approximate value of property, etc.

Promissory Note

Appendix C includes many worksheets and other aids to help you evaluate property selections. Before you fill in any of these worksheets, be sure to make lots of copies so you'll have more for future use.

From reading the notices, you know how much is owed on the property. Now you must determine its value. By subtracting the amount owed from its market value, you can get a rough idea of the gross profit potential. This figure represents the known equity in the property.

How do you figure out the home's market value? Well, if you've followed our advice and carefully studied your target area, you can probably at least make a rough guesstimate based on the prices of similar homes on the market in that area.

Or you can call your advisors or real estate agents and get market values for comparables homes in the neighborhood. These figures—commonly referred to as comps—are similar to what an appraiser uses when determining a home's value.

Land Lingo

Comps or **comparables** are the prices of recently sold properties that are used to determine the value of a similar property.

Here's a system we like to use: obtain current prices for three homes in the neighborhood, comparable in size, style, age, construction, etc. to the home you're interested in buying. Add the three prices and divide that total by three, which will give you an average market value.

Take the amount owed on the property (including any liens or other obligations that must be satisfied) and subtract this figure from the home's market value. This will tell

Watch Out!

When using comps, make sure you're using the selling prices of recently sold homes, not the asking prices. Also be sure to use current prices. If possible, avoid using data that's more than a few months old.

you the potential profit of buying the home. If there is little difference between the property's debt and its value, walk away. On the other hand, if there's a sizable difference between the two figures, this may be a promising property. It may even have the potential for earning you a really nice profit—such as in the case of a $100,000 property with $40,000 in debt.

Contacting Homeowners

You've identified a property, confirmed it's in your target area, and run the numbers to make sure it could be a profitable investment. Now what? At this point, you must try to contact the homeowner. Many beginning investors find this to be the toughest and scariest part of the whole process.

Some people feel uneasy about the idea of "preying" on people in distress, or trying to profit from someone else's hardship. That's the wrong attitude. Remember, you didn't put the homeowner in this situation and—unlike the lender—you don't have the power to simply "forgive" the loan or ignore the default. However, you can try to make the most of a bad situation. Keep in mind the objective we stated in the "Investing Overview" section of this chapter: finding a solution that benefits everyone involved—the homeowner, lender, and you. You're not an unscrupulous scam artist trying to swindle the homeowner into blindly signing their home over to you for nothing. (And if by chance you are, please do us a favor and find a different book or infomercial, because that's not what we're about.) You want to try to make the resolution as beneficial and painless for the homeowner as possible.

Search Methods

Now you are ready to try to help the homeowner, but you must first contact them. This is, admittedly, easier said than done. Remember, facing the loss of their home is often the last step of a family's financial crisis. At this point, they're probably fighting off numerous creditors, lawyers, and others who are hounding them for money. Most likely, they've become very cautious about answering the phone or opening the door to a stranger. If you lived in fear of the repo man coming to claim your car or the electric company arriving to shut off your power, you'd be apprehensive about strangers, too. In addition, one of those unscrupulous swindlers who want to take advantage of the homeowner (you know, the shady people we don't like) may have already paid them a visit, causing the homeowner to be even more leery of strangers.

All this explains why you may find fear, suspicion, paranoia, or a host of other emotions when dealing with the homeowner. Be prepared!

So how do you find people who may not want to be found? You can through free online "people search" services and through fee-charging services.

There are some free services that we've been pretty successful with in the past:

◆ **Addresses.com** lets you search for addresses, phone numbers, and e-mail addresses.

◆ **Freepeoplesearch-online.com** lets you do various searches online, plus gives tips on searching techniques.

◆ **Einvestigator.com** has links to lots of different search engines and other tools.

Depending on how badly you want the property, it may be worth investing a small fee to locate the owner. Here are some of our favorite fee-charging search sites:

◆ Intelius.com allows you to search by name, address, Social Security number, or other criteria.

◆ KnowX.com is considered one of the best personal search tools on the Internet. You can search criminal records, property records, etc. The cost is pretty reasonable (many services cost only a few dollars).

◆ Querydata.com is one of the least expensive ways to locate someone online. You can search driving records, conviction records, civil judgments—even possibly locate the person's relatives or neighbors.

Promissory Note _____

Ever notice how bill collectors never seem to have trouble finding people? If you really want to have an advantage when it comes to locating people, make friends with some who works for a collection company.

Foreclosure Fact

In an effort to cut down on swindlers who prey on distressed homeowners, California has enacted legislation regarding the purchase of foreclosures or the equity of loans in foreclosure. One section of the civil code addresses "equity purchasers" who use schemes to entice a homeowner to sell his property for a small fraction of its value. Another section refers to "equity consultants"—those who claim they'll help homeowners stop foreclosure for a fee.

Good Old Snail Mail Searching

Given that the homeowner may be afraid to answer the door, your best bet is to start by mailing a letter. In this letter, clearly spell out how you can help the homeowner. The person who gets your letter will immediately wonder, "Who are you, and why are you bothering me?" so you must answer those questions right off the bat.

> **Promissory Note**
>
> When contacting a home-owner by mail, we suggest addressing the envelope by hand. Not only will this help the envelope stand out from among stacks of bills, it'll also add a personal touch. Also don't use a company name in the return address. The home-owner may assume the letter is from a creditor.

To overcome a skeptical homeowner, you must immediately convince them you have their best interests at heart, and that you want to help them. Don't insult their intelligence—be upfront about the fact that you also want to make a profit, but explain that you can accomplish both goals at the same time.

So what exactly should you say in your letter? Explain that you may be able to stop the foreclosure, save their credit rating, and allow them to walk away with some cash—cash that is probably desperately needed to pay off other bills, relocate, etc.

Foreclosure Fact

Co-author Todd was once involved in the test marketing of a new product geared toward apartment renters. There was some interoffice debate about the best way to mail the offers. The loudest argument was for the cheapest way, whereas Todd and others favored a more effective way.

The company took 1,000 names from a mailing list. All 1,000 offers were mailed in plain white envelopes and contained the exact same letters and offers. The mailings were then split into three groups. The envelopes in Group 1 featured mailing labels and metered postage. Group 2 also featured mailing labels, but featured unusual, oversized stamps applied by hand. Group 3 envelopes were hand-addressed, with unusual stamps, plus a sticky note atop the letter inside that read, "(Person's name), I thought you might be interested in this."

The results? Nine people from Group 1 responded, 25 from Group 2, and an impressive 41 from Group 3. The point: creativity and a personal touch yield much better results.

Your first letter should be friendly and simple. Say you're interested in buying a home in the area, and noticed this house may be sold at auction. You'd like to discuss buying the home, while preventing foreclosure and helping the homeowner. The actual wording you use in your letter will vary. Develop a letter that matches your individual style.

In states where the foreclosure process moves along quickly, you'll want to send a series of letters in rapid succession—perhaps twice a month.

Watch Out!

When dealing with homeowners, it's vital to avoid using any kind of fancy terms or jargon. Rattling off terms such as "shared equity transaction" and "home-equity conversion mortgage" won't impress the homeowner—just the opposite, it's likely to scare them away. Even worse, it gives the homeowners grounds to later claim they didn't understand what you were offering or what they agreed to.

Sample Introductory Letter

Here's an example of what your first letter to a homeowner might look like:

> Ms. Trustworthy Investor
> 123 Homebuyer Lane
> Anytown, USA

Dear John Smith:

We're contacting you because we may be interested in buying your property should you consider selling it.

We know from the county records that foreclosure proceedings have already begun against your property. We are not real estate agents or lawyers—simply investors who buy and sell property.

We can help you resolve this unpleasant situation by stopping the foreclosure process and avoiding further damage to your credit rating.

Should you wish to discuss this matter, please contact me at 1-800-000-0000.

Sincerely,

Trustworthy Investor

The Phone Call

Ideally, your well-worded letters will do the trick and prompt the homeowner to call you. If not, you can always make the first move and try calling them. Either way, always be professional and courteous on the phone. Never misrepresent yourself or your intentions.

Tell the homeowner that it's important for you to meet with them at the property, in order for you to properly assess both their situation and the property itself.

> **Promissory Note** _____
>
> Don't try to conduct an in-depth interview by phone. Just get the basic information, and arrange a time when you can meet in person. As with all your other interactions, this meeting time should be scheduled for whenever is most convenient for the homeowner. Remember: This person is already under a major amount of stress. Anything you can do to make the process a tiny bit easier or less unpleasant would be a big help.

Getting Homeowners to Come to You

You can eliminate much of the legwork involved in buying pre-foreclosures if you can get homeowners to make the first step and seek you out. How do you do this, exactly?

Classified Ads

Place classified ads in your target area's newspapers, with wording along these lines:

> "I Buy Foreclosures! Quick Closings. No need to file bankruptcy. Get cash to pay off bills. Call 1-800-123-4567."

Signs, Flyers, and Postcards

You can also get "I Buy Homes!" signs—make sure they're brightly colored and placed in high-traffic areas. Similarly, you can print up flyers with similar wording and post them in various area businesses.

Many investors also print up postcards announcing their interest in buying foreclosures, and mail these out to the homeowners whose names appear in local court records or on foreclosure lists.

The Toll-Free Number with Voicemail

Get a toll-free number (they're pretty cheap these days) and have it forwarded to an answering machine or voicemail. This is important for several reasons. First, you don't want your home number ringing of the hook at all hours of the day or night. Second, your outgoing message will help you prescreen callers. What should your message say? Explain that you're interested in pre-foreclosures in a specific area. Ask callers to leave as much information about their situation and property as possible—amount owed, condition of property, any additional liens, and exactly what the seller hopes to get out of the deal. Say you'll be in contact with callers whose property/ situation meets your needs or criteria.

The In-Person Meeting

However you make contact, the homeowner has agreed to an in-person meeting. Congratulations! You've accomplished an important feat. This first in-person meeting is perhaps the most crucial point in the whole process, so be sure to be prepared.

CAUTION   Watch Out!

Some investors get all decked out for their initial meeting with the homeowner— sporting fancy clothes and jewelry and driving a fancy car. Presumably, they hope this will impress the homeowner. In reality, we think this approach is much more likely to alienate the homeowner, or make them feel even worse about their financial distress. However, don't go to the other extreme, either. Showing up at their door dressed like a bum will only make the homeowner suspect you're planning to rob the house, not buy it. Our advice: be as "generic" in appearance as possible. Although you may not bowl anyone over with your style, it's unlikely that you'll scare anyone off or offend anyone.

Be sympathetic, but not overly emotional. Remember, your goal is to make a profit, and if you try to "save" every unfortunate homeowner you meet, you'll quickly find yourself facing financial hardship of your own. The following sections discuss ways to make the meeting go smoothly.

Ask Questions

The main purpose of the in-person meeting is to assess the homeowner's needs, while also evaluating the home's profit potential. Ask questions. Find out how much is owed on the property (although, if you've done your research, you probably already know). Are the homeowners planning to move? Hoping for a last-minute miracle to remain in the home? Do they need cash? Are they considering declaring bankruptcy? Record all of this information in the Property Owner Questionnaire located in Appendix C.

Here's one of the most important questions to ask: find out what the homeowner thinks the property is worth. More importantly, what amount are they willing to accept?

It's important that you don't make any promises at this initial meeting. We know that's easier said than done—especially if you really like the property, or if the homeowner is practically pleading with you to help them. However, it's important not to get the homeowner's hopes up until you've had a chance to go home and review all the information, crunch some numbers, and determine if this is a property you should pursue.

Inspect the Property

When setting up the in-person meeting, warn the homeowner that you'll need to inspect the property, and therefore would like access to as much of the property as possible.

Be sure to conduct a careful inspection. Any damage or decay of the property will have a negative impact on your bottom line. Use the Property Inspection Checklist in Appendix C to record the results of your inspection.

Watch Out!

If the homeowner accompanies you on the inspection tour, be sure to keep any comments as nonjudgmental as possible. Although it's okay to comment on damage or things that need repair, derogatory remarks about the wallpaper pattern or other matters of style or taste will only offend the homeowner.

Turn all the faucets on and off, open and close all the windows and doors, flush every toilet, etc. Note all damaged or missing appliances, fixtures, etc.

As you become more experienced in buying and selling properties, you'll start to get a feel for some of the more common home repair problems, and the average cost to fix them. We also include a list of rough estimates of the cost of various repair projects in Appendix C.

Here's how to do a quick estimate of the profit potential. Add the amount in default (as indicated on the foreclosure notice), plus any liens or judgments, and the estimated costs of repairs to bring the home to a sellable condition. If the total of these three amounts is close to or over the average market price you calculated earlier, there will be no money left over as profit (or worse, the home could actually end up costing you money). If it's blatantly obvious there's no profit to be made, you may just want to be upfront with the owner at this point and admit that, much to your dismay, you don't think you can help them. Thank them for their time and hospitality, wish them luck, and be on your way.

Promissory Note

Co-author Bobbi also has written the *The Pocket Idiot's Guide to Home Inspections*, which may prove helpful to you in evaluating and estimating the cost of home repair problems.

Obliterating the Competition

If your first meeting with the homeowner is a positive and pleasant one, you will have simultaneously accomplished a secondary goal—obliterating the competition's chances of elbowing in on your deal. Spilling their guts to a virtual stranger isn't something most people enjoy doing. If they feel comfortable that you can help them, they won't want to embarrass themselves by confiding in another stranger.

Preparing Your Offer

You've seen the home, gathered all your information, researched the property and its related debt, and you believe you can make a decent profit on the property. You rush to the phone and blurt out an offer the homeowner, right? Wrong! Although experts vary on how they like to proceed from this point, most agree that you need to check, double-check, and triple-check all of your information and figures before making an official offer.

Verify that there are definitely no other liens or *encumbrances* on the property. Check with the local tax collector to make sure there are no delinquent taxes. Take the list of damages from your Property Inspection Checklist and have your handyman teammate calculate the cost of repairs. Ask him if there's anything on the repair/improvement list that is optional or can be fixed in a more cost-efficient way.

Land Lingo

An **encumbrance** is anything that may restrict the value or use of a property. Common examples include liens, judgments, and unusual zoning restrictions.

Finally, assemble and record all of this information in the Equity/Profit Calculation Worksheet in Appendix C.

Sample Scenario

You have located a property, and found a Notice of Default indicating the loan is in default to the tune of $55,000. You've gathered the comps and determined the property has an average value of $100,000. Subtracting the $55,000 in default, you get $45,000 in gross equity. However, suppose the home needs $8,500 in repairs. Subtracting that figure from the comps, you now put the home's current maximum value at $91,500. Subtracting the default amount, you get a gross profit margin of $36,500. Sounds pretty good, but there are still more expenses to consider. A preliminary title search must be performed to verify there are no other liens or judgments. If there are, you must collect the specific details (name, contact information, date filed, amount, type of lien, and *position*).

Land Lingo

The **position** of a lien is basically its position in the debt hierarchy. In other words, the order in which it would be satisfied or paid off among the various liens or judgments against the property. The mortgage holder is generally the first lien holder, with additional mortgages or lien holders known as junior lien holders.

Using the property in our example, we found $22,500 in additional liens on the property. They were:

- ◆ Second mortgage: $15,000
- ◆ Mechanics lien: $2,800
- ◆ Other lien: $4,700

Generally speaking, if this property went to auction, the trustee or courts would have established the default amount and added all other charges. This would be the initial bid amount, or upset price.

The default amount in our example is $55,000, so the bidding would start there. Suppose the bidding continues and the property is eventually auctioned off for $71,300. In this scenario, the lender bringing foreclosure has been bought out for their $55,000. This leaves $16,300. The second mortgage holder would get their $15,000, leaving only $1,300 in proceeds from the sale. There are two other liens on the property, though. In this case, the lien holder owed $2,800 would be next in position. However, all they would receive is the remaining $1,300 from the sale.

The rest of their claim would be lost forever. And the poor final lien holder wouldn't see a single penny.

We examine the auction process in greater detail in a later chapter, but we wanted to touch on it briefly here to illustrate the profit potential associated with lenders and lien holders.

Negotiating with Lien Holders

By investigating other liens or clouds on the property before making an offer, you not only make yourself aware of potential hazards, you also put yourself in a better position to negotiate with the homeowner.

If you believed the deal wasn't strong enough initially, you might find that working with a lien holder can provide you with an additional source of profit.

In our example, there was enough of a bid to take care of the first and second mortgage holders. There was enough left over to cover a portion of the third lien holder's amount due, whereas the fourth party got nothing. This is very common. The more lien holders or the higher lien amounts involved, the more likely it is that at least some of the lien-holding parties will end up with nothing. This is where you come in.

Our prospective property was valued at $91,500 (after deducting the cost of repairs). The gross equity was $36,500. After discovering the additional $22,500 worth of liens on the property—liens that you'd need to pay off—you realize you'd only be left with a profit potential of $14,000. Keep in mind that to close on the property, you'd also need to pay for title insurance, inspections, delinquent payments, transfer fees, and assorted other expenses. If, say, these expenses totaled $5,100, you'd now be looking at a profit of $8,900. If you enlisted the help of a broker to sell the property, you'd have to pay a commission of $6,000, which would bring your profit down to $2,900. Suddenly this deal isn't looking so profitable, is it?

Most lien holders understand what they're doing by filing a lien. They take that step because they've been unable to collect a debt. They realize there's a good chance they may never see their money.

Contact these lien holders and tell them you're interested in buying the property and are aware of their lien(s). Be sure they're aware there are other parties also holding liens against the property. By stressing the existence of other liens—especially any liens in a higher position—you make this lien holder aware that there's an increasingly slim chance they'll ever see their money.

Tell the lien holder you've met with the homeowner and are trying to arrange a solution that would benefit everyone involved. Mention, though, that you're weighing whether it'd be worth your trouble, given the repairs needed and liens involved. Explain to the lien holder that if they'll consider accepting a discounted amount for their lien, the odds that you'd be able to go through with the deal will increase. Be sure to remind the lien holder that the lender or primary lien holder will get first dibs on the sale proceeds should the property go to auction and junior lien holders have a very good chance at getting nothing.

> **Promissory Note** _____
>
> If possible, try to meet with the lien holders in person. This way, you can bring pictures of parts of the home needing repairs, proof of other liens and judgments, etc. This will help you make a stronger case in convincing the lien holder to work with you.

Start your negotiations at 25 percent of the original debt amount and work your way up if necessary.

Take our example of $22,500 in liens. If you could negotiate down to 60 percent of the totals, you'd add $9,000 to your potential profit. Ah, this deal is beginning to look up. There may be hope after all!

Maximizing Your Profits

Returning again to our previous example, suppose you're unable to convince any of the lien holders to accept less. You're once again looking at a potential profit of around $2,900. Plus you haven't even paid the homeowner anything yet! Many investors would explain to the homeowner that after all the expenses and debt involved, there is only $2,900 of equity left, and that's the exact amount they'd offer the homeowner. (Keep in mind, though, that the homeowner gets additional nonmonetary benefits, such as a salvaged credit rating, relief from debt, etc.)

But wait! If you give that money to the homeowner, where do your profits come from?

Well, you have to start cutting corners in the expenses listed in our example. Perhaps you only make the most urgent repairs or take another shot at negotiating with lien holders. You might also decide to sell the property yourself, thus saving broker's fees.

Helping the Homeowner

There are other ways you can put your negotiating skills to work. Remember, one of the basic goals of the in-person meeting was to learn about the homeowner's needs.

Say, for example, you discovered that Heather Homeowner is upset about a $2,000 debt she owes to the auto repair shop where her brother works. Perhaps you can negotiate with the shop owner to accept a lower amount. Or maybe there's another creative solution. If you have a low-interest credit card for example, you could pay off the full amount with your charge card, and then simply make the minimum payments for the few months until you sell the property. This way, you only need to lay out a small amount from you own pocket. However, this isn't something you'd want to consider if you have a credit card with high interest rates, as it wouldn't prove financially wise.

The point is, a little creativity—combined with some imagination, good negotiating skills, and a bit of legwork—can often turn a not-so-great deal into a pretty darn good deal.

> **Promissory Note**
>
> You know the old saying, "One man's trash is another man's treasure?" Well, it's the same with foreclosure investing. What one investor thinks is a great deal may be something another investor feels isn't worth their time. Some investors don't want to bother negotiating with lien holders, making repairs themselves, etc. Other investors won't bother with properties under a specific market value. Only you can determine your own investment interests and parameters. Don't worry about what others think— find the investment strategy that's right for you.

Negotiating with the Lender

You also sometimes can successfully negotiate with the lender. The loan officer often has some leeway in this situation, especially if it means a fast closing with minimal hassle. If you're going to live in the property, and will let the bank hold the mortgage (assuming you have good credit and are a low-risk borrower), it's obviously in the bank's interest to cooperate with you.

Presenting Your Offer

Before presenting your offer to the homeowner, do a final check to make sure all of your worksheets and forms have been filled in completely and correctly. Then phone the homeowner, letting them know you're interested in presenting an offer and would like to meet in person to discuss it.

At the meeting, show the homeowner all your worksheets and supporting documents. Start with the Property Inspection Checklist, including estimates for any damage repairs. Make sure you've used a reputable professional contractor. Don't ruin your credibility by getting some figures from your cousin Charlie.

Next, show the homeowner your Property Appraisal Worksheet and Loan Analysis Worksheet. Some homeowners may not even be interested in seeing all the details, but it's to your advantage to make a strong presentation and be able to have documentation that backs up any statements you make, especially when it comes to lowering the price of the home.

If the homeowner wants to think about your offer, tell them your offer is only on the table until a specific date. You may want to remind them of the impending foreclosure sale date, if one has already been set. Leave a copy of your offer with the homeowner, thank them, and leave.

The Competition

Most likely, there will be several other interested parties—some legitimate, some shady—circling the property, also trying to make a deal with the homeowner. How do you handle that? As they say, the best defense is a good offense. Rather than pretending these people don't exist, discuss them with the homeowner, explaining why each of these parties may not be able to help the homeowner as much as you can. Some examples follow.

Credit Counselors/Debt Agencies

Like many people in financial distress, the homeowner may have been contacted by a credit counseling company offering to reduce or eliminate their debt. Explain to the homeowner that there are many scams involving outfits that call themselves "credit counselors" and only leave the debtor in worse financial shape. Even if the company is legitimate, if the homeowner is in severe financial straits and unable to make even a nominal monthly payment, there may be little or nothing the agency can do to help.

Bankruptcy

The homeowner may be considering bankruptcy, or may have been contacted by an attorney specializing in bankruptcy. Depending on state and local laws, bankruptcy may still not stop foreclosure proceedings or eliminate the mortgage lien. Point this out to the homeowner. At most, bankruptcy may be a quick temporary fix—but one that comes at the cost of their credit rating for the next seven years or so.

High-Interest Lenders

The homeowner also may have heard about lenders who work with people in financial crisis. Point out that these lenders will try to get the homeowner to agree to a very high-interest loan, which will only land the homeowner in deeper trouble in the near future when they soon find themselves unable to pay this new loan.

Other Investors

What can you do about other investors who may have contacted the homeowner? Become the homeowner's first choice by presenting yourself in a professional, friendly manner, making it clear that you have a sincere concern for the homeowner, and are trying to help them. Odds are, many of the other investors haven't asked about the homeowner's problems or tried to figure out creative ways to help them. You can also win the battle through organization and preparation. By showing the homeowner clearly with your documentation that all your numbers are legitimate, they'll know you're not trying to rip them off.

> **Promissory Note**
>
> The process of getting a homeowner to say "yes" to your offer is often really a process of reducing their odds of saying "no." By removing any negatives in your offer, you'll get to the "yes" answer much faster and more often.

The Purchase Contract

With your attorney's help, prepare an Equity Purchase or Real Estate Purchase Agreement that clearly spells out all the terms of your offer and the agreement. (You may be able to find a standard Equity Purchase Agreement at your local office-supply store that you can use as a guideline.)

All parties recognized in the mortgage contract must sign the agreement—meaning, if both spouses are listed on the mortgage, they must both sign the agreement.

> **CAUTION**
>
> **Watch Out!**
>
> Never sign—or show the homeowner—any agreement that hasn't been prepared or examined by your attorney first.

Depending on your state, there may be laws stipulating the type of contract you can use, or the requirements governing this type of purchase.

No foreclosure-buying book would be complete without stressing the importance of knowing the laws regarding this matter as it pertains to your state. We've said it before, but we'll say it again: Carefully study your local and state laws and enlist the help of an attorney who is very familiar with these laws.

Terms of the Agreement

This is a critical part of your agreement. You must clearly—very simple language—state the terms of the agreement.

Your agreement will state the purchase price, the portion of that amount that goes directly to the homeowner (sometimes known as "net to seller"), the closing date, and terms in which you'll buy the property.

Your purchase agreement should contain the following:

♦ Always include a "subject to" clause that allows you to get out of the deal if everything is not as has been agreed upon—if new damages occur to the home, for example.

♦ Include a statement allowing you to show the property as soon as possible, if you plan to resell quickly.

♦ Specify that the agreement depends upon the property being appraised at or above a certain amount.

♦ Stipulate the occupants—and all their belongings—must leave the home by a specific date.

Watch Out!

Many states require you to provide the seller with a Notice of Cancellation. This gives the homeowner a period of time—usually a few days—to change their mind.

♦ Clearly state the amounts due on current loans for the property.

♦ Stipulate the sale is subject to the conditions of the title and loans or liens against the title.

♦ Agree that the buyer is responsible for all costs incurred at the closing.

♦ Stipulate that the seller shall: deed the property to the buyer; be aware the buyer may resell the property; be aware the purchase price is below market value; leave the premises in its current or agreed-upon condition; and vacate the property on the date specified.

Additionally, you should also get lien holders to agree in writing to the deal. Don't count on verbal agreements.

Ready, Set, Close!

Some investors like to give the homeowner a good-faith deposit upon signing the contract. Should you decide to do this, keep the amount small, no more than $100.

Make the financial arrangements. If you're assuming the seller's existing loan, and have made prior arrangements with the lender, make sure they can stop the foreclosure process before the sale date. Have your attorney coordinate a Release of Lien to be recorded at closing for all lien holders.

Order all necessary inspections and appraisals as required before closing.

From the seller you'll need the deed to the property, all insurance policies, loan and payment books, and their signature on a Property Insurance Transfer document.

If anything shows up in the title search at the last minute, you can accept it, deal with it, renegotiate or walk away. That stipulation was built in to your purchase agreement.

Have your attorney, title company, or escrow agent handle the actual closing. At the closing, all documents will be collected, signed, and distributed. Debts will be paid, and the applicable agencies and parties will get their money—as will the seller. You will then be the proud owner of a property that you bought for well below market value.

The Least You Need to Know

- ◆ Complete a thorough inspection of the property and itemize every single expense or cost for repair. Use your contacts, such as a handyman, to help you come up with these figures.

- ◆ Ask the homeowner lots of questions and take note of their concerns. This will help you come up with an agreeable solution and help you negotiate.

◆ After the homeowner has agreed to work with you, you may be able to negotiate with the lender and lien holders. They may be willing to accept less, meaning more profits for you.

◆ Use members of your advisory team as much as possible. Their input and expertise is vital at this stage.

◆ Be creative and learn to think outside the box to come up with ways to satisfy the homeowner and help increase your profits.

◆ Draw up your purchase agreement carefully and make sure you understand all of the terms and issues it contains.

Chapter **10**

Buying at Auction

In This Chapter

- ◆ Pros and cons of auction buying
- ◆ Beware of bidding frenzies
- ◆ Calculating your maximum bid

The second phase of the foreclosure investing stage is the auction. After the pre-foreclosure phase has passed, and after proper notification and in adherence with local laws, the property will be sold to the highest bidder at a public sale. In this chapter, we tell you how to find out about auctions, and what you need to do before you go. We'll also give tips on getting the best possible deal at an auction.

Introduction to Auction Buying

Some of the highest profits in foreclosure investing are generated at these sales, so there are plenty of opportunities for great deals. However, some big pitfalls lurk at the auction, so it's important to be fully prepared and informed before you attend the auction or cast your first bid.

Remember, the sale is the final step in terminating the property owner's rights. By this time, the property owner may have deserted the property or been evicted, leaving the property a prime target for vandals or looters. Alternatively, the homeowners may have stubbornly refused to leave, and may in their emotional state have deliberately damaged the property.

Typically, the lender and investors show up at the auction. Sometimes, lien holders also attend. The number of others investors (in other words, your competition) is an unpredictable variable. If there are any factors that may hinder people's ability to attend—bad weather, for example—you may get a lucky break and find yourself with little or no competing bidders.

The lender shows up to bid on the property to protect its interest. Depending on state laws, the lender may bid or merely present its claim to start the bidding process.

Generally, the minimum bid will be the amount owed on the mortgage loan.

> **Land Lingo**
>
> A **deficiency judgment** is a court order requested by a lender when the foreclosure sale doesn't raise enough money to satisfy the mortgage debt. The lender would seek the difference between the amount owed and the amount received at auction.

The highest bidder at the auction wins the property. The funds are distributed to the primary lien holder (the one bringing the action) first. Then the remaining balance is paid to the secondary lien holders, in order of their position. The homeowner gets the money (if any) left over after all liens and judgments have been paid.

Most of the time, nothing is left over and the homeowner walks away empty-handed. If the amount earned at the foreclosure auction isn't enough to satisfy the mortgage debt, the lender can ask the courts for a *deficiency judgment* for any amount still owed.

Some states set minimum bids for properties being sold at auction. This is partly to protect homeowners from very high deficiency judgments. Say, for example, a homeowner defaults on a $50,000 loan for a property worth $100,000. If the property is sold at auction, and for some reason only gets a high bid of $20,000, the lender could still pursue a deficiency judgment against the homeowner for $30,000. This poor homeowner would not only have lost the approximately $50,000 in equity they had in the home, they may also be facing a judgment of $30,000. Worst of all, they're still without a home!

Investing Overview

At the foreclosure sale, you won't be negotiating with the homeowner (or the lender or lien holders, for that matter). Instead, a neutral third party, such as a sheriff or trustee, performs the auction. Foreclosure auctions are governed by very strict and specific laws, which vary from state to state. Always consult your attorney for a refresher course on related laws before attending an auction.

Whether you buy at the pre-foreclosure, auction, or REO stage of the foreclosure game, the basic principle of making money in foreclosure investing is the same: buy low and sell high.

No matter what your investment strategy, never lose fact of the basic concept: You're buying distressed or discounted properties to be resold at higher prices. Your main goal is to make money—and that can only happen if you buy properties with enough profit margin to allow you to walk away with a tidy sum in your pocket after expenses.

Even before attending the auction, you must locate, research, and evaluate the properties that interest you. You also need to research the auction itself to find out whether there are any requirements such as minimum bids.

Be sure to calculate your potential profit before leaving home. Arriving at the auction unprepared is a big mistake—one that can cost you big money.

Disadvantages of Auction Buying

Buying at auctions can be fun and profitable. It also can be risky and dangerous if you're not careful.

Be prepared for some disappointments. You may not even get the chance to enter a single bid. Foreclosure auctions are frequently postponed or cancelled at the last minute. After all your research and preparation, your big day may never come. This is all part of the rollercoaster ride of the exciting life of an investor. Don't let this discourage you from trying again.

Right of Redemption

The *right of redemption*—available to property owners in some states—can be a real thorn in investors' sides. Imagine going through all the trouble of researching the property, attending

Watch Out!

Be sure to arrive at the auction early. You'll probably need to complete some paperwork and meet bidding qualifications. Plus, many auctions proceed very quickly, with the whole thing often wrapping up in a matter of minutes.

Land Lingo

The **right of redemption** is a defaulting homeowner's right to reclaim their property after it has been sold at auction by paying all amounts past due on the property, plus any applicable fees.

the sale, submitting the highest bid, arranging financing, and possibly even repairing the property, only to discover that six months later the former owner can get the property back. Unfortunately, this is a situation some investors find themselves in. Although they get a refund for their bid amount, they lose any money they've invested into the home since the sale.

Financing Your Auction Buys

Financing is another auction-related headache. Payment and deposit policies vary, but generally you need to bring a cashier's check for a portion of the sale price with you at the time of the sale. If you don't bring this check, you often can't even be approved as a qualified buyer. Generally, a deposit check is for at least 5 percent or 10 percent of the purchase price, but sometimes it's a flat fee amount, such as $10,000.

The balance of the winning bid is usually due within 30 to 60 days following the auction—sometimes within just a few days of the sale. Generally, these purchases are on a cash-only basis. This need for an immediate chunk of cash is perhaps the biggest drawback of buying at auction.

Title Problems

The other major problem is the condition of the title, as well as the condition of the property itself. As the winning bidder, you may find you've not only gotten the property, but you've also inherited all the debts and obligations that go with it. This is the biggest risk when dealing with auctions forced by second mortgage lenders or other "junior" lien holders. Remember, the primary lien holder has "first dibs" on the property. So if a junior lien holder forces a sale, the primary lien remains in effect, even after the property is sold.

Promissory Note _____

Don't assume that the primary mortgage lender is forcing the foreclosure sale. If the holder of a second mortgage or junior lien forecloses, it doesn't wipe out obligations to the primary mortgage lender or other higher-position lien holders. This is why it's so important to do a full title search—and as close to the sale as possible. Lenders and other creditors who hear about the sale may decide to file a last-minute lien in an attempt to collect their money.

Say you attend a foreclosure sale and—to your delight—your $10,000 bid on a home worth $100,000 is the top offer. You think you've won the foreclosure lottery, right? Not so fast. You might soon discover to your horror that the home has a $75,000 mortgage and $10,000 in liens attached to it. Sadly, this happens to naive investors all the time. Don't let it happen to you!

Property Damage

Then there's the condition of the property. Although you may be able to tour or inspect the property prior to the sale, often you are not able to uncover damage before the auction. You then face the risk of buying a home, only to discover it needs massive repairs or cleanup work.

Evicting the Homeowner

Another auction-related problem: emptying the home of people and their contents. Unlike a pre-foreclosure deal where you work with the homeowner and have their cooperation, an auction sale may involve homeowners who are angry or upset about the sale and may not want to leave their home without a fight. The eviction process can be time-consuming, especially if the homeowner enlists the help of a good attorney who can cause the process to drag out for six months or more. Meanwhile, you're now the proud owner of a home you can't access. How easy do you think it'll be to quickly sell a property that has a hostile occupant in it?

Promissory Note

If the foreclosing lender doesn't bid on the property—or worse, doesn't even show up at the auction—then you shouldn't bid on it either. This is generally a sign that the lender or their attorneys know something about the house—something bad enough to convince them it's smarter to simply walk away and risk losing the entire amount owed, rather than try and sell the house as an REO property.

There's another danger present at foreclosure sales that is inherent at any type of auction: buying fever, which tends to be highly contagious. There's a real risk of getting caught up in a bidding frenzy, only to find yourself spending way more than you'd planned or buying a home you know nothing about. If you're at all prone to impulse buying or getting caught up in auction excitement, it's a good idea to bring along a friend or advisor—ideally, the real estate expert on your advisory team—who can serve as your voice of reason.

CAUTION | **Watch Out!** _____

Beware of shills at foreclosure auctions. In the world of auctions, a shill is a person who works with or is hired by the auctioneer. The person is a plant sent out among the crowd to pose as a bidder. They place bids, but they have no intention of actually buying the property. Instead, this is a ploy to drive up the price of the property. Although shills are somewhat rare at foreclosure auctions, you should still be on the lookout. Additionally, veteran investors sometimes try to "initiate" newbies by driving up the price of a property they don't really want, hoping the new investor will get stuck with an overpriced buy that will scare him away from future auctions.

Finding Out About Auctions

To find foreclosure auctions, you'd use many of the same methods outlined previously: searching newspapers, watching legal ads, checking with the local courthouse, etc. Also touch base regularly with local auctioneers, real estate agents, and others involved with auctions who can keep you updated on upcoming sales.

Evaluating Properties

You can use the forms supplied in Appendix C to research and evaluate all types of property, no matter how you buy it—including whether you buy it at an auction. Use the Property Evaluation Worksheet to calculate the default amounts and determine the property's fair market value. Then use the Property Appraisal Worksheet to further help you assess the property's potential.

Have your title company do a preliminary search on the property. If the search reveals too many liens or encumbrances—as in, enough that would make the property financially unattractive, walk away.

Inspecting the Property

As already mentioned, inspecting a property scheduled for auction can be difficult or even impossible. At the very least, you should drive by the property and do a visual inspection. Perhaps you can even chat with a neighbor who can give you the scoop on any known problems with the property.

CAUTION

Watch Out! _____

Exercise caution when visiting the auction property. If you know the place is occupied, keep your distance. An already-distressed homeowner won't be thrilled to see you peering in the windows. Remember, at this point the property still technically belongs to the homeowner, who can accuse you of trespassing.

If the property is available for inspection, double-check that you have the right date and time. Inspections are often held for a very short period, and you don't want to miss your chance. Use the Property Inspection Worksheet to record all relevant information.

Calculate Your Profits

It's imperative that you determine your preset spending limit before pursuing an auction property. To calculate your potential profits, first estimate a price at which you believe you can sell the property in good condition. Subtract the estimated cost of repairing any damage. Then you must also factor in the costs you'll incur by obtaining and holding the property: insurance and tax payments, loans, maintenance, etc.

Also include the closing costs you'll incur when you sell the property, along with a broker's fee if you plan to use a real estate agent. The resulting figure is what you can expect to receive when all is said and done, after you've bought and sold the property.

Here's an example:

Your sale price: $100,000

Deductions:

Repairs: $8,500 (This figure will obviously be less if you do the work yourself than if you pay for labor.)

Holding costs: $2,325

Closing costs: $1,000

Agent's commission: $6,000

Your net after the sale: $82,175

Keep that figure handy. It's the first important number in your calculations. Now assume your search discovered one lien on the property for $13,500. You also know the default amount is $55,000. You need to subtract these figures from your potential profit.

Now the figures look like this:

> Net to you after sale: $82,175
>
> Liens or judgments: $13,500
>
> Default amount: $55,000
>
> Gross profit potential: $13,675

The bidding for the property will start at the *upset price* of $55,000.

Land Lingo

The **upset price** (also known as a reserve price) is the starting minimum bid for a property at foreclosure sale. This is generally the amount in default to the mortgage lender.

You have already determined that there's $13,675 in potential profit in the property. So how much should you bid? Bid the lowest amount you can, of course. If the sale starts at $55,000, bid $55,100. Remember, anything you bid in excess of the upset price will then lessen your profit potential. Keeping these figures in mind, it's pretty easy to set your predetermined bidding parameters. You have $13,675 worth of "wiggle room" in your bidding. Your bidding range would be $55,000 to $68,675. Obviously, the closer you get to that top number, the less profit you'll see.

Promissory Note

Although we think title insurance is a "must have" with any real estate transactions, it's absolutely vital when buying via a foreclosure auction. Title insurance protects you from any claim against the property that happened before you bought the property. The title company performs a search of the title, and then agrees to cover costs or damages related to any claims or judgments that it failed to discover. The title company will include a list of things that aren't covered, though, so be sure to read these exclusions carefully.

There are often hidden expenses associated with auction properties—unexpected repairs, last-minute liens, etc.—so it's a good idea to build an extra cushion of at least a few thousand dollars into your calculations. If you're the winning bidder and are lucky enough not to encounter any unpleasant surprises, you'll end up with some extra cash in your pocket.

Use the Equity/Profit Calculation Worksheet and fill in all items relevant to buying at the auction.

What You Need to Bring

As we've already stressed, you need to be fully prepared when entering an auction situation. So what exactly do you need to bring with you? Bring any paperwork you've gathered related to the property—most importantly, your predetermined bidding range and maximum bid limit.

You also need to bring your deposit check (be sure to confirm the requirements beforehand) and possibly some kind of verification that you have access to the remaining sum, should you be the winning bidder.

Prequalifying Bidders

To save lots of time and aggravation, auctioneers weed out the real bidders from the wannabes by prequalifying bidders. To actually bid on a property, you need to meet the criteria to become a qualified bidder. The process varies widely—in some cases, you simply need to complete some paperwork. In others, you may have to provide financial information that proves you have the resources to pay for the property. In virtually all cases, you have to show the certified check in the amount of the required deposit.

Practice Before You Purchase

It can be risky—some might even say foolish—to plan on buying a property at your first auction. Instead, many experienced investors advise attending several auctions as a spectator before actually buying anything. Nelson Zide, senior vice president of ERA Key Realty Services in Framingham, Massachusetts, offers this advice: "Develop relationships with the auctioneers and other important people, so they'll give you inside information. In order to do this, you must be a registered bidder—which usually involves bringing a check. If you're not a registered bidder, the bigwigs won't even talk to you. So you have to bring a check in order to be recognized as a serious contender, but for your first few auctions you should bring someone along who will keep you from actually bidding. Don't think about making a bid until you've attended at least three or four auctions."

Success!

You're the winning bidder—congratulations! Now what? Upon completing the transaction, you receive a copy of the deed. You want to record the deed in your name as soon as possible. You should also get title insurance as quickly as possible.

You also need to go about removing any tenants or property that are still in the home. Ideally, you can convince the residents to vacate the property peacefully and without causing damage. If not, your best bet is to start legal eviction proceedings, which will most likely result in the sheriff or constable removing the occupants from the property.

Next you go about the process of repairing and selling the property, just as you would with property you obtained through the other foreclosure methods. We discuss selling the property in much greater detail in Chapter 16.

Tax Sale Auctions

For the bulk of this chapter, we've discussed property auctions as they pertain to auctions forced by foreclosing lenders and other lien holders. However, there is another common type of property auction—the tax sale. The following sections discuss the tax sale auction.

Risks and Complications

We haven't devoted a lot of space to the topic of tax sale auctions because this type of sale involves specific risks and complications that many investors may not want to bother with. For one thing, last-minute cancellations are common. If the property has a mortgage, the lender isn't going to let its interest in the property slip away because of some back taxes. Instead, the lender will usually advance the amount of overdue taxes and then tack that amount onto the debt owed by the property owner. Also the bidding will usually start at the total amount of taxes owed, but can quickly escalate from there (any "extra" amount will go to the next lien holder in line, with any remainders going to the property's former owner).

Finding Out About Sales

Most municipalities hold tax sales once or twice a year. They're usually advertised in the classifieds or legal notices of large local newspapers. You can also find out about upcoming sales by contacting your county tax collector's office.

Using Tax Information to Your Advantage

Even if you're not interested in attending tax sales, you can use information on past due taxes to your advantage by using the information to contact the homeowners with an offer to buy the property before the tax sale. Many homeowners in this situation won't want to take the chance of losing their home in the tax sale and will try to find a more attractive solution. People who are delinquent on their taxes are often also behind on their mortgages, so they may have already accepted the fact that they may lose their home.

Promissory Note

You *might* be able to find a good deal on a property at a tax sale if the sale involves bare land without a building, or if the property is owned free and clear without a mortgage.

The Least You Need to Know

- Be sure to fully research any property that interests you before you get to the auction.

- Confirm all the auction rules and policies—especially the amount of any checks you need to bring—well in advance.

- To avoid getting caught up in bidding frenzies or making impulsive bids, bring along a friend or colleague to act as your voice of reason.

- Carefully calculate your budget and spending limits before attending the auction.

- The biggest drawbacks to auction purchases are the need for available cash and the possibility that the homeowner may exert their right of redemption.

- Tax sale auctions can offer good deals, but be sure to carefully research any liens or other judgments against the property.

Chapter 11

Buying Bank Foreclosures and REOs

In This Chapter

◆ What is an REO property?

◆ Pros and cons of buying from lenders

◆ How to negotiate the best deal

The third method of foreclosure investing involves buying properties directly from the lender after they have assumed ownership of the property. In this chapter, we tell you how to find out about bank-owned properties, and what to expect if you want to buy one.

Investing Overview

Buying lender-owned property, also known as *REOs*, is the most popular method of foreclosure investing. It is also the easiest and safest method.

Land Lingo

An **REO,** or real estate owned, property is a property that the lender acquired at auction if no one bid higher than the default amount.

On the other hand, bargain buys tend to be less common and competition is heavier.

With REOs, just as with the other two phases of foreclosure buying, you still need to use many of the same basic skills: locating properties in your target area, researching properties, calculating profits and expenses, and negotiating your best deal.

Myths and Misconceptions

In dealing with aspiring foreclosure investors, we realize that there are several common myths and misconceptions about buying REOs.

Only Banks Own Foreclosed Properties

Buying a home "from the bank" is actually a phrase commonly used when referring to an REO property. In actuality, though, a bank is just one of several institutions that lend finance loans for home buying. Credit unions, finance companies, mortgage companies, and other businesses all lend money, and all will foreclose on a home if the loan goes into default. So what is a "bank foreclosure"? It's a common term for an REO—a property held by the lender.

Lenders Can Profit from REOs

Calling an REO property a "bank foreclosure" is a common and harmless mistake. A bigger—and potentially more costly—mistake is the commonly held belief that a lender who owns an REO property cannot now profit from it. When a lender forecloses on a nonperforming loan, the lender's goal is to recover the original loan amount plus any added fees and other costs. Under most laws, during the preforeclosure and auction phase, all the bank can try to collect is this original loan amount plus these additional fees and costs. The lender is entitled only to their losses and expenses. They can add on every single legitimate expense—and, trust us, they will. However, they can't try to get a single penny profit.

However, when the lender has taken ownership of the property after the auction, it's a whole new ballgame. As rightful owner of the property, the lender can now do whatever it wants with it. The lender can rent or hold on to the property—or sell it for whatever amount the lender chooses.

Bottom line: While in foreclosure, the lender can't make a profit or take advantage of the property owner in any way. After the lender *becomes* the property owner, though, it can sell and make as much profit as possible from the property.

Lots of Cloudy Titles

Prospective foreclosure buyers are often concerned about the property's title, as any wise investor should be. However, when dealing with REOs, you're virtually assured that there are no liens or judgments clouding the title. The lender will bid at auction only if it wants the property. The lender, typically the senior lien holder, wipes out all junior lien holders or judgments in the process. Upon successfully winning the property at auction, the lender will also satisfy all back taxes, bringing the property taxes up-to-date. No lender will go through all the trouble of buying the property at auction only to then risk losing it for a few thousand in back taxes.

Naturally, you'll want to do the usual title search and research on the property, just to be on the safe side, but in general most REOs come without any title-related strings attached.

Advantages

So what are the advantages of buying REOs as opposed to pre-foreclosures or auction properties? There are several. First, it requires much less effort to buy REOs. Most likely, the homeowner is long gone from the property at this point. Any liens or encumbrances (except possibly for tax or IRS liens) have probably been erased, because the lender is typically the primary lien holder. Usually the lender must bring the property taxes current when acquiring the property at auction, so the taxes will generally be up-to-date.

The amount of cash required upfront to buy an REO can also be less than in other situations, because you don't need money to pay off liens, bring past-due loans current, give homeowners money, etc.

Instead of the normal down payment of up to 20 percent, an REO purchase can often be yours for a lot less money down. The lender is generally eager to sell the property quickly and will usually work with you to increase your odds of getting the property. Chances are good you'll be able to buy with very little down. In addition, the lender may offer other incentives—such as waiving the closing costs, offering a reduced interest rate, and so on.

Disadvantages

With any type of investing, the potential reward generally is directly proportional to the amount of risk. REO investing tends to involve minimal risk—consequently, your potential reward may not be as great as with other types of foreclosure investments. An REO investor should have no trouble finding properties at 10 percent or even 20 percent below market value, but greater deals are tougher to find.

The conditions of properties in REO inventories run the gamut from dilapidated to delightful. Some may be heavily damaged, possibly the victims of vandalism while vacant. Generally, you should assume you're buying the property in "as is" condition. Any repairs the lender intended to do will likely have already been done before you inspect the property.

Another frustrating aspect: The process of buying an REO property can sometimes be time-consuming. Buying at an auction can take as little as five minutes. Negotiating with a homeowner for a pre-foreclosure may take a month or so. Buying an REO can take much longer. Lenders are often big businesses, and anyone who has ever dealt with big corporations knows how much bureaucracy and red tape can be involved in even the simplest transaction. Many different departments or staff members may need to sign off on the deal before the REO property can be sold, and thus can slow the pace to a crawl.

Buyer Beware

In previous chapters covering pre-foreclosures and auction sales, we explained that you typically are competing against at least a few other interested investors at various points along the process. So if the property is still available at the REO stage, you may start to wonder why nobody else has snapped it up yet. It's very likely that several pre-foreclosure investors showed at least a passing interest, and possibly even made contact with the homeowner. You can also assume there were some shrewd investors at the auction, as well. Yet the property wasn't sold at that point, either. So there may be a nagging thought in the back of your mind: "Okay, what's wrong with this property, that nobody wanted it? What do they know that I don't?"

Indeed, it's possible that there is something "wrong" with the property—some flaw that you're overlooking. On the other hand, perhaps the homeowner deliberately remained unavailable to avoid dealing with investors. Perhaps the property is in an area that doesn't interest many investors. Possibly, an investor had planned to buy at the auction but his financing fell through at the last minute.

In short, you may never know the answer. Thus, although REO purchases may be less risky than other foreclosure investment, there's always the possibility of some "unknown" factor in the equation. This could be the jackpot property—or it could end up a big money pit.

How Lenders Dispose of the Properties

Depending upon the amount of foreclosures in inventory, the size of the organization, and the in-house policies, lenders typically handle foreclosure properties in one of two ways.

The first option: having a real estate agent handle it. Lenders often enlist the help of brokers to sell their properties. The broker may mix these properties in with the rest of their listings for sale. A prospective homebuyer my be shown a recently foreclosed property and not even realize it.

The other option: The lender may handle REO transactions internally. The lender may have an employee—or even an entire department—devoted entirely to REO properties.

If a real estate agent is involved, you can expect to pay more. The lender needs to pay the agent's commission, which generally translates to a higher price for you.

Perhaps the lender is a small banker in a rural community who is embarrassed about this problem on their books—not to mention inexperienced at dealing with REOs—and may be so eager to unload the property that they'll practically give it away.

On the other hand, you may also encounter a hard-as-nails REO officer in a big bank who takes a no-nonsense approach, knows her market inside out, and who fights you tooth and nail for any discounts you try to get.

Most likely, the situations you encounter will be somewhere in the middle of both these extremes.

The Lender's Asking Price

A lender bases their asking price on several factors. First and foremost, they must consider the amount of the default that prompted the foreclosure in the first place.

Remember, the lender still hopes to recoup its losses on that nonperforming asset. Not surprisingly, the lender is going to seek something at or above that default amount.

Next, the lender will add in the expenses related to foreclosing on the property—legal fees, court costs, advertising, etc.

The lender will then tally up the costs of repairing and maintaining the property, and any broker's fees incurred.

Lastly, the lender will try to build in some profit for itself in the deal. They'll probably consider the property type, condition, local market, etc. when determining the amount of "profit padding" they can add onto the price.

> **Foreclosure Fact**
>
> If the property's a run-down old home in a bad part of town, the lender may set a low sale price, even it means taking a loss. However, don't expect to get a spacious four-bedroom newer home in a nice suburban development for almost nothing.

Locating REOs

Finding REOs requires many of the same skills we've already outlined earlier in this book. Although looking at the Lis Pendens or Notice of Default may be interesting, it's really not necessary at this stage. You're no longer interested in contacting the homeowner or preparing for an auction.

The Notice of Sale can still be useful, even though you won't be buying at the sale. Start contacting the lender as soon as possible following the sale to find out whether they were the successful bidder, because this happens the majority of the time.

Once again, the county courthouse is a wealth of information. When the lender acquires the property, the deed will be recorded and the transaction filed at the courthouse, where you can easily find and read it.

 **Promissory Note**

Maintain a contact list of the person or department who handles REOs for lenders in your target area. Periodically send them a friendly letter saying you're looking for a home in a specific area within your price range. Ask them to let you know if they should happen to foreclose on a property meeting your criteria. Also ask if they could forward your information to any real estate agents they use.

Newspapers are once again another source of helpful information. Most print a general list of real estate transactions periodically. Pay attention to the buyers' names, taking note of any banks or other lenders whose names appear. Newspapers may also contain ads from lenders and real estate agents announcing their listings of REO properties.

Foreclosure Fact

Banks maintain a list of REO properties for their internal records, clients, real estate agents, and others involved in handling these properties. The banks aren't required to provide this list to the general public and may decide not to give you this information.

There's no standard format for keeping or presenting REO information. One bank may give you a nice computerized report, whereas another may give you a handwritten list of one or two properties that a secretary quickly jotted down from information last updated six months ago.

Narrow Your Selections

After you've gotten leads on some potential prospects, begin narrowing your selections. You do this just like we've explained in previous chapters, by determining which properties meet your specific criteria and fit your investing needs.

Contacting the Lender

After you've done as much advance research as possible, it's time to contact the bank and start playing "Let's make a deal." How you make initial contact depends on your personal preference, but there are some important lessons to be learned about this first meeting that will help make your investment experience much more fruitful.

Promissory Note _____

If the lender is selling an REO property through a broker or real estate agent, there's a reason for that. Perhaps the lender doesn't want to spend the time or effort dealing with buyers and worrying about inspections and other details. If a broker is handling the property, don't try to circumvent them by trying to contact the lender directly. You won't get a better deal, and will probably just annoy the lender.

Watch Out!

When dealing with an REO officer, don't demand to know how much the lender has shelled out for the property and subsequent repairs. The numbers will probably reveal themselves as you work through the process. If not, find out for yourself by doing research at the courthouse and other avenues. Demanding this information from the lender will only put them on the defensive.

Foreclosure Fact

The REO phase is the easiest and least-stressful foreclosure phase in which to inspect properties. The home is almost always vacant, making it easier for you to spot any damage or structural problems. Plus you don't have to worry about the uncomfortable situations involved with inspecting a property while the homeowner watches.

Promissory Note

In your inspections, you may sometimes encounter properties that have already been repaired to varying extents by the bank. This isn't a freebie. Expect to have the cost of those repairs passed on to you in the asking price.

When making initial contact with a lender, the attitude of your approach can make or break the deal. Remember, the lender is already aware that this non-performing asset is a "black mark" on their books. They don't need you to rub it in or criticize them for this situation.

Lenders and their employees also hate dealing with rude, arrogant investors. Don't act like you're doing the bank a favor by taking this property off their hands (even if that's how you really feel).

When meeting with the lender, your main objective is to find out how much it wants for the property. You should also request a copy of the most recent appraisal of the property. If you're still interested at this point, request a chance to inspect the property.

Inspecting the Property

Just as with any investing method, it's important when considering REOs that you make a careful and thorough inspection of the property. Most likely, the lender or broker handling the property will be agreeable to allowing you to inspect the property.

Use the Property Inspection Checklist in Appendix C to assist you in noting important details during the inspection. Be very thorough in your inspection. Remember, every negative item you miss will be something you'll have to pay for later. Be sure to point out any damage or disrepair to the lender or broker who accompanies you on the inspection. Jackie Lange, president of Texas Home Solutions, Inc., recommends hiring a home inspector to go over the property. "It usually costs around $200, but you'll know exactly what you're getting into. These guys will almost always find *something* negative, and you can use that as ammunition to negotiate the price down."

Don't Expect Huge Discounts

Although you can get many good deals on REO properties, don't expect to find many "steals." The price is often less than market value, but it's almost never as cheap as buying at auction or at pre-foreclosure stage.

Foreclosure Fact
Nelson Zide, senior vice president of ERA Key Realty Services in Framingham, Massachusetts, says buying REO properties is strictly a numbers game. "Unlike a defaulting homeowner, the lender isn't emotional about the house. If you hit their price, they'll sell you the house. It's that simple. But most likely you'll be dealing with someone who is pretty savvy about the home's value. You might get a good deal, but don't expect miracles. In a nice residential area, you're not going to get it for 90 percent off, unless it's on a nuclear waste site."

Obstacles That Can Work in Your Favor

There are a few "problem" conditions that may make a lender more agreeable to negotiating. Ward Hanigan is a California foreclosure expert who runs the website www.foreclosureforum.com. He describes a few conditions that tend to make lenders open to lower offers:

♦ The lender incurs an ongoing expense after taking control of the property. (Perhaps there's some kind of major maintenance problem, such as a water leak, for example.)

♦ The former owner refuses to move out without a fight, making it difficult for the lender to show or sell the property. (Obviously, if you buy the property, then you will inherit the problem of evicting this person.)

♦ The ex-owner strips the home of features or amenities that contributed to its value, such as carpets, additions, prefab buildings, and so on.

♦ The lender is out of the area and must have one or more agents or other experts handle the property, adding to the cost.

Calculate Your Profits

At this point, you reach the number-crunching part of the process. The basic principle is the same as we've described in previous chapters: Add the price of the property plus any expenses or fees and deduct that figure from the amount you think you could get from selling the property.

Use the worksheets and forms included with this book in Appendix C—especially the Property Appraisal Worksheet and the Equity/Profit Calculation Worksheet—to determine your profit potential. Don't rely on your casually determined average market price—be sure to get the most recent appraisal from the lender or broker.

Watch Out!

When calculating your profit potential, be sure to factor in the costs of insurance, maintenance, and other expenses you'll incur during the period you anticipate it'll take for you to sell the property.

Keep in mind that the lender's asking price is just that—an *asking price*. If you find a desirable property with an asking price of near market value, you need to somehow reconfigure the equation to increase your profit potential. The most obvious place to start? Getting the lender to lower their asking price.

Calculate the profit several times, each time lowering the asking price by, say, 5 percent. If you find, for example, that you must reduce the asking price by 10 percent to make even a small profit, you know that new figure is your absolute highest offer. Each subsequent discount that you are able to get from the lender will mean an added profit in your pocket.

Study your expenses to see where you can cut costs. Can you sell the property personally without the help of an agent or broker (assuming you're not an agent yourself)? If so, you'll save a nice sum that you would have paid in commissions.

Making the Offer

If you're working with a real estate agent, you'll probably have to do most of your negotiations with that person. Your offer will most likely be recorded on a standard sales agreement, which will then be relayed back to the bank along with your deposit check. Generally, it's tougher to talk the price down when dealing with a broker or agent. Remember, this person works on commission—the lower the final selling price, the less money they make.

Try to get the agent on your side. Point all damages to them as you do your expenses. Stick to legitimate damages and problems—trying to "invent" damages or making a big deal out of minor cosmetic details will only annoy the agent and won't motivate this person to help you.

You should make your offer in writing. This offer should include the following:

◆ A statement indicating intent to purchase real estate

◆ The property address

◆ Your offer (purchase price)

◆ Financing terms

◆ Closing date(s)

◆ Any contingencies or conditions of the sale

◆ Deposit

◆ Your name, contact information, and signature

 Promissory Note

You may be dealing with a veteran REO officer who has handled countless purchase offers. Make yours stand out—but not in a negative way (so forget the neon pink paper). Your offer will be notable simply for its clean, neatly typed professional appearance and wording.

As with any type of financial negotiation, your initial offer should be the lowest price or best terms that you think the bank would realistically entertain. In other words, leave yourself room for negotiation, but don't completely insult the lender's intelligence to the point that your offer makes a quick trip straight to the trash can.

We suggest you start with an offer about 20 percent or 25 percent below average market value for comparable properties. You might want to leave specific terms out of this first offer. Give the lender time to mull over just the dollar amount. As this initial offer will probably be less than what the bank wants to accept, they may counter your offer with a higher dollar amount but with an attractive financing package thrown in.

You may want to accept their financing offer, and only give a little on the price. This way, the lender may come back with another figure, but still more attractive financing terms.

Your ultimate goal—after all this back-and-forth negotiation is over—is to get the whole enchilada: a lower selling price, lower closing costs, and the best possible terms.

Sample Offer Letter

Here's a sample of what a letter containing an offer on an REO property might look like:

Mr. Ben Buyer

Anyplace, USA

Mr. Ben Franklin

Special Assets

City Bank

Anycity, USA

Date: May 1, 2004

Re: Offer for Property Located at 1001 Main Street

Dear Mr. Franklin:

I would appreciate your consideration of my offer to purchase the property described above. I have included some documentation that shows the costs of necessary repairs to fix damage caused by neglect and abuse.

Price: $125,000

Down Payment: $6,250 (5%)

Terms: 30-year, fixed-rate @ 7.75%, City Bank waives points

Closing: June 1, 2004

Conditions: Subject to appraisal @ $150,000 and clear title

Deposit: $100.00 (enclosed)

Please contact me at your earliest convenience, as I'm looking forward to discussing purchase of this property.

Sincerely,

Ben Buyer

Financing

One of the main factors in considering buying an REO property is financing. This can be a major hurdle for new investors without a lot of money at their disposal. Exactly how much money you'll need varies widely with the individual circumstances. Most likely, you'll need at least a few thousand dollars to cover the down payment and closing costs.

Remember, one of your main goals in the negotiating process is to get the best possible financing terms. Which specific aspect of the financing package is most important to you? That depends on your needs and what you plan to do with the property. If you plan to resell the property quickly, you may not be so concerned about the lifespan of the loan or the fact that the interest rate may increase at a future point. On the other hand, if you intend to hold the property as a rental situation, you want to make sure your monthly payments are less than your rental income from the property.

Closing

When the bank accepts your offer, you'll want to be ready to close as quickly as possible. Make sure you have all the necessary documents prepared and ready to be signed. Also be prepared to assume physical possession of the property. Be prepared to address any immediate concerns involving repairs and maintenance. Be ready to evict any tenants or homeowners if necessary. Know what kinds of paperwork (occupancy certificates, rental permits, and so on) you're required to have.

The Least You Need to Know

♦ The advantages of buying an REO usually include a clear title, no dealing with a homeowner, and the lender is eager to finance.

♦ The downside: Don't expect huge discounts, but do expect lots of red tape and possible delays.

♦ Conduct a thorough inspection of the property, carefully noting any problems or negative qualities that can help you negotiate a lower price.

♦ It's often possible to negotiate a very attractive financing package, especially if the lender is eager to unload the property.

Government Properties

In This Chapter

- ◆ Lots of agencies, lots of properties
- ◆ The bidding and buyer process varies by agency
- ◆ Special financing is available

We've discussed buying distressed properties from the owner, at the auction, and from the lender as an REO. However, no book on the fore closure investing industry would be complete without mentioning the government agencies that also play a role in foreclosures.

The properties owned, managed, and sometimes sold directly by these agencies are commonly called government foreclosures. In this chapter, we'll tell you how to find these properties and what to expect before you try to make an offer.

HUD Properties (Department of Housing and Urban Development)

The Department of Housing and Urban Development (HUD) is a federal agency originally established to manage federal housing and community-development programs.

HUD properties are sold when an FHA (Federal Housing Administration)-insured mortgage goes into default and is foreclosed. HUD pays the original lender the amount of the loan due plus additional expenses. HUD then resells the property, usually through a private contractor.

HUD homes are typically "blue-collar" types in the lower- to moderate-value range. They're often in better overall shape than the average government-owned property.

Finding the Properties

You can find HUD properties by calling local real estate agents or watching the newspaper for HUD property sales. You can also call HUD directly at their HUD Homes Hotline (1-800-767-4483). You can also find information and home listings online at www.hud.gov/homesale.html.

The Bidding Process

The red tape involved in buying HUD properties can be frustrating. Sometimes offers are accepted only by *sealed bid*. You need the help of a HUD representative or HUD-registered real estate broker to conduct any transaction. Sometimes the required deposit is as low as $500, but it can also be as high as 10 percent of the bid amount. Terms and conditions vary from state to state.

> **Land Lingo**
>
> When an auction is conducted by **sealed bid**, this means that all bidders submit their offers at the same time. The bids are the opened at a pre-determined time and date, with the person submitting the best offer usually declared the winner.

As always, inspect—if only from the outside—any property you are interested in buying. HUD properties are generally first offered to "owner occupant" buyers—that is, people who want to live in the property themselves. Owner occupants get first dibs on the property for a short initial period, usually around 10 days. After that, the property becomes available to everyone.

Financing

All HUD properties must be financed through a conventional mortgage lender or through other outside means. HUD doesn't finance the purchase of any of its properties.

FHA (Federal Housing Administration)

The Federal Housing Administration (FHA) was created under HUD to assist home-buyers in reaching their goal of becoming homeowners. The FHA mainly helps low to moderate income families and first-time homebuyers by offering lower down payments and below-average interest rates.

Originally established in 1934 under the National Housing Act, the FHA was granted the authority to insure mortgage loans made by private lenders. The FHA issues an insurance policy—the premium of which is paid by the borrower—and works only with approved lenders. The FHA doesn't actually grant loans itself.

The FHA insures that a loan granted under its terms will be paid back in full to the lender should a default occur. Thus, a lender who may have initially been reluctant to approve a loan is now reassured by this guarantee of payment by the federal government. If an FHA-insured loan goes into default, the FHA steps in, pays the lender, and conveys title of the property to HUD.

FHA loans are made more liberally than the average loan, with less qualifying criteria and better deals. In the past, all FHAs were *assumable*, making them even more attractive. That aspect has changed, and a buyer may have to meet certain qualifications to assume an FHA mortgage.

Land Lingo

An **assumable** loan is one in which the buyer can take over the existing loan with the original borrower's terms, often without going through the approval process required for an original loan.

The advantages of FHA properties are the lower down payment and relative ease of assumability. Huge discounts are pretty rare. Unlike REO properties owned by lenders, properties owned by the federal government tend to be widely advertised and—as a result—usually attract more attention from investors and potential buyers.

Watch Out!

The FHA isn't under the same pressure to sell a property quickly as a lender is. In the case of the FHA, no depositors or shareholders are breathing down the agency's neck to dispose of the property, as there would be in the case of a lender or other corporation. Government agencies have the luxury of moving very slowly in selling properties—and trust us, they often take full advantage of that luxury.

VA (Department of Veterans Affairs)

The VA—or Department of Veterans Affairs—was originally called the Veterans Administration and was established in 1930. Its involvement with home loans began in 1944 with the Servicemen's Readjustment Act. This act, commonly known as "The G.I. Bill," authorized the VA to guarantee a certain percentage of loans to eligible military veterans. (The bill also included previsions for educational benefits for veterans.)

If a veteran with a VA loan goes into default, the original lender will start the foreclosure process. The VA—which guaranteed the loan—will then step in and buy the property from the lender. This is done during the foreclosure process, before the auction phase.

> **Foreclosure Fact**
>
> From 1944, when VA began helping veterans purchase homes under the original GI Bill, through January 2004, about 17.4 million VA home loan guarantees have been issued, with a total value of $812 billion. VA began fiscal year 2004 with 2.7 million active home loans reflecting amortized loans totaling $213.2 billion.
>
> In fiscal year 2003, VA guaranteed 508,436 loans valued at $65 billion. VA's programs for specially adapted housing helped about 550 disabled veterans with grants totaling more than $22 million last year.

Ocwen

These acquired properties are marketed through a property management services contract with Ocwen Federal Bank FSB, West Palm Beach, Florida. VA properties are sold through approved brokers via local multi-listing systems (MLS). Check with local real estate agents to see which brokers in your area handle VA properties. A list of properties for sale may also be obtained from Ocwen's website at www.ocwen.com.

Bids are accepted from the public. Properties are sold as is, but the listing often contains warnings alerting potential buyers to some possible existing conditions—such as lead-based paint, mold concerns, and so on. In some cases, you may get lucky and find a property that has already been repaired and brought back to good condition.

Don't expect to find huge discounts, though, especially for properties that are in good condition.

Vendee Financing

If you're interested in buying a VA-owned property, you may be able to take advantage of the Vendee Financing program. Unlike traditional VA loans, which are guaranteed by the VA and are strictly for veterans and their spouses, Vendee Financing is available to both veterans and nonveterans alike.

Vendee financing requires fewer fees and less out-of-pocket money than traditional mortgage loans. You need a lower down payment—possibly no down payment, especially if you plan to occupy the home yourself—than with a traditional mortgage. Information on the Vendee Financing program is available on the Ocwen website.

SBA (Small Business Administration)

The Small Business Administration (SBA) was created to advise, counsel, and assist America's small businesses. The SBA either grants loans directly or guarantees loans from other lenders. Often these loans are for the purchase of commercial real estate. Similarly to the VA foreclosure process, the SBA will buy a property from the lender when a loan guaranteed by the SBA goes into foreclosure. The properties are usually sold by an auctioneer. Obviously, this is mainly of interest to investors seeking commercial properties, because it's rare for the SBA to have residential properties available.

On the plus side: Investors seeking commercial buildings or raw land can often find good bargains through SBA auctions.

The drawback: SBA properties may be tough to find. Contact the nearest SBA office, who can probably tell you which auctioneer(s) in your area handle SBA sales. You can also search for properties online at http://app1.sba.gov/pfsales/dsp_search.html.

FDIC and FSLIC (Federal Deposit Insurance Corporation and Federal Savings and Loan Insurance Corporation)

The Federal Deposit Insurance Corporation (FDIC) and Federal Savings and Loan Insurance Corporation (FSLIC) were both created as bank insurance corporations. Their purpose is to collect and set aside insurance premiums from member banks to protect the banks' depositors from loss. If an FDIC or FSLIC member bank failed, the depositors' funds would be paid back by the federal government.

The FSLIC became insolvent in the last 1980s, and its responsibilities were transferred to the FDIC.

Promissory Note

It's not uncommon to obtain FDIC properties for 10 percent to 25 percent off the market price.

If the FDIC closes a bank and takes it over, it must sell the bank's assets. FDIC properties are sold through brokers and at auctions. Again, the best way to find out about these auctions is through building a solid contact network among your local real estate agents and auctioneers.

You can also view the FDIC's real estate sales website at www.fdic.gov/buying/owned/index.html.

Fannie Mae Repossessions

The Federal National Mortgage Association (Fannie Mae) is the nation's largest source of financing for home mortgages. Although it doesn't loan money directly, it offers various mortgage programs through a national network of approved lenders.

Properties owned by Fannie Mae are sold by local real estate agents. You can search for available properties at www.fanniemae.com/homes/.

You can also check with your local real estate agents. (Many of the same agents who handle other REO and government properties will have information on Fannie Mae homes.)

Freddie Mac

The Federal Home Loan Mortgage Corporation (Freddie Mac) buys residential mortgages from lending institutions.

Finding Properties

You can search for properties owned by Freddie Mac on its specially designated website at www.homesteps.com.

Properties are sold through local real estate agents across the country. The property listing will provide information on the agent you need to contact about that specific property.

Financing

There's a special financing program available for buyers of Freddie Mac–owned properties. This program, called HomeSteps Special Financing, offers low down payments, competitive interest rates, and doesn't require an appraisal or mortgage insurance.

IRS Properties

The Internal Revenue Service (IRS) sometimes forecloses on a property in an attempt to collect overdue unpaid taxes owed by the property owners.

Locating Properties

You can find listings of IRS sales and upcoming auctions on the IRS website at http://www.treas.gov/auctions/irs/real1.html.

Right of Redemption

Owners of properties sold by the IRS have a redemption period, generally 120 days, during which they can reclaim their property by paying the amount due to the IRS.

CAUTION

Watch Out! _____

Again, we stress the importance of doing diligent research before considering the purchase of any property. With IRS sales, you must watch out for liens and other claims against the property, some of which may be superior to the IRS claim and therefore will be inherited by the buyer. In its sale listing for the property, the IRS will include information on any encumbrances or liens it is aware of, but don't take it for granted that there may not be others against the property.

Payment

You might not be surprised to learn the IRS doesn't offer financing assistance. You must be prepared to cough up the full purchase price in the form of a cashier's check, certified check, or cash. Generally, you need at least 20 percent for a deposit on the day of the sale, with the remainder due within 30 days.

Government Properties for a Buck?

When discussing buying government properties, inevitably someone will ask about the popular belief that you can buy government properties for a dollar. Well, we're sorry to burst your bubble, but that's not exactly true. Uncle Sam likes to make a profit on its properties, just like anyone else. However, we have seen cases where government entities—generally small local municipalities—have distressed nuisance properties they're eager to unload. Often these properties have suffered serious neglect and vandalism and in many cases need to be demolished. In cases such as this, sometimes the municipality will decide it can benefit financially from giving the property to an investor or other buyer who agrees to bear the cost of demolition or repair, thus alleviating the municipality's burden. In these cases, the municipality sets the one dollar price, which is the standard token fee in real estate transactions where the property is basically being given away for free.

The Least You Need to Know

◆ You can find out about most available government properties for free online.

◆ Many real estate agents specialize in selling properties from numerous government agencies.

◆ Several agencies offer financing assistance to investors seeking government properties. Others, such as the IRS, operate on a "cash-only" basis.

Chapter 13

Financing Your Purchase

In This Chapter

- Why your credit rating is so important
- Mortgage companies and other lenders
- The pros and cons of partnerships
- Understanding wholesale flipping
- Additional sources of funding

Like any new endeavor, investing in foreclosures can be a little challenging in the beginning, until you get the hang of it. In our opinion, though, nothing is more difficult than trying to buy a property with no money. Many people want to invest in foreclosures but are discouraged because they think they can't come up with enough cash. In reality, although they may not have piles of cash lying around, most people have access to more capital than they realize.

Before You Get Started

Before you pursue any type of financial assistance or loans, make sure you have all necessary paperwork and documents in order. Items you will probably need include your tax returns for the past few years, recent pay stubs, a list of your current loans or other financial obligations, information on property or other assets you own, and similar documentation. It's a good idea to have several copies of all these important documents where you can easily locate them. You don't want to risk having a great deal slip through your fingers because your tax return is buried under a mountain of paperwork somewhere in your house.

Borrowing Money

The objective in buying investment property is to try and shell out as little out-of-pocket money as possible. If you are unable or unwilling to get a bank loan, try alternate ways of borrowing money. Loans and lines of credit can come in many forms. Most credit card companies offer lines of credit, which may essentially allow you to charge your cash purchase and defer the cost. Some credit cards allow cash advances as high as $5,000 or $10,000. We know of numerous cases in which investors tapped several of their credit cards for cash advances to gather up the necessary funds to purchase a property.

> **Promissory Note**
>
> If you decide to use credit cards for your down payment and other costs, look for cards with the lowest possible interest rate. We've seen many offers recently for cards with very low rates. Be careful, though, because often these are "introductory rates" that rise dramatically after the first few months. However, if you're confident you can flip—or resell—the property very quickly, the interest rate may not be such a big factor, because you'll be paying off the debt in a short period of time.

> **Land Lingo**
>
> A **line of credit** is an established, pre-approved loan that is available whenever the borrower needs it. After the line of credit has been established, the borrower can withdraw any amount up to the preset limit without filing a new application.

Lines of Credit

Many investors name the *line of credit* as one of their favorite financing techniques. You should be able to access your line of credit quickly. This is important to investors who tend to find deals they must snap up on short notice.

Donna Brown of RE/MAX First NE Asset Pros in Plainville, Connecticut, has years of experience in buying REO properties and is a big fan of this type of financing. "A line of credit is the easiest way to purchase," Brown says. "It solves the time needed to get a mortgage."

A great thing about lines of credit is that you don't pay a thing unless you actually use them. So they can serve as kind of a security blanket, available just in case you need it.

Finance Companies

You could also consider a commercial finance company such as CitiFinancial or Beneficial. These companies tend to charge considerably higher interest rates than banks—but again, if you're confident you'll be able to flip the property quickly at a nice profit, you'll be paying off the debt before the interest has a chance to pile up. Just be sure you borrow from a company that allows early repayment without charging you penalties. An added bonus: each loan that you pay off quickly will boost your credit rating, making it easier to borrow money the next time.

Promissory Note

If you're seeking a relatively small loan, we suggest simply saying you need the money for debt consolidation or personal reasons. If you mention buying a home, the lender may want to do an appraisal, put a lien on the property, etc.—all of which will drive up the costs and drag out the process. There is nothing illegal about being vague as to how you plan to use the money. If a lender is willing to loan you money, the lender really can't dictate or control how you spend it. Of course, this only applies to small loans. For larger loans, the lender will want some kind of security (as in, the property), so obviously in that case the lender will be well aware of how you're spending the loan.

If you're already a homeowner, you might consider getting a home-equity loan or refinancing your property.

Your Personal Credit

Your credit rating is probably the best weapon in your quest for investment cash. If you have good credit and stable employment, you can probably qualify for a loan without much trouble.

Suppose you want to buy a house for $100,000. Your down payment will be 15 percent, or $15,000. If you have good credit and stable income, the bank will be likely to approve your loan, especially given that the down payment—plus the property valued at $100,000—is considerably more than the $85,000 the bank would need to lend you.

Loan to Value Ratio

Banks use several complicated formulas to determine whether you qualify for a loan. One such formula is the loan-to-value ratio (LTV). This is determined by dividing the loan amount by the property's appraised value.

In addition to a down payment, the borrower is expected to make regular monthly payments on the property. This, coupled with the value of the property, reduces the bank's risk in granting a loan. Given that, you may wonder why the bank cares about your credit rating at all. Well, as we've already explained, banks want to do everything in their power to *avoid* foreclosing and selling the home. They want to be proactive, weeding out potential "problem borrowers" way before they get the chance to default.

Sure, even people with good credit can default on a loan, but—statistically speaking— it's less likely than with people who have shaky credit.

The Credit Report

Because a good credit rating is important in obtaining financing, it's vital that you keep a close eye on your credit report. You should contact the three major credit reporting agencies, and get a copy of your report from each. (Each agency collects different information, so your report may vary from one agency to another.) We include contact information for the top three agencies in the resource section in Appendix B. With identity theft rising rapidly, it's becoming more and more common to find errors—sometimes major ones that can really hurt your credit. Recent legislation allows U.S. residents to obtain one free copy of their credit report per year. You're also entitled to a free copy of your credit report if it played a part in your being denied a loan. Even if you have to pay a small fee for a copy of your report, it's well worth it.

Watch Out! _____

It's fairly common to find errors on your credit report. Most are tiny mistakes, fortunately. However, with identity theft skyrocketing, it's becoming more and more common to find shocking information on your report—the result of someone illegally hijacking your identity. Co-author Bobbi was once the victim of identity theft when someone lifted her personal information from her mail (which had been stolen). She can tell you from personal experience that it can be a time-consuming and frustrating process to fix these errors, so the sooner you spot anything amiss in your credit report, the better.

Mortgage Companies

Mortgage companies are another great resource for financing foreclosures. Unlike banks and other traditional lenders, these companies focus solely on making loans for buying homes. With more and more people getting involved in real estate investing, mortgage companies seem to be cropping up everywhere these days.

There can be several advantages to using a mortgage company. For one thing, these are private companies—so you generally don't face nearly the amount of red tape as with highly regulated lending institutions. Often times, there's a manager or other boss onsite who can make the decision as to whether to approve the loan. Sometimes your application is forwarded to a main office with the final say, but you'll still almost always get a quick answer.

Also these companies are very well-versed in everything related to mortgages—after all, that's all they do. They're also very accustomed to dealing with investors. So they can help expedite your financing process and may also be able to suggest creative solutions to any specific obstacles you may face.

Check your local phone book for mortgage companies in your area. However, as with most other things these days, you can also apply for a mortgage online from wherever you live. Some national companies that allow you to apply for mortgages online include HomeLoanCenter (www.homeloancenter.com) and Market Street Mortgage (www.marketstreetmortgage.com). Both companies offer conventional loans as well as construction loans, FHA/VA loans, programs for borrowers with credit problems, and many other services.

Promissory Note _____

We find that the phrase "investment property" seems to open doors at mortgage companies. Firms that may have been hesitant to lend money for an owner occupant are more than happy to help an investor. Presumably, this is because investment properties are often flipped quickly, meaning the loan gets paid off quickly. On the other hand, insurance companies often take the opposite view of investment properties, because presumably these properties involve a higher risk of claims.

Friends and Family

If you have very generous friends or relatives with some available money, they may be willing to float you a loan for your down payment and other expenses. Offer to give them a cut of whatever profits you make, in addition to whatever interest you agree to pay. Should you borrow money from friends and family, this isn't something you need to tell your lender. The lender doesn't care where your down payment came from—and probably shouldn't be told anyway, as it's none of their business.

This option, though, is one that many people avoid like the plague, even if they have friends with deep pockets. Some people hate the idea of asking loved ones for a loan. Also you really need to be confident in your ability to make a profit on the deal—or at least break even—so you can repay the loan quickly. Should Uncle Larry take a major loss when you fall through on the loan, you're guaranteed to have some stressful family gatherings.

Partnerships

Partnerships—like marriages—can be really great or really bad. In a good partnership, one partner will usually do most of the "legwork"—finding, investigating, and researching the property, and possibly preparing all the necessary paperwork. The second person usually has cash to invest but doesn't want to be bothered with all the work.

If you can find yourself a good money partner, you may be sitting pretty. The specific terms of your partnership arrangement are up to you and your partner. You should make sure, though, that each partner is entitled to a reasonable and fair share of the profits in relation to the effort or money they've invested, so that nobody ends up feeling like they got the bad end of the deal.

You can form partnerships with friends, relatives, or colleagues. It may be easier to enlist several partners, thus lessening the investment—and risk—that one person would carry. Suppose you need $15,000 to buy a property that would return a 100 percent profit (meaning, another $15,000) in 120 days. Wouldn't it be easier to find three people to each chip in $5,000, as opposed to one person financing the whole $15,000? Everyone involved would still take a risk, but it would be a much lower risk. Likewise, everyone would profit, but only by one third of the dollar amount—although their return on investment would still be 100 percent ($5,000 invested, $10,000 returned).

How are partnerships handled by lenders? In the case of a simple partnership—as in, two people are "in on the deal," both can apply for the loan and the debt—as well as the deed and other related documents—would be in both names. The lender would simply do a background check on both parties.

In partnerships involving a group of people, it's common for the group to select one person to be the borrower/buyer for a specific deal. That person would apply for the loan and the property would be in their name, but the group would have a private agreement in writing detailing their interests in the property.

Investors

In the classified sections of larger daily papers, you'll often spot ads posted by people who want to loan money, generally under a category called "Money to Lend" or something similar. Contact these individuals to find out what kind of lending they do. Some only lend in large amounts, whereas others may require major collateral, such as your house. Many of these lenders charge high interest rates, so be sure to use caution, shop around, and compare terms.

Promissory Note _____

Be prepared with a carefully thought-out plan of how you will use this money wisely—and be ready to explain this plan in an articulate way. The fastest way to turn off an investor is by looking like an amateur. On the other hand, you can impress an investor by having your facts and details ready. Explain that you want to borrow money for a quick and profitable return. Convince the investor you know what you are doing, just as you would if dealing with banks or other lenders. Have your documentation ready and be prepared to back up your strategy with numbers and facts.

You can also take a proactive approach and place an ad of your own in the "Money Wanted" or "Investment Opportunities" sections.

Hard-Money Lenders

There's a type of lender that specializes in making loans to investors and others who need a big chunk of money quickly, but can't—or won't—go to traditional lenders, for whatever reason. These are called *hard-money lenders*. If you have bad credit, are self-employed, or otherwise have trouble documenting your income, or simply don't

Land Lingo _____

A **hard-money lender** is a firm or private investor who makes high-interest loans to people who can't borrow money elsewhere. These lenders often pay little or no attention to the borrower's credit, instead focusing on the property's equity and potential profit of the deal.

want to deal with banks, you may want to consider a hard-money lender. However, give this a lot of thought before you proceed. There's a joke that these places are called hard-money lenders because the money doesn't come easy. Or at least, it doesn't come cheap. Generally, hard-money lenders charge high interest rates. However, they're geared toward investors who only need financing for a short time while they buy, fix, and flip the property, so interest charges may not be a big problem.

Promissory Note

Although there are some major downsides to using a hard-money lender—mainly, the high interest rates—there can also be some advantages. Loans are usually approved quickly, without all the red tape involved in many traditional loans. Plus, these lenders will consider loans that banks won't touch—cases where the property is in a remote area, for example, or needs a lot of repairs.

This definitely isn't an option you want to consider if you're seeking someone to finance your 30-year mortgage. In fact, many hard-money loans are granted only on a short-term basis—the entire amount of the loan is often due within six months or a year.

It can be a challenge to find a good, reputable hard-money lender. Many only operate within a limited geographical area. Your best bet is word of mouth. Ask your contacts in the real estate business whether they know of any hard-money lenders they can recommend. One firm that makes hard-money loans nationwide is www.ezinvestormoney.com.

FHA Loans

The FHA offer several loan options that might help you finance your foreclosure purchase.

203(b) Loans

The most popular FHA loan program is the 203(b). You can use this program to buy new or existing 1-4 unit properties in both urban and rural areas. A 203(b) fixed mortgage can be repaid in monthly payments over terms of 15 or 30 years. You can pay off the entire balance of the loan at any time, without any prepayment penalties.

Interest rates on FHA loans are slightly above market rates, but down payment requirements are lower than with traditional loans.

You don't need to be a first-time homebuyer to qualify for an FHA 203(b) loan. For more information, contact the FHA at 1-877-342-8632.

203(k) Loans

The FHA also offers a 203(k) loan. How does this differ from the 203(b) loan? Well, the (k) version is a rehabilitation loan. You can borrow money above the purchase price of the property to pay for home improvements.

Wholesale Flipping

One common principal in profitable foreclosure investing is the practice of buying, fixing, and flipping (or reselling at a profit) properties quickly. Basically: Get in, get out, get your money. However, there's another type of "flipping" in which *you* never actually own the property at all. This is possibly the best way of financing a foreclosure deal: letting someone else pay for it. This is known as *wholesale flipping*. (It's sometimes also called assigning the contract.)

In this type of arrangement, you do all the steps up to the point of actually buying the property—meaning, you find and research the properties, contact the owners (or lenders, in the case of REOs), negotiate with any lien holders, inspect the property, do the title search, negotiate the best possible price ... and then you turn the deal over to someone else. In this scenario, you're acting more as a scout or negotiator for someone else. You get a pre-set fee for your services. You won't earn as much as if you actually bought and flipped the property yourself—but then again, you're not investing any money or taking any risk, so it balances out.

Who do you flip these properties to? Bigger investors, contractors seeking a rehabilitation project, or people looking for fixer-uppers. Ask around or place ads in the local classifieds announcing that you have fixer-uppers for sale.

> **Land Lingo**
>
> **Wholesale flipping** is the practice of acquiring an interest in a property, or the right to buy that property, and then signing over your interest to another investor at a profit. You do all the negotiations and legwork, but don't actually buy or pay for the property.

> **Promissory Note**
>
> "I actually think whole flipping may be the best and safest route for a new investor who wants to break into foreclosures," says Jackie Lange, president of Texas Home Solutions Inc. and founder of www.SellYourHousein7Days.com. "They don't need to get approved for financing, they're not investing any of their own money—plus they get valuable experience as to the foreclosure-buying process."

> **Watch Out!**
>
> The most important factor of wholesale flipping is making sure you have a qualified buyer lined up before you put too much work into the deal. You don't want to go through all the trouble of lining up this great deal, and then find yourself stuck without anyone to buy it.

The amount of profit you make from a wholesale flip will vary. When determining your fee, figure in the amount of time and effort you put into the process of finding the property and negotiating the deal. Generally, you should expect to make at least a few thousand dollars on a typical wholesale flip deal.

Other Sources

There may be other available sources of funding you can tap into. Many states have a Homebuyer's Program. This may go by one of several different names—the state's Housing Finance Program, for example, or the state's Residential Financing. Check your state's website for information on any available programs that may be of help to you.

These agencies specialize in assisting first-time and low-income homebuyers, and are especially eager to help people willing to buy properties in low-income or distressed neighborhoods.

The biggest benefit of working with these agencies is the low interest rates and low down payments.

Advanced Financing Options

We've already outlined the financing strategies that we believe are the easiest (and least risky) for new investors to use and understand. However, there are other financing options that are popular with many foreclosure gurus and investors. We advise "newbies" to proceed with caution when considering these techniques. However, if you've gotten some experience under your belt—or if you're comfortable and confident working with fairly complex or risky financial transactions, you may want to tackle some of these tactics.

We explain these techniques in greater detail in later chapters, but want to briefly mention a few of them here.

Subject To

Buying a property "subject to" basically means you're taking the property *subject to* the existing loan or financing. In other words, you simply take over the payment arrangements that were put in place by the person selling the property. The tricky part? Although the payments remain in their name, the title is now in yours.

Lease Option Sales

With a lease option arrangement, you rent the home to a person who is kind of a combination tenant and future buyer. In simple terms: in exchange for a down payment and monthly rent (a portion of which is usually credited toward future purchase of the property), the tenant gets the option to buy the property at a specified price within the given time limit. Not only does this provide you (as the seller/owner) with a lump sum of cash, but you should also set the rent at an amount exceeding your mortgage payments, allowing you to make a monthly profit.

The Least You Need to Know

- Good credit can be a key to getting financing, so be sure to keep a close eye on your credit report.

- If you're sure you can resell a property quickly, a higher interest rate on a loan or line of credit might not be a big problem.

- It's easier to find partners if you can reduce their risk and required financial investment.

- Wholesale flipping can be an easy, low-risk way to break into foreclosure investing.

Part 4

After the Sale

Congratulations, you've successfully bought your first foreclosure property. You work is not done yet. In the next few chapters, we explain your options at this after-the-sale stage. We describe your most important first steps and share tips for getting the property in the best possible shape. We help you decide whether you want to be a landlord, and—if not—how you can sell the property for the most profit.

Chapter 14

Details, Details

In This Chapter

◆ Why vacancies can be a blessing

◆ The first important post-purchase tasks

◆ Handling existing tenants

◆ What the redemption period means to you

Okay, you've done the deal and signed on the dotted line. Now you can relax, right? Not so fast. You must do immediately several important things upon taking ownership of a foreclosure. In this chapter, we'll discuss important post-purchase issues, such as removing occupants from the property and making sure the property is officially yours.

Is It Officially Yours?

You're the proud owner of a new foreclosure property—or are you? How do you know that the property is truly, officially yours?

When it comes to buying foreclosures, ownership can—as some new investors are disappointed to discover—be kind of a gray area.

Right of Redemption

Some states give defaulting borrowers the right of redemption. This means they can get their property back, even long after it has been sold at auction. Hopefully, you've followed our advice and researched what—if any—redemption period applies in your state.

Should you live in a state with redemption rights, you basically have to hold your breath and keep your fingers crossed until this time period ends. Theoretically, if the defaulting homeowners can come up with enough cash to bring their mortgage current—plus any added costs and fees—they can reclaim their home during this redemption period. This is rare, but it is a possibility that you need to keep in mind.

If this were to happen, the administrating authority that handled the sale would contact you to inform you that Mr. Homeowner has redeemed the property according to all proper procedures and that your purchase price will be refunded. If you do buy a property in which a redemption period applies, we'd suggest checking in periodically to make sure the homeowner hasn't exerted their right of redemption (or expressed plans to do so), to avoid being caught by surprise.

Pre-Foreclosures

If possible, you should hold the closing at—or very near—the property itself. This way, you'll be able to inspect the property's condition at the very last minute, to verify that it's the same as it was when you made the offer. Plus you can (hopefully) make sure the homeowner vacates the premises immediately upon closing, if they haven't already done so.

You essentially become the property owner once the title has been transferred into your name. But if you haven't completely taken control of the property—if any loans or other documents or obligations remain in the defaulting homeowner's name, for example—things can get a little tricky, because the seller is still the homeowner in the lender's eyes.

This is why it's vital to make sure—and have your attorney confirm this—that all paperwork and legal documents have been filled out completely and correctly and filed/recorded with all necessary departments and agencies.

Auction Buys

If you were the successful bidder at a foreclosure auction, you can't officially claim the property until you've paid the full purchase price, completed all the necessary paperwork, and fulfilled any other legal obligations. You will have already paid a portion of the price—probably at least 10 percent—as a deposit at the auction. You need to quickly gather the rest of the amount. Generally, you only have about 30 days—possibly less—to pay the balance of the purchase price. Contact your lawyer and accountant or financial advisor immediately after the sale so they can assist you with whatever arrangements need to be made.

Contact the person who handled the sale and confirm the total amount you need to bring, as well as any documents or other paperwork you need.

Be sure to fulfill all the obligations and conditions of the sale, or you may find yourself without the property—and without the deposit (which you'll forfeit).

REO or Government Property

If a lender or government agency accepts your offer to buy an REO property, be sure to have your attorney review the final contracts before you sign them.

What to Do First Following the Closing

You need to take care several important things immediately after closing on a foreclosure property.

Signed, Sealed, and Properly Filed

Make sure that you (or your attorney) have filed all paperwork related to the closing and that it has been received and recorded by the proper person or department at the courthouse.

Insurance Coverage

This is perhaps one of the most important things you need to do after closing on a property. It would be heartbreaking to go through

Watch Out!

As unbelievable as it sounds, co-author Bobbi once suffered a total loss when the home she had just bought burned down *the day of the closing*. Trust us, insurance coverage is one thing you can't put off—get it taken care of right away!

all that time and effort to buy the property, only to see it go up in smoke—and then realize you have no recourse because you hadn't gotten it insured yet.

Take Care of Any Necessary Red Tape

Contact the local municipality to find out about any permits or other paperwork that needs to be transferred or issued in your name.

Inform the utility companies that the bills should now be in your name.

Contact the tax collector or tax bureau to confirm that they are now listing the taxes in your name.

Promissory Note _____

Before the closing, you should have already contacted the utility companies to ensure that the bills are all current, or that any outstanding bills will be the responsibility of the seller or previous owner. You don't want to take control of the home only to discover you've "inherited" an electricity bill for several thousand dollars!

Address Serious Safety/Maintenance Issues

You probably plan to repair any damage or problems with the home in due time, but you must immediately address any serious hazards or safety issues that pose a significant threat to the property or the people around it. Are there windows that are broken or missing? Replace them—or at least board them up—to keep animals and children out, and to prevent weather damage. Wiring problems? Have the utilities disconnected until an electrician can make repairs.

Watch Out! _____

Keep in mind that as of the moment you signed the transfer of ownership papers at closing, you are now legally responsible for the property. In other words, you can be held liable for any injuries or damages caused by anything related to the property.

If the home will be vacant, make sure it is locked and secure. Taking this a step further, consider installing a security system or hiring a security company to at least make periodic checks on the property. This is another instance where nosy neighbors can come in handy. If you've made friends with any of the locals, ask them to be your "eyes and ears" and let you know if they notice anything amiss at the property.

Eviction

Perhaps you have the opposite problem—the home isn't vacant, but you wish it were. You, my friend, are about to become way too familiar with the eviction process. This is one of the most common complications of buying a foreclosed property—and one of the tasks investors dread most.

Evicting a stubborn tenant or former homeowner can be a time-consuming and costly process. It can take several months, lots of money, and several court hearings to force someone to leave the property. Worse, they can inflict a tremendous amount of damage upon the property—*your* property—while you're trying to remove them.

If you must initiate the eviction process, enlist the help of an attorney who is experienced in these types of proceedings. There are many rules related to this process, and one misstep or missed detail can delay the timeline even longer.

> **Watch Out!**
> Evictions can be a financially and mentally draining process. This is why many investors refuse to consider properties that are occupied. Other investors wisely withhold any money to homeowners until they've vacated the property.

Ideal Eviction Scenario

Ward Hanigan is a California foreclosure expert and founder of ForeclosureForum. com. He has perfected an eight-step process for handling evictions. Thanks to this technique, Hanigan says he's never had a case of vandalism by ex-owners in the 300+ foreclosure deals he's handled in the past 20 years. Here's an example of his technique, reprinted with permission from ForeclosureForum.com:

(Assume the homeowners are a couple named Ronald and Susan Crawford.)

#1. I knock on the front door and introduce myself, and extend my business card. "Mr. Crawford, my name is Ward Hanigan and this is my son, Eric Hanigan. I'm in the real estate business and last Tuesday I participated in a foreclosure auction and when the dust settled I discovered I was the new owner of the property here at 123 Elm Street."

"At the moment I'm somewhat nervous and apprehensive because I don't know how you're going to react to this news, but if we can talk things over for 5 minutes or so I know I'll feel a lot better and I think you will, too. May I come in please?"

#2. Once I enter the house I continue with, "Mr. Crawford, it's important to my peace of mind that you acknowledge that I'm not responsible in any way for causing your foreclosure. I guess what I'm saying is that if you have a list of people you're upset with concerning your foreclosure that I don't belong on that list, okay?"

#3. Then, with his agreement with #2, I continue: "Mr. Crawford, please feel free to call me Ward, okay?" (my hand is held outstretched for a handshake). If he just shakes my hand, but doesn't reciprocate with his first name then I ask him, "Mr. Crawford, what do your friends call you?" And he responds with "RJ." Then I'll ask, "May I call you RJ?" and he says "Sure." And I'll say, "Thanks, RJ."

Then I turn to his wife and say, "Mrs. Crawford, please feel free to call me Ward, okay?" (my hand is held outstretched for a handshake). Almost always she will shake my hand and say, "And feel free to call me Sue". To which I respond, "Thanks, Sue."

#4. Then I'll say, "RJ, the state of California seems to think that at this juncture I only need to give you a 3 Day notice to vacate, due to foreclosure. I disagree with our legislature on this point because I don't think they've thought out how most people actually move. I think most people are like me and move with the help of their friends, co-workers, neighbors and relatives, right? And they're the ones that need more than a 3 day notice to come help you move. So I'm prepared to extend this 3 Day notice (hand it to RJ) to a week from this coming Sunday at 4:00 P.M. if we can come to agreement on two points.

Now, from the public record I can see that you've lived here for about 9 years. During that time you've probably accumulated a lot of gadgets that you no longer use because their novelty has worn off. For example, in my garage right now you'd find a perfectly good bread machine I no longer use. It works fine, but we don't eat much bread any more, so there it sits, along with a lot other unused stuff.

So what I'm asking is that when you move that you leave the property in broom clean condition. So any stuff you don't care to move with you just give, sell, donate, or throw away, okay? And Sue, by broom clean I just mean no debris or unwanted stuff left behind, that's all.

And the second point I'd like to agree on is this. I'd like your permission to come visit the outside of the property with a contractor to start getting quotes on some possible exterior work if the opportunity presents itself, okay? We won't be coming in or even bother you with knocking on your door. We'd just be looking at the property from the outside that's all. But I bring it up now so you aren't wondering why I'm out on the sidewalk with somebody just a couple of days from now, okay?

#5. Sue, do you have a calendar of upcoming family activities, perhaps in the kitchen or somewhere close by? I wonder if you'd be so kind to get it so we can be in clear agreement as to the move-out date I'm willing to extend things to? Thanks."

When Sue is out of the room take out your camera and start taking pictures without asking permission while you explain to RJ that another lucky break we've received is that the insurance company that's issued the new insurance policy for fire and vandalism has agreed to let us take the pictures they need rather than sending someone else out to the property and bothering them in the next 10 days or so.

When Sue comes back with the calendar and starts to go ballistic over the fact you're taking pictures, just keeping clicking away while you repeat to her what you told RJ concerning the picture taking. Then abruptly stop for a moment and ask her, "Sue, I hope I'm not rubbing salt into a wound, but why did the foreclosure happen, what went wrong?" And while she and RJ are caught off stride, continue clicking away as you walk from room to room.

Ask RJ if they have any dogs, and if they do, ask him to put them in the garage temporarily while you go in the back yard to take a picture of the exterior of the house.

#6. When you're done taking pictures tell Sue that she'll be happy to hear that you have reinstated her delinquent first loan (if you took title at the sale of the 2nd) and that it's going to be a very positive reference on their credit record since the loan is in their name even though you're paying it every month about 5 days before it's due. Soon that credit item will be rated "Better than agreed" because of the consistently early payment routine you practice. Therefore, inquire if she would look for the loan payment book or monthly payment statement in order to effect a change of address that will route it to your address so you can make the monthly payments as promptly as possible.

#7. Then while both RJ and Sue are together with you tell them that you can also help them in a very important way: "Folks, let me share with you an important boost I can arrange for you as you start out in the rental market once more. You're probably aware of the importance potential landlords place on making sure you've kept your promises with other landlords and that you don't have any recent evictions attached to your names in the Unlawful Detainer Registry (UDR), especially not any recent ones. So if you keep your promise to be out when agreed and don't force me to evict you, you'll be able to sidestep several years of being blackballed by the rental industry. On top of that I'll be happy to give you a good reference and report that you gave me adequate notice when leaving and that you left the premises clean and neat."

#8. "Now RJ and Sue, one more item and I'll be on my way. Please keep my business card for your future reference. That's because some day, no matter how improbable it seems right now, you will have put this foreclosure business behind you and will be on your feet once again, capable of buying another home. When that day comes please give me a call and I will sell you any house I have in inventory for just 10 percent over my winning bid. I will even show you my actual purchase receipt to certify the deal you'd be getting. I plan to be in this business a good long time to come, so remember to give me a call whenever you feel ready and I'll do my best to make you an outstanding deal, okay? Oh, by the way, can you tell me where you'll leave the key for me to use once you're gone?"

Firm Up the Financing

Right before the closing, you should have verified that your financing is approved and officially ready. Following the closing, double-check that everything is in order and that there's nothing else you need to do to finalize the financing arrangements.

Find/Maintain Tenants

If you plan to hold on to the building as a rental property, and there are already tenants in place, you may want to maintain the status quo and keep things as they are. If possible, ask the seller or broker for as much information as possible about the tenants. Obviously, if they've been late with their rent every month for the past year, you might want to rethink the idea of letting them stay. However, if they've been good tenants, you can make things easy on yourself by keeping the tenants in place. You'll want to execute a new lease or rental agreement in your name, specifying any changes you've made or plan to make.

Get Ready to Sell

Assume you intend to resell this property for profit. How soon should you start preparing to sell? As soon as you've walked out of the closing. The longer you hold on to the property, the more costs you incur and the lower your profit potential. The faster you flip it, the sooner you make your profit. Bonus: Quickly selling the property will allow you to repay any loans or other financing, thus adding a major "gold star" to your credit rating.

The Least You Need to Know

◆ If your state gives defaulting borrowers a right of redemption, don't assume the property is completely yours forever until any redemption period has expired.

◆ Evictions can be a big hassle and should be handled by a qualified attorney.

◆ The longer you wait to find buyers or tenants for the property, the less profit you'll make.

Maintenance and Home Improvement

In This Chapter

- ◆ Home inspectors can be helpful
- ◆ Repairs that can't wait
- ◆ Don't overlook the little stuff

Once you've actually purchased the foreclosure property, what do you do with it? Unfortunately, the answer often involves rolling up your sleeves. Many foreclosures have been damaged or neglected and are in need of repair. In the case of major problems that pose a safety hazard, these repairs need to be done right away, regardless of your plans for the property. In this chapter, we'll discuss common maintenance problems and concerns, and tell you which ones can spell big trouble if not addressed right away.

Selling vs. Renting

The amount of time and money you invest in repairing the property will depend in large part on your plans for the place. If you're selling, you want to start showing the property as soon as possible, so you may not want to tackle time-consuming repairs unless absolutely necessary. You'll probably be more concerned with quick cosmetic fixes—and perhaps one or two larger repairs that might significantly affect your asking price.

On the other hand, your approach will differ if you plan to keep the building and rent it out. Major structural systems—such as the heating unit(s) and the roof—will be more important in this case, as you don't want all your profits going down the drain as you finance constant nickel-and-dime repairs. It's much wiser to invest a lump sum at the outset, to make sure everything is up to par and will be running smoothly. You also don't want to risk putting your tenants in an unsafe building. Sparing yourself a middle of the night phone call from irate tenants who find themselves with no heat on a January night would also be a good thing.

Foreclosure Fact

Some of the most successful foreclosure investors are those with construction or maintenance skills/experience who can do at least some repairs themselves, resulting in considerable savings. At the very least, you should take a basic home repair class so you'll know how to do simple repairs. Another option: Find a trustworthy contractor and agree to throw as much work as possible his way in exchange for a reduced rate.

Where to Start

Regardless of your plans for the property, you must take care of any pressing maintenance problems right away, especially those that present a safety hazard or are huge money-wasters. Anything that leaks, sparks, squeals, or sways should probably be at the top of your "needs repairs now" list.

Generally, electrical problems should get attention first, followed by heating problems. (You should definitely have someone check out the chimney, especially if the home's been vacant for a while, as blockages can cause deadly fumes to back up into the home.) Structural problems such as holes in the floor, broken stairs, leaks in the roof, and flooding in the basement should also all be addressed right away.

Promissory Note _____

One good way to find out what home repair/maintenance issues exist in your property is to have an inspection done by a qualified home inspector. They'll evaluate the major systems and components of the home, and point out things that could hurt your chances of selling. An inspection will probably cost around $200 or $300, but it can be well worth the price if it helps you spot some maintenance problem that will give your home a black eye. Shameless plug: For more information on home inspections, check out co-author Bobbi's book entitled *The Pocket Idiot's Guide to Home Inspections* (Alpha Books).

The Major Issues

Unless you plan to sell the house in "as is" condition as a true fixer-upper that would probably interest only the most ambitious handyman, there are some basic repair and maintenance issues that must be resolved. These are problems you will also need to address if you plan to rent out the property.

Foreclosure Fact

According to a study done by HouseMaster (one of the largest home inspection companies), electrical problems were the deficiencies most frequently found in home inspections. In homes 30 years and older, almost half of all houses had electrical problems. Shocking, isn't it?

Wiring Problems

Faulty wiring and other electrical problems are nothing to take lightly (no pun intended). An electrical fire can easily destroy the whole property, sending all of your potential profits up in smoke.

Structural/Framing Issues

Structural and framing-related defects and damage are among the most serious and potentially dangerous conditions a home can have. If you see any signs of possible structural damage—floors that slope or sage, major cracks in the walls or ceilings— have it evaluated by a contractor or engineer immediately before letting any tenants or buyers inside the home. Major structural problems are big undertakings that shouldn't be handled by a do-it-yourselfer. Unfortunately, they're also expensive problems to fix; so if you discover structural problems with the property, you may have to try to find a buyer who is willing to completely gut the property.

Faulty Furnace

A new furnace can easily cost $2,000 or more, so few buyers want to face the prospect of having to replace a furnace right off the bat. Hopefully, any problems with your property's furnace are minor and can be easily fixed. Small parts such as belts and filters are cheap and can generally be installed easily by the average person.

> **CAUTION**
>
> ## Watch Out!
>
> Be sure to keep an eye on the furnace's air filters and change them regularly. It's a simple job you can do yourself, and filters are pretty cheap (usually no more than a few bucks). On the other hand, *not* changing the filters can be costly. A clogged or dirty filter can cause your furnace to run less efficiently—and can even cause the furnace to overheat, possibly ruining the entire unit.

We want to repeat our previous advice about having a professional check the furnace vents and chimneys. Blockages or damage can cause carbon monoxide fumes to back up into the home, which can be deadly.

Kitchens and Bathrooms

Here's an unscientific fact: buyers *love* to look at kitchens and bathrooms. A modern, spacious kitchen can be a big selling point for a home—as can an attractive bathroom or two.

> **CAUTION**
>
> ## Watch Out!
>
> If you add or upgrade the kitchen appliances, be sure the electrical system can handle the new setup. Also all kitchens and bathrooms should be equipped with GFCI (ground fault circuit interrupters), special outlets that are designed to guard against electrical shock in case of a short circuit. They're especially important in areas such as kitchen counters where water may be present.

Pay special attention to "hot spots" in the bathroom. A wobbly toilet will be sure to bother a would-be buyer—it's usually an easy fix, so take care of it before buyers arrive. Ditto for leaky faucets. Make sure the tub and shower look their best, with no signs of leaks, loose tiles, or rust.

In the kitchen, it's all about the cabinets and appliances. Some nice shiny appliances and beautiful wooden cabinets can compensate for a multitude of other things the home may be lacking. If the cabinets are in bad shape, it's a good idea to have them repaired or replaced. Likewise, if the appliances are old, don't work properly, or just plain don't look very nice, spending the money on some new appliances can be a wise investment. Common kitchen problems include poor ventilation, appliances that are too old or don't operate properly, and inadequate electrical supplies to handle all the appliances.

Doors and Windows

Doors or windows that are broken, worn, or otherwise in disrepair will give the whole property a black eye. More importantly, they spell a financial loss—and not just because buyers may submit lower offers. Windows that are loose or broken will offer no protection against heat loss. If you are paying the heating bills, you'll literally be throwing money out the window if you don't take care of this right away.

Also doors or windows that are buckled or crooked can also signal more serious structural problems. This is something a good home inspector or contractor should be able to analyze for you.

The Roof

The roof is a very important part of the home. It acts as the protective skin—keeping elements out and heat in. Savvy buyers will zero in on any signs of roof problems. Repair any leaks immediately, and watch out for discoloration, scaling, and other signs of water absorption problems. A leaky roof can spell a bigger problem than a few drips falling from the ceiling. If water gets into the roof, it can cause the shingles to loosen or fall off. In areas with cold weather, this can also cause ice to build up on and under the roofing materials. Repeated cycles of freezing and thawing can eventually cause a faulty roof to deteriorate or collapse completely.

Basements and Foundations

Because the basement and foundation are basically what holds up the rest of the house, this is obviously a pretty important area of the home. Most buyers' main concern in the basement will be the possibility of water damage. Act quickly at the first sign of basement water problems and you may be able to solve the problem with little expense.

Often basement water problems are the result of poor drainage or improper grading on the property. Installing gutters and drains or making landscaping changes that help water flow away from the house can often solve the problem.

With the foundation, watch out for red flags such as cracks in the foundation walls. Horizontal cracks are especially worrisome, because they can sometimes be a sign of a serious structural problem. Consult a qualified contractor—ideally, a structural engineer—to check it out.

Do You Really Need to Fix It?

Exactly which repairs you choose to make is your decision. In this chapter, we tell you which home maintenance problems will generally concern buyers most, but it's up to you whether to address those problems. You're free to leave a damaged or run-down house as is, of course, but you must realize that this will significantly affect your asking price. You need to weigh your priorities when it comes to selling this house. Which is more important to you, a higher asking price or a quick sale? Ideally, you'd get both, but that's not always possible. If you mainly want to flip the property quickly, your best bet might be to fix one or two of the most visible problems, and leave the rest—lowering the price accordingly.

> **CAUTION**
>
> **Watch Out!**
>
> If the property does have maintenance problems, damage, or related issues and you conceal that fact from the buyer, you could risk facing a lawsuit or other problems, depending on your local and state laws. Consult with your attorney and/or real estate broker to find out exactly what your responsibilities are concerning full disclosure.

Make the Home Buyer-Friendly

If you plan to sell the property, you must think like a buyer and consider the issues that may attract her attention.

A Maintenance-Free Image Is Key

Many people do not have good imaginations when it comes to homes. They can't easily envision what a run-down home will look like in good condition. More importantly, they don't want to envision themselves doing the considerable work required to get the home in that condition.

The only thing they'll see is the broken window, the hole in the wall, and the cracks in the bathroom tile. You can spend an hour spinning a great tale of how gorgeous the home will look after repairs, but you'll never be able to get those first-impression images out of the buyer's head. Don't underestimate the importance of fixing any obvious imperfections, even if they are actually minor flaws that the buyers could live with or easily fix on their own.

Creepy Crawlers

The home may be a gorgeous mansion, but a potential buyer who spots an ant colony in the kitchen—or worse, a mouse scurrying across her feet—isn't likely to make an offer. Strongly consider having an exterminator give the place a once-over, especially if the home has been vacant, is near the woods, or is in a climate where insects and other pests are a problem.

If the buyer will be getting a mortgage, their lender may insist on a termite inspection—in which case, an unresolved termite problem can kill the whole deal. Better to nip that problem in the bud before it ends up biting you in the … bottom line.

Curb Appeal

Some buyers make their decision about a property before they even step through the front door. The house's outside appearance can make or break a deal, so you should do everything possible to improve the home's "curb appeal." Clean up the front yard, clear the walkway, make sure there's adequate lighting, and maybe even add a nice colorful mailbox or a decorative planter at the end of the driveway.

> **Watch Out!**
>
> Yes, it's important to flip the property as quickly as possible to maximize your profits. However, be careful not to jump the gun and show a property before it's ready. If the property hasn't been repaired to an acceptable level, you may scare off any would-be buyers. In this case, a little delay may be a smart move, if it gives you time to get the repairs done. Besides, you'll only end up wasting time and money advertising and showing a property before it is really "ready for its close-up."

Garages and Sheds

Garages and sheds can earn big bonuses points for a house, but only if they're in tip-top shape. An old, half-collapsed shed is an eyesore that will definitely turn off buyers. Better to tear it down before buyers spot it.

A nice garage in good condition can be a big asset, so make sure it's clean, well lit, and that all doors open and close properly.

Underground Gas Tanks

In some parts of the country, buried oil tanks are a big deal. Minimal mitigation costs $2,000, and if they've leaked, it can spell big trouble. If a house is heated with oil (or has been), it's always a good idea to find out if there's a buried tank. This is one of those disclosure issues that can really come back and bite you in the behind. If the buyer finds himself with a leaky tank, he can come back and in many states successfully sue you for damages if you knew or should have known the tank was there and didn't tell him.

Little Improvements Mean a Lot

Little things can make a big difference. Some relatively inexpensive improvements can really help you make a good impression on prospective buyers.

Paint

One of the easiest ways to spruce up a home is with a fresh coat of paint. Stick with neutral colors. Sure, you may a big fan of purple walls, but some of your buyers may not be so thrilled with that choice. Plus, one of your main objectives is to encourage buyers to envision themselves living here—which will be tough for them to do if they are preoccupied with thoughts of how badly their furniture will clash with this unusual color scheme.

> **Foreclosure Fact**
>
> As an investor, you have a big advantage over someone selling their own residence: You have no emotional connection to the property. Be sure to remain objective and view the home with the same critical eye as a buyer. Sure, the previous owner may have loved hot-pink walls, but odds are good that this won't be a hit with buyers.

Landscaping

A well-manicured lawn can instantly make any home look much nicer. By contrast, a home featuring weeds, lots of unruly stray branches, and overgrown grass can kill a deal. You know what buyers see when they spot an ugly yard? Well, yes, they see an ugly yard—but they also envision the countless weekends they'll have to spend trying to get this yard under control. Bottom line: An ugly yard equals work, and the last thing buyers want is to do a lot of work.

Do You Need a Professional?

It's true that you can save lots of money by doing as many repairs as possible yourself, but it's also important to know your own limits. Certain jobs should be handled only by experienced qualified professionals. Don't tinker with the electrical system, for example, unless you happen to have considerable experience as an electrician. A home inspector can probably clue you in as to which of your property's problems should be left to a pro.

An Expert's List of Hot Spots

Janet Wickell is a real estate expert who runs the Home Buying/Selling site at http://homebuying.about.com.

She says there are a few basic problem "hot spots" that will definitely scare buyers away. Fortunately, most of these can be remedied fairly easily/cheaply, but you should be sure to address any of these problems before letting anyone tour the property.

Mold and Mildew

Wickell says, "Mildew stains and odors scare buyers, especially now that toxic black mold is such a hot topic. Chances are you won't even get an acceptable offer if mold and mildew are present."

Wet Basements and Crawlspaces

Wickell points out that making sure the basement and any crawlspaces are dry is important to the home buyer. She says, "Buyers and inspectors will look closely at the walls and floors for patches of mildew and signs of dampness. Cover exposed earth in basements and crawl spaces with plastic to help keep moisture levels down. Leaking walls in the basement may be expensive to repair. If serious problems exist, and you do not want to make repairs, you can consider lowering the price of the house upfront, with the understanding that the price reflects the problem."

The Roof and Its Neighbors

The roof will be inspected, so it is a good idea to take a close look at it before the home buyer does. Wickell says, "Deteriorated shingles or other roof coverings are one of the first things home buyers and home inspectors notice. If the elements underneath the shingles are moist or rotted, you can bet repairs will be requested."

Clean the gutters and make sure downspouts are positioned so that water runs away from the house.

Flashing around the base of chimneys should be watertight. Mortar and bricks should be in good condition.

Inadequate or Inferior Electrical Systems

The electrical panel and circuit breaker configuration should be adequate for the needs of the house. A 125-amp electrical panel works for most homes. Individual circuits should not be overloaded.

General Repair/Maintenance Costs

Your actual repair/maintenance costs will vary widely depending on the specific problems and the size/type of home involved. However, here are some basic general guidelines of costs for common repair problems (figures courtesy of HouseMaster, a national home inspection company).

Plumbing

Some basic plumbing costs are as follows:

- ◆ Replacing sections of pipe: $300 to $500
- ◆ New water heater: up to $900
- ◆ Replacing entire piping system: $3,000 to $5,000

Roofing

Supplies only, for a 1,500-sqaure-foot home:

- ◆ 30-year asphalt shingles: $1,000
- ◆ 24-inch cedar shakes: $3,000

Hiring a professional:

- Installing new asphalt shingles over existing layer: $1,500 and up
- Removing several layers of shingles and replacing with plywood and shingles: $4,000

Bathrooms

Some potential bathroom repair costs:

- Replace shower pan: $1,000 to $1,500
- Reset toilet: $100 to $250

Framing

Costs you may encounter if you have framing problems:

- Replace main beam: $30 to $75 per foot
- Reinforce exposed joists: $10 to $20 per foot

Chimneys

Some possible expenses with chimneys and fireplaces:

- Flue cleaning: $100 to $150
- New fireplace with two-story chimney: $8,000 to $15,000

The Least You Need to Know

- Major problems—such as faulty wiring and structural deficiencies—need to be handled immediately by a professional.
- It may be wiser to lower the price on the property or sell it "as is" instead of tackling major expensive projects.
- Buyers tend to be especially interested in kitchens and bathrooms, so make sure these rooms look their best.
- There are several "hot spots" in a home that are particularly prone to scaring off buyers—such as a leaky roof or a moldy basement.

Chapter **16**

Holding On to the Property

In This Chapter

- ◆ Are you cut out to be a landlord?
- ◆ Avoiding common rental headaches
- ◆ Depreciation and other big tax breaks for landlords
- ◆ Finding good tenants takes work
- ◆ Getting the property tenant-ready
- ◆ Preparing and understanding a lease agreement

Once you've addressed any urgent repair and maintenance issues, it's time to start making this investment property pay off. In this chapter, we'll discuss using a foreclosure property for rental income. We'll show you how to decide whether you even want to be a landlord, and—if so—how to find good tenants.

Owner Occupancy

Generally, most people buy a foreclosure property as an investment, meaning that it has one of two goals: flipping it for a quick profit, or renting it out for a steady monthly income.

It's fairly uncommon for foreclosure buyers to keep the property as their own residence. However, it does happen occasionally—especially when you first start out, or if you happen to discover a property that is the exact image of the "dream house" you've been seeking your entire life.

There's nothing wrong with buying a foreclosure as an owner occupancy. It can be a smart way to get a nice home for a good discount from market prices. However, be sure to give some thought to your plans before you obtain financing or sign on the dotted line. You won't be getting any rental income from the property, so you need to be sure you can afford the monthly payment from your own income. Also because you won't be flipping the property, you should avoid hard-money lenders or mortgages with balloon payments that can spell financial disaster down the road.

As we said, though, most investors who hold on to their foreclosure properties do so with the intention of renting them out, so that's the focus for most of this chapter.

Are You Landlord Material?

Not everyone is willing or able to be a *landlord*. It can be a stressful and time-consuming job, sometimes accompanied by plenty of headaches. If the furnace dies at 3 A.M. on a frigid January morning, guess who gets the angry calls from frantic (not to mention freezing) *tenants?* Or if a resident trashes the place or causes problems for the neighbors, who will have to foot the bill for repairs or field the complaints? That's right—the landlord.

If you plan to rent out property, be prepared for emergencies and unexpected phone calls. We can practically guarantee you that emergencies never happen on a good day—say, when it's sunny, warm, and you have nothing better to do.

Land Lingo

A **landlord** is someone who rents or leases his or her property to someone else. The occupant who rents the property is called the **tenant**.

If you want the investment benefits of rental property without the round-the-clock responsibility, you might want to consider hiring an individual or firm to manage the property on your behalf. If you have numerous properties, it can be worthwhile to have a full-time property manager on the payroll.

Some landlords provide a manager or building superintendent with free or reduced rent in exchange for keeping an eye on the property and handling minor repairs and maintenance issues.

Depreciation

Everyone likes to be appreciated, but for land-lords, *depreciation* is the name of the game.

Depreciation is important to landlords because Uncle Sam allows you to write off a certain amount on your taxes. The exact figure depends on several factors, such as when you started renting out the property. Still, this is generally a very nice tax break.

Parts of your property that aren't real estate—such as appliances, electronics, furniture, land improvements, etc.—can also be depreciated, but over a shorter time period, which translates to a bigger deduction on an annual basis.

Keep in mind, the depreciation expense that's allowed on your tax return (use Schedule E) goes by the total cost of the property, not just what you've paid you so far. If you buy a $100,000 rental property and only put down $20,000 (20 percent), your depreciation is based on the full $100,000. If 90 percent of your property tax bill is allocated to improvements (assuming you paid $2,000 in closing costs) then your yearly deduction for depreciation is around $3,300.

Even if you don't depreciate a property, if you are entitled to do so, you must *recapture* it when you sell. So it's kind of silly not to take it. Yet lots of people don't because they don't understand all the complicated issues involved. This is why you really need a good accountant on your advisory team.

Land Lingo

Depreciation is the reduction of value over time of an item that is usually large or expensive, such as a house, car, appliance, etc.

Foreclosure Fact

Only the building is eligible for depreciation, not the land. To find your depreciable figure, check your property tax bill for the percentage breakdown between land and improvements. So if 90 percent of your bill is for improvements, then 90 percent of your total cost for the property is allowed as a deduction, spread out over 27.5 years.

Land Lingo

To **recapture** depreciation means included part or all of the depreciation you deducted in prior years in this year's taxable income.

More Tax Breaks

You can also deduct every single penny that you spend improving, advertising, cleaning or inspecting your rental property.

> **Foreclosure Fact**
>
> According to figures from the 2000 U.S. Census, around 35 million homes or apartments in this country are rental properties. Meaning, one out of every three households has a landlord.

Any money you've spent for building maintenance, upkeep expense, and interest on mortgage payments is subtracted from your profit figure before taxes are paid.

Depreciation, deductions, and other tax issues can get pretty complicated, so we strongly recommend using a professional accountant. Even if you plan to use some of that do-it-yourself accounting software, you should still do a lot of research and studying about tax related issues.

Before Seeking Tenants

There are some things you need to do before you actually start looking for tenants. By addressing these issues early in the process, you'll spare yourself many headaches and have the best chance of getting quality tenants quickly.

Learn the Law

The laws concerning landlord-tenant issues vary from state to state. Be sure to research and study the laws in your area. Better yet, find a lawyer who specializes in real estate law, specifically as it relates to rental situations.

Spruce the Place Up

Just like sellers, tenants often make snap decisions as to whether they like a place immediately upon laying eyes on it. There are a few quick and easy things you can do to greatly improve the property's "curb appeal." Mary Tyler, a Virginia investor and landlord, is a big believer in the power of pretty landscaping. "It's human nature. When they walk up to the house and see beautiful, colorful flowers and nice trees, they automatically get a good feeling." Tyler says you should also make sure the hardwood floors are in tip-top shape. "People love hardwood floors. But dirty, dull floors are a turnoff. On the other hand, if someone walks in and sees nice shiny hardwood floors, they'll really perk up."

Call Your Insurance Agent

Consult with your insurance agent to make sure your homeowner policy covers rental occupants. Also ask about any special conditions you may need to be aware of. For example, some insurance companies charge extra to cover certain kinds of dogs who are prone to be aggressive.

Network

You can learn a lot by chatting with veteran landlords. Join local real estate groups—you may even be able to locate a group specifically for landlords. If there's none in your area, there are plenty of websites for landlords that you can visit online. Many—such as www.landlord.com and www.mrlandlord.com—have lots of free resources, such as sample leases and other forms. These online groups generally also offer message boards where you can connect with other landlords.

Determining Your Rent

Before you can advertise the property or seek tenants, you need to figure out exactly how much rent you plan to charge. A good place to start is by scanning the classifieds to see the rents for similar properties in the area.

Still, don't rely too heavily on that information. You have no idea what kind of expenses the owners of those properties have, or what their mortgage payments may be. Your main goal as an investor is to try and make a nice profit after covering all the expenses for the property. Add up your total expenses for the property—including mortgage, insurance, taxes, utilities, etc. For you to make a profit, you must charge tenants a rent that is higher than this amount. Ideally, you did these calculations *before* buying the property, to determine if this would be a profitable investment.

CAUTION

Watch Out!

If you own rental property in California, Maryland, New Jersey, New York, or Washington, D.C., you need to be aware that some communities in these areas—such as New York City and San Francisco—have laws limiting the amount of rent a landlord can charge. Many rent control laws also require landlords to have a valid legal reason for evicting a tenant.

Promissory Note _____

Mary Tyler, a veteran landlord from Virginia, says she likes to try and make at least a $100 monthly profit from renting a property—meaning, $100 left over after the mortgage payment and other expenses. Keep in mind, though, that Tyler keeps that $100 monthly balance in her fund for capital expenses. "If the dishwasher breaks or the pipes flood, it can cost a pretty penny. You need to have a fund to cover those expenses."

Of course, if your property is in a low-income area where rents tend to be pretty low, it can be tough to build in even a $100 cushion without pricing yourself right out of the market. "You're generally lucky to break even, from a monthly income point of view," Tyler says. "The real profit in rental properties lies in the equity of the property."

Advertising

Your advertising strategy can be as simple as posting signs on or near the property. This can be especially effective if the property is in an area that gets a lot of foot traffic. Most likely, though, you'll have to work a bit harder than that to find good tenant candidates.

Which Tenants Will You Attract?

Certain kinds of properties tend to attract specific types of people. By evaluating your property—and thinking about the type of people who'll be likely to gravitate toward it—you can determine the best way to advertise it.

If the building consists mainly of studio or one-bedroom units, your prospective tenants will most likely be singles or couples who aren't that concerned with the local schools. In this case, would-be tenants may be most interested in price—especially if the apartment is near a university and would interest college students with a tight budget.

If the apartment is small but in a nicer part of town, tenants will want to know about the property's condition and amenities. Play up any "perks" such as fireplaces, whirlpool tubs, decks, etc. Also be sure to stress that the place is clean, safe, and well maintained.

Online Outlets

These days, it's very easy to find tenants the modern way—by posting ads online. We think Craigslist.org—a very popular online community where people can post various ads for jobs, apartments, etc, in numerous major cities across the country—is by far the most high-traffic site (in fact, we know many people who have found apartments or tenants on that site), but there are many others. Try www.rentalhousehunter.com.

Brokers/Agents

Many real estate agents don't handle rental properties, simply because the relatively small profit isn't worth their time. Even if you do find an agent who handles rentals, think carefully about whether you want to give someone else a chunk of your profits.

If you live a distance away from the property, or don't have the time or energy to screen tenants and show the property, it may be worthwhile to enlist the help of an agent or broker.

> **Promissory Note**
>
> We advise always mentioning the price in your ad or online post. This way, you automatically weed out people who can't afford the rent. On the other hand, we strongly advise against including the exact address, for obvious reasons.

Classifieds

The tried-and-true method of renting out an apartment or house is by placing an ad in the classified section of the local newspaper.

Would-Be Tenants: The Good, the Bad, and the Ugly

You've advertised the property, and hopefully you've gotten a great response. Lots of people are anxious to see the place. So how do you separate the good from the bad, and avoid finding yourself with a nightmare tenant? There's no surefire way, but there are certain categories of tenants who automatically come with built-in advantages or disadvantages.

Military Tenants: A Mixed Blessing

If your property is near a military base, call the housing office and ask to be added to their listing of available properties.

> **Watch Out!** _____
>
> It's illegal to discriminate against potential tenants based on their race, gender, color, religion, sexual preference, or disability. To avoid inadvertently landing yourself in legal hot water, be sure to study the Fair Housing Act, which can be found on HUD's website at www.hud.gov.
>
> Also, the Miami Valley Fair Housing Center has compiled a list of words and phrases that you should avoid using in rental ads. You can check out the list here: http://www.mvfairhousing.com/pdfs/ad-word-list.pdf.

Military personnel can make great tenants. First and foremost, you can feel like you're doing your tiny part to help support our wonderful servicemen and women.

From a financial perspective, military tenants can also be wonderful. The military has a rental program in which the housing allotment is automatically deducted from the paycheck and submitted via direct deposit into the landlord's checking account.

One drawback: Military personnel can legally cancel or terminate their lease without prejudice if they are transferred or deployed—which can sometimes happen on short notice.

Section 8 Tenants

Section 8 is a program in which the government pays some or all of the tenant's rent. The rent checks arrive like clockwork directly from the government every month. However, some landlords believe that Section 8 tenants are more likely—perhaps because they aren't personally footing the entire rent bill—to damage the property or become problem tenants. However, if you screen Section 8 tenants properly—just as you would any other tenant—we see no reason why you should have a higher chance of problems than you otherwise would. Section 8 has a limit as to the maximum rent it will cover—usually determined by the number of people in the family and the number of bedrooms they need.

Disabled Tenants

Allen Watkins is a real estate investor whose website is www.homebargains.com. He and his wife have a disabled son. Concern for his son's future housing needs prompted Watkins to establish Housing Resource Center, Inc., a not-for-profit organization with a focus on providing housing and related assistance for people with disabilities.

Many landlords worry about the costs involved in making a property handicapped accessible. You may be surprised to find that it's much cheaper than you thought. If the home is, say, a ranch with no stairways, very few changes may be required. Also keep in mind that a disability doesn't necessarily involve a wheelchair. People with disabilities may be blind, deaf, coping with breathing problems, or facing any one of a number of physical challenges. In addition, if a ramp or other wheelchair-related additions are required, community or government grants may be available to help with part of the costs.

Promissory Note ___

When people with disabilities find a suitable place to live where they feel comfortable—especially if they require specific special accommodations—they tend to stay put for a long time. Having a reliable long-term tenant is definitely a plus for any landlord.

Your Perfect Tenant

Before you start dealing with potential tenants, it's important to spend a little time envisioning your perfect tenant. Is the person quiet and single? A family willing to do some of the smaller maintenance tasks themselves? By identifying what you're looking for, you can better target your dream tenants.

It might also be a good idea to make a list of your requirements, broken down into "must have" and "nice, but not essential."

If you absolutely don't want pets, state that clearly in the ad or mention it upfront when a would-be tenant calls. This will save you—and the tenants—a lot of time and aggravation.

However, if you prefer someone without a pet—but it's not a definite deal-breaker—this is a possible area of negotiation. If an otherwise perfect tenant has a small well-behaved cat, perhaps you can work out a deal where the person agrees to a slightly higher security deposit to move in with the cat.

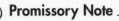

The Application

If a tenant likes the place and seems like the kind of tenant you want to have, the next step is to have him fill out an application. You should have these printed up in advance. You can make up a form of your own using your computer, or use one of the ready-made forms available for free on various landlord websites.

What kind of things should you ask for on the application? It varies, but we recommend all applications include some basic things.

Employment Information

Obviously, it does no good to find the perfect tenant if he's unable to pay the rent. You need to make sure he has a stable job with sufficient income to cover the rent. Ask to see several pay stubs from the past month or two. In the case of someone who is self-employed, ask for his recent tax returns.

Recent Landlord Information

You should ask for contact information for the applicant's current and former landlords—basically, the landlord(s) he has had for about the past five years. Call and ask if the tenant paid the rent on time, and if he ever caused any problems.

Foreclosure Fact
If possible, try to contact one of the tenant's previous landlords; they will likely be much more honest than the current landlord in the case of a not-so-great tenant. Think about it: if the current landlord is eager to be rid of this person, do you really think he's going to fess up about what a nightmare the person has been? More than likely, the landlord will come up with all kinds of false praise for his terrible tenant, in the hopes that you'll take this headache off his hands. If you do contact the current landlord, Allen Watkins of www.homebargains.com suggests that you simply describe yourself as someone seeking a credit reference, without letting on that you're a potential landlord.

Credit Report

We also recommend checking a prospective tenant's credit report. This is fairly easy to do these days, because the major credit reporting agencies all make it pretty easy to order a credit report online. There is a fee involved. We think it's a small price to pay to find a good tenant, but to save money, we suggest only doing credit checks on would-be tenants who have already passed all your other screening checkpoints.

Playing Detective

Even if a prospective tenant looks perfect on paper, you may still want reassurance that he is in fact as good as he seems. This is a good time for you to brush up on your investigative skills. You can use some creative techniques to try to get the true picture of what this person may be like as a tenant.

Irene Montalban, author of the *Be Aware of Real Estate Handbook*, offers this tactic for getting the real scoop on prospective tenants. "I think the most concrete way to learn about them is driving by the prospective tenant's previous rentals. You can judge the type of neighborhood and home or apartment complex the tenant was 'comfortable' living in. Chances are if it is not a desirable home or area, the tenant probably will not upkeep your home either."

Allen Watkins of www.homebargains.com takes that one step further, suggesting you do a surprise in-home inspection at the tenant's current residence. "Say something like, 'We've narrowed it down to two people, and you're one of them. I just wanted to drop off this lease for you to look over.'" Watkins suggests that you then ask to use the phone or bathroom, which will give you an excuse to enter his home and see what kind of condition it is in. "I've been in homes where I've literally had to watch where I was stepping to avoid urine or feces from the dog or cat. Boy was I glad I did an in-home inspection!"

> **Promissory Note** _____
>
> In your lease with the tenant, it is wise to spell out exactly what maintenance issues the tenant will be responsible for. For instance, if you expect him to mow the law every week during the summer and shovel the snow in the winter, you ought to include that as well as a mention of who will supply the lawn mower and the snow shovel. We suggest also including a clause that the first $100 of every repair will be paid for by the tenant. That discourages damage. You don't have to collect it upfront; you can just deduct it from the security deposit.

The Lease

You've found a great tenant who loves the property, has glowing references, and passes your screening process with flying colors. Congratulations! You're the envy of landlords throughout the land. Now it's time to seal the deal and sign on the dotted line. You and your tenants need to sign a lease, in which you clearly spell out each and every clause and condition governing the rental agreement and their use of the property.

> **Promissory Note** _____
>
> An important issue to cover in the lease is occupancy—meaning, who actually has the right to live in the house. Generally, this includes the tenants and their minor children. It's vital that you clearly spell out who is—and isn't—allowed to live in the property. Many landlords have been burned by tenants who sublet the property without permission or allow their entire extended family to move in.

You can find basic lease forms at office-supply stores or on many landlord-related websites online. Important aspects that should be covered include the amount of the monthly rent, the due date, any late charges that will be imposed, the length of the lease, and any security deposits that you will charge. It should also spell out who is responsible for utilities and other costs.

Be sure to spell out in very specific detail any special rules or conditions you want the tenants to follow. For example, if you don't want them to paint the walls or change the landscaping, be sure to include those details.

> **Foreclosure Fact**
>
> How much of a security deposit should you charge? Generally, a figure equal to one or two months' rent is standard. Again, it's important to study local laws—about half the states have set maximum limits as to what kind of security deposit you can legally charge.

Security Deposit

We strongly recommend that you charge tenants a security deposit. This is extra money that the tenant gives the landlord as kind of an insurance policy that he won't trash the place. When the tenant moves out—assuming he leaves on good terms and doesn't damage the property—he gets the security deposit back.

Although this doesn't guarantee the tenants won't damage the property, it may decrease the odds. Plus, it gives you at least a small financial cushion to help cover any damages that may occur.

> **Promissory Note**
>
> Eva Rosenberg of taxmama. com suggests always doing some routine maintenance in the apartments yourself. For instance—put into the lease that you will inspect all smoke alarms every three months, and replace batteries, as needed. This will give you a regular excuse to enter the apartment and see the condition.

Entering a Tenant's Property

You always have the right to enter your rental property without warning or advance notice in emergencies (fire, flood, etc.). In nonemergency situations, though, you need to abide by any relevant state laws designed to protect tenants' privacy. Be sure to research the laws in your area.

Renters Insurance

We suggest strongly advising your tenants to obtain renter insurance. This covers their personal belongings in case of theft, fire, etc. Generally, your homeowner policy would only cover the structure itself, not any personal belongings. Rental insurance can also cover them for liability in situations where they can be held responsible. For example, if they own a dog that bites someone, it would be they, as owners of the dog (not the property owner), who could be held responsible. This insurance can also cover the expense of short-term housing costs in the case of emergency.

Promissory Note _____

One of the things people often hate most about being a landlord is playing the "bad guy" role—enforcing the rules, cracking down on late payments, etc. Some landlords have found it's easier if they present themselves as the manager of the property, rather than the owner. This way, when they need to deliver bad news, they come across simply as the unfortunate messenger acting on behalf of the big bad mysterious landlord.

Eviction

Sadly, no matter how carefully you screen and select tenants, it's still possible to find yourself with a problem. Maybe the tenants violated a major clause in the lease, or perhaps they "forgot" to pay the rent for three months. Whatever the reason, the bottom line is you want them out. You're now facing the most dreaded of all landlord tasks: the eviction.

Watch Out! _____

Before beginning the process of kicking out a tenant, be sure to check the laws regarding eviction in your state or consult a lawyer with expertise in this area. This is especially important in cases involving problems other than nonpayment of rent—if you believe the tenant has violated the lease in some way or is doing something illegal in the property, for example.

We warn you, this can be a stressful and time-consuming ordeal. You need to file a complaint at the local courthouse or magistrate's office. Generally, a hearing will be set, at which point you can present the facts and state your case. Often the tenants don't even bother to show up for this hearing, usually resulting in the case being ruled against them by default.

If you win the case, the judge issues a court order requiring the tenant to vacate the property. If they don't leave, the sheriff or constable usually comes and removes the tenants and their belongings.

Promissory Note _____

After you win your court case, your property still may not be vacant immediately. The court often allows tenants a certain period of time—usually at least a week— to get out. Even after this period has passed, you might still need to get the sheriff or constable to remove the tenants—meaning more delay and more expense. At this point, Allen Watkins of www.homebargains.com sometimes proposes what he calls a "cash for keys" trade. He offers the unwanted tenant a small amount—say, $100—to hand over the keys and leave the property. It sounds crazy to *pay* tenants who owe you money, but at this point, you need to cut your losses. And for Watkins, paying the tenant a hundred bucks is still cheaper than paying several hundred to get the sheriff involved. However, the deal is contingent upon the tenant leaving the property in clean and undamaged condition.

The Friendly Departure

Ideally, your tenants will leave under more positive circumstances—if they've bought a house, for example, or accepted a wonderful new position in another town.

In this case, make every effort to keep your parting of the ways as mutually pleasant as possible. After the tenants give their notice, give them what we like to call the "moving out memo." You can also think of this as the "let's wrap this up without any problems" document. Basically, this can be a short and sweet note thanking them for being a good tenant, and spelling out your expectations for the condition of the property when they leave. If you want them to shampoo the rugs, for example, you should clearly state that—especially if it's a condition for the return of any security deposit the tenant may have paid.

Record Keeping

As a landlord, it's vital that you keep detailed, organized records of everything pertaining to your property and its tenants. Be sure to keep copies of all rent receipts, leases, and other important documents.

These records will also be very important in calculating your taxes and relevant deductions. Trust us, if you're ever in the unenviable position of experiencing an

IRS audit, you'll be thankful you kept good records. These days, financial software programs make it easier to keep track of all your records, but if you doubt your book-keeping skills, it's worth it to pay an accountant to take care of this for you.

The Least You Need to Know

◆ Being a landlord is a round-the-clock job with lots of responsibility, so it may be worthwhile to hire a property manager.

◆ Laws governing landlord-tenant issues vary widely from state to state. Be sure to research the laws in your area.

◆ It can be a nightmare to evict tenants, so it's important to screen prospective tenants as thoroughly as possible before handing over the keys to the property.

◆ Spend some time preparing your property for viewing by prospective tenants. This will make it more likely that you'll attract quality tenants.

◆ Be creative in advertising your property or trying to locate would-be tenants. The more people you reach, the bigger a tenant pool you'll have to choose from.

Chapter **17**

Selling Your Property for a Profit

In This Chapter

- ◆ Go it alone, or use a broker?
- ◆ Spreading the word
- ◆ Helping your house make a good impression
- ◆ How to handle an interested buyer

If you don't intend to use your foreclosure property as rental income, most likely you plan to try and sell it for a nice profit. In this chapter, we discuss what you need to do before putting up the "For Sale" sign, and tell you how to spread the word about this available gem.

Selling Strategy Overview

Most successful investors follow this basic formula for selling properties quickly:

1. Buy the property wisely.

2. Hold the property no more than three to four months.

3. Start marketing your property as soon as possible.

4. Aggressively market the property.

5. Price the property to sell.

6. Present the property in good condition.

Working With Brokers

One of the first decisions you need to make is whether to enlist the help of a broker to sell your property. Generally, this usually comes down to a financial decision. Remember to consider not just the cost of the broker's commission, but also the price you'll pay for holding a property too long and not being able to sell a property with low demand.

Brokers can prove especially helpful with fixer-uppers or properties that may otherwise be a tough sell—an office building in the warehouse district, for example.

If you have a property that doesn't show good promise for a quick resale, consider getting a broker to help. You'll have to pay a broker fee, of course, but you may be able to cut costs in other areas. Perhaps you'll decide—with the broker's input—that you'd be better off discontinuing repair work and selling the property "as is" as a fixer-upper. True, you'll have to lower your asking price—but you'll have a better chance of a quick sale, thus reducing your costs of holding on to the property.

Choosing a Broker

As we advised earlier in this book, it's a good idea to have a real estate broker as one of your "teammates." That way, you already have someone you trust at the ready. However, if that's not the case, you need to seek a broker who has the right connections—and the right attitude—to suit your needs. Look for someone with experience and understanding of the foreclosure and REO process.

Some tips:

◆ Always work with a broker who has a good local reputation.

◆ Pick a broker familiar with your area.

◆ Pick a broker who will aggressively market your property.

- Ask how soon they expect to start showing your property.

- Ask what price you can reasonably expect for the sale of the property.

Necessary Conditions

Part of your decision in choosing a broker should be based on these conditions:

- Make sure the broker lets you sign a short-term contract (for, say, three months) that states a minimum amount the property can be sold for.

- Don't sign any contract that gives the broker exclusive rights to advertise and promote your property. It's okay to negotiate a listing agreement, where the broker is the exclusive listing agent, but you want to reserve the right to market the property yourself simultaneously.

- Make sure the broker will list your property in the MLS listing service.

- Use your best deal-making skills to try and negotiate the best possible selling commission arrangement.

Price It Right

Hopefully with the help of the information we've already shared—plus the help of your team—you'll have a solid idea of what the property is worth and what you can make for its sale—*before* you buy it.

Go back and review your initial figures. Compare the repairs you actually made versus what you had anticipated, and adjust your figures—and your asking price—accordingly.

Compare the prices of houses in the area, taking into consideration size, type, condition, age, and amenities of comparable properties. In other words, gather up a list of comparatives. When you are armed with all this information, consult with your teammates and/or broker to determine a fair asking price.

Take some time to get familiar with your property and its surroundings. Find out if there's anything special about your property that might justify a higher-than-average price. Similarly, find out about any problems that might cause the property to attract lower offers.

Foreclosure Fact

Your best hope for selling the property quickly will be to price it attractively. Everyone wants to find a great deal, so you should consider the idea of selling the property at 3 percent, 5 percent, or even 10 percent below market value. Sounds crazy, right? Not really. Remember, if you picked up a bargain property at 20 percent below market value and flip it for 7 percent below market value, you can still make a bundle.

Advertising the Property

To sell the property, you need to attract buyers—which you won't be able to do if nobody knows the property is for sale. You need to advertise it, using as many different techniques as possible.

For Sale Signs

The most basic tool in a home-seller's arsenal is the good old-fashioned "For Sale" sign. You can find some nice signs at hardware stores or large chains such as Home Depot or Wal-Mart. Look for a sign that says tours are *By Appointment Only*. If you're using a broker, they will take care of this and other details involved in advertising/marketing, so you probably won't have to worry about it.

Foreclosure Fact

Study your local newspaper to determine when the biggest section of real estate ads appears—generally, it's either Saturday or Sunday. You want your ad to appear on the busiest day. If possible, include photos or at least ask to have the ad's headline printed in bold or a special font to catch the reader's eye.

Classifieds

Not long ago, the classifieds were pretty much the only way to advertise a home for sale. These days, there are many options—but you still shouldn't underestimate the value of this tried-and-true method.

Including some nice pictures of the home can help. However, if you don't want to spend a lot on the ad, stick with a to-the-point ad and choose your wording carefully. Include just a few of the most important tidbits—say, the number of bedrooms (especially if the home is large) or the fact that there's an in-ground pool. If the home is in a desirable neighborhood, be sure to mention that, as well.

By mentioning the neighborhood and including your price, you will have indicated to the prospective buyer that the property is a good deal. Serious shoppers will have at least a general idea of what properties in specific neighborhoods are selling for. If your property is in a good neighborhood and is reasonably priced, you should get plenty of calls.

Here's an example of an effective classified ad:

> Newly Remodeled in Eagle's Landing Country Club
>
> Gorgeous Golf Course Views
>
> 4 Bedroom / 3.5 Baths on quiet interior lot
>
> New Paint and New Carpeting
>
> Large Modern Kitchen
>
> New Cabinets and Appliances
>
> Sold by owner
>
> Call 201-555-1212 Today!

Online Ads

Many people search for homes online these days, so it can be very helpful to advertise the home on a website—either your own site or one that lists many homes for sale.

If you have a site of your own, try to make the name something short and catchy. It's very inexpensive to register a domain name, and something memorable can really attract buyers' attention. For example, www.mansionwithpool.com would certainly catch someone's eye. If you frequently sell property in one area, perhaps you can maintain a site that lists your current inventory in that area—for example, www.GreatOakdaleHomes.com.

If you don't want to create a site of your own—or you want to advertise on a site that gets a lot of traffic—you can go with one of countless websites devoted to selling homes. Some of the more popular sites include www.fsbo.com and www.postyourproperty.com.

Flyers

Irene Montalban of BeAwareOfRealEstate.com is a big fan of flyers in helping to advertise a home. It's pretty simple to design a nice-looking flyer on your home computer.

What should you include in the flyer? The basic information, of course—location of the home, price, etc. More importantly, play up any unique or attractive qualities or amenities the home offers. Here's a list of features Irene included in one of her recent flyers:

◆ Lakeside views

◆ Gunite pool

◆ New ceramic tile

◆ New Berber carpet

◆ Newly landscaped

◆ Newly painted in and out

◆ New window treatments

◆ New light fixtures

◆ All appliances included

◆ Central air conditioning/heating

◆ Covered shaded patio

◆ Fireplace

Promissory Note

You can also use your flyers or classified ad to announce an open house. Buyers tend to like the open house scenario, because they often believe it won't be as high-pressure as if they were touring the home individually.

As you can see, she included just about anything that might attract a buyer's interest.

You can go to your local print shop or copy center to get a hundred or so copies of your flyer. Try using colored paper (in a pale shade, so the text is still clearly visible) to help your flyer stand out. Distribute your flyers where the people most likely to buy your property will see them. Leave small stacks at grocery stores, beauty salons, daycare centers, and in the lobbies of office buildings.

Be creative. It would be great to leave your flyers in the rental offices of apartment buildings (after all, odds are good that at least some of those tenants are sick of paying rent), but most likely you won't be allowed to do that. However, you may be able to leave some flyers in the common areas of the building, such as the laundry room or lobby.

Here's a sample of what your flyer might look like:

Home for Sale

An Outdoorsman's Dream!

(Insert some tempting pictures of the property here.)

Don't miss your opportunity to own this fabulous property, nestled in the lovely mountainside, and surrounded by 10 acres of unspoiled nature.

Here, you give your best sales pitch for the home, playing up its special features.

Price: $000,000

Bedrooms:	Age of Home:
Bathrooms:	School District:
Square Feet:	Garage:

Irresistible Feature #1:

Irresistible Feature #2:

View this home online at www.website.com

Phone: 555-222-3333

Presenting Your Property

When it comes to showing your property, presentation is critical. An otherwise good deal can fall apart at this stage, possibly just because you neglected a few important details.

The home should look its absolute best when any potential buyers come calling.

Curb Appeal

Perhaps the single most important visual aspect of a home is its *curb appeal*. This is the first—and possibly last—look a buyer will get of the home.

It's common for buyers to drive past the home in the evening. Be sure to do a nighttime check of your home's after-dark curb appeal. Pay attention to the lighting and other factors that may be especially important at night.

Land Lingo

Curb appeal is the first impression you get of a home when viewing it from the street.

Neatness Counts

Nothing will turn off buyers faster than a sloppy house. Clutter, dirt, grime—any of these are a seller's mortal enemy. We hope this goes without saying, but your home should be spotless and clutter-free before you even think about letting prospective buyers take a look.

Promissory Note

Anything you can do to really make an unforgettable first impression on potential buyers will earn extra points in your favor. Setting the right mood can be a big help. If the home has a pool, perhaps you could have a few people lounging in or near it, to give buyers the idea that this would be a nice place to relax. Lighting some candles and playing some soothing music can also be good techniques to set a relaxing tone. Hey, maybe you can even recruit your sweet grandmother to come over and bake some of her irresistible blueberry muffins! Who knows how many buyers will be lured in by that tempting smell.

Play It Safe

When it comes to decoration and décor, it's best to stick to safe—yes, even boring—colors and styles. You can't predict the tastes or preferences of buyers who'll tour the home, and you don't want to risk losing a sale simply because Bonnie Homebuyer isn't a fan of "shabby chic" design elements. Also you want buyers to be able to easily envision themselves—and their belongings—in the home. That may be a challenge if their furniture is green and you've painted the walls a lovely shade of neon pink.

> **Foreclosure Fact**
>
> If you're going to paint the home's interior, consider using an off-white flat paint—also sometimes called antique white or eggshell white. You prefer blue or yellow? Too bad. You're not selling the home to yourself. We've heard that off-white is the top selling shade of interior paint. It's definitely the safest choice—few people can object to a light, neutral color scheme. Worst-case scenario: They think it's a bit too plain—in which case, they'll realize that it's much easier to paint over a light color than it would be if the walls were, say, lime green.

What's That Smell?

Of course, dirt and clutter won't bother buyers if they're already running out the door, and any funky or strange smells are sure to have people heading for the hills. Follow your nose, and be sure to find—and eliminate—the source of any bad odors. Smells with any hint of a mildew odor can be especially dangerous, because they may cause would-be buyers to suspect a mold or dampness problem.

 Watch Out!

Remove any personal belongings left in the home by the previous owner/occupant. The point is to help buyers envision themselves living there. Reminders of another family who lived there will only be a distraction.

Small Repairs

You don't want a small problem to give buyers the mistaken impression that the house is falling apart. So try to handle any minor repairs before showing the property.

Irene Montalban of BeAwareOfRealEstate.com offers these suggestions:

- Repair leaky faucets and toilets.
- Tighten doorknobs, switch plates, cupboard latches, etc.
- Repair any holes or unsightly patching of drywall.
- Clean and repair windows.
- Repair seals around tub and sink.
- Replace dead light bulbs.
- Oil any squeaky door hinges.

Ten Ways to Make Buyers Hate Your Home

Janet Wickell, veteran real estate agent and the guide to the Home Buying/Selling section of About.com, offers this list of the top 10 things that will make prospective buyers run the other way:

- ◆ Odors
- ◆ Dogs that meet you at the door or on the driveway
- ◆ Dirty bathrooms
- ◆ Dimly lit rooms
- ◆ A house full of busy wallpaper
- ◆ Damp basements
- ◆ Bugs
- ◆ Poor curb appeal
- ◆ Gutters with plants growing in them
- ◆ Sellers who hang around for showings

Use Competition to Your Advantage

Whenever possible, arrange to have several potential buyers tour the property at one time. This allows you to take full advantage of human nature to become competitive. If you're lucky, one of the visitors will get the ball rolling by making it obvious that he likes the property. If any of the others are also interested, they may start to worry that someone else will snap up the place first. As a result, they may become eager to submit an offer quickly. We've even heard of buyers who enlist friends or family to wander around their open house chatting about their interest in the property in front of the real buyers.

Get It in Writing

If all goes well, at least one person who tours your home will want to make an offer. Great! Now be sure to get it in writing, making sure he spells out any conditions that may restrict or cancel his offer.

You can get standard purchase agreement contracts from most office-supply stores or various real estate websites.

The Deposit Check

A buyer who submits a formal offer on the property should also be willing to present a deposit check. This is usually a small token amount, and is basically just a gesture of good faith. They can make the check payable to you or the lawyer or title company who may be handling the transaction for you.

The First Screening

Your screening process should begin the minute the phone rings with a call from a potential buyer. Irene Montalban of BeAwareOfRealEstate.com suggests having a pen and questionnaire right next to the phone. In her questionnaire, Irene asks things such as "Do you own a home now?" and "Have you already been pre-approved by a mortgage company?" This only applies, of course, if you're selling the property yourself. If you are using a broker, you generally wouldn't have contact with prospective buyers at this point.

Sometimes the answers to these questions immediately allow you to weed out callers who don't fit the bill. For example, a single person seeking his first home probably wouldn't be interested in your four-bedroom with a hefty mortgage. Likewise, you can probably rule out the elderly buyer with health concerns as someone who'd be willing to take a fixer-upper off your hands.

Beyond that initial screening, you can also qualify buyers by asking them some basic questions about employment and income, which should give you some idea if they can afford the property.

> **Promissory Note**
>
> If you have a lender among your team of advisors, now would be a good time to use them. If potential buyers haven't yet sought financing, offer to have your lender friend take their information and pre-qualify them. This way, you'll know they've passed financial muster—and you'll also be throwing some business your friend's way.

Negotiating Price and Terms

In a perfect world, the first interested buyer submits an offer that is exactly your asking price and meets all of your desired terms. In reality, it very rarely happens that way. More likely, you'll have to go through a period of back-and-forth negotiations. Perhaps they want to offer lower than your asking price. Or maybe they want to change some of the terms—perhaps asking you to cover some of their *closing costs*, for example. Like most good business deals, the sale of a home often requires some compromises. This is a good opportunity for you to sharpen your negotiating skills.

Promissory Note

Closing costs are expenses incurred by the buyer and/or seller related to the purchase of a home (not including the actual price of the property). Examples of typical closing costs include attorney fees, transfer fees, recording costs, and appraisal fees.

Land Lingo

FSBO is short for For Sale By Owner. This means the owner is selling the property personally, without the help of a broker or real estate agent.

Land Lingo

A **property disclosure** is a statement to a prospective buyer listing information that relates to a piece of property, such as the presence of hazardous materials.

Make sure you have carefully thought your goals through in advance. You should know exactly what you hope to gain from the deal, and what the bare minimum you're willing to accept. Establish your priorities—know which aspects of the deal are most important to you. This way, you can choose your battles and know where to stand firm, and where to allow the buyer some wiggle room.

Often this process involves several trips back to the "bargaining table." This may involve actual sit-down meetings—more often, though, it's in the form of revised contracts or new offers relayed back and forth through lawyers or real estate agents.

Common "For Sale by Owner" Mistakes

Maybe you've decided to save yourself the cost of a broker's commission and sell the home on your own. This is what's known as a *FSBO* situation.

This is very common—many owners sell their properties solo. However, you need to watch out for some pitfalls. Janet Wickell, the home buying/selling guide at About.com, describes some of the most common FSBO mistakes.

Property Disclosures

State law may require you to give potential buyers one or more *property disclosures* when you sell a home.

Examples of conditions you'd be required to divulge in property disclosure may include any major structural problems with the property; the presence of radon, asbestos, or other harmful materials; or the fact that the property is located in a flood plain or earthquake zone.

Lead Paint Disclosure

For homes built before 1978, federal law requires sellers to disclose information about any lead paint test results and give buyers the opportunity to do further testing. Most buyers won't actually take you up on this, but by giving them the opportunity, you're fulfilling your legal obligation.

Buyer's Deposit

Your contract should spell out what happens to the buyer's deposit money if the deal falls through. Generally, the money is refunded to the buyer if the deal is broken for good cause—such as if he's unable to get the financing he expected—or for something that wasn't his fault. Don't count your chickens before they hatch—that money isn't yours until the sale goes through or the buyer breaks the contract for no good cause.

Qualifying Buyers

To avoid wasting their time, most real estate agents will *pre-qualify* buyers before showing them properties. Unfortunately, when selling a home yourself, you're basically stuck dealing with pretty much every buyer who expresses interest. You need to be on guard, because people who know they'd never pass muster with a real estate agent due to bad credit or other negative factors will often deliberately zoom in on FSBO properties.

Land Lingo _____

To **pre-qualify** a buyer simply means putting him through some kind of basic initial screening process. Often this involves asking his basic income information and plugging it into a standard income/debt formula. This differs from **pre-approval**, in which a lender takes detailed income information—which the lender then confirms—and does a credit check to approve the borrower for a preset loan amount.

Accepting the Offer

After you reach a mutually acceptable agreement with a buyer regarding price and terms, you can formally accept their offer. Your sales agreement should include the following:

◆ Price of the property

◆ Down payment

◆ How the balance will be paid

◆ Date of closing

◆ Date of possession (if different from closing)

◆ Other contingencies

Closing

Upon receipt of the deposit check and sales agreement, you can begin the "closing" process. This is where you will utilize your team members the most. You need your title company representative or attorney to establish an *escrow account*. This is where the money stays until the sale has been finalized and all necessary fees and costs have been paid.

> **Land Lingo**
>
> An **escrow account** is money that is held by a third party—not the buyer or seller—during the real estate transaction.

The escrow agent handles most of the details of this transaction. Still, you should keep a close eye on things to make sure no details are overlooked.

The Least You Need to Know

◆ Rather than relying on one means of advertising your property, take advantage of as many publicity avenues as possible.

◆ Little details can make a big difference when it comes to showing a home.

◆ A broker can often be worth their commission if they can help you sell the property quickly and for maximum profit.

◆ Be sure to consult your advisors and team members for as much insight and advice as possible during the negotiation and closing phases of the sale.

◆ If you decide not to use a broker, there are some common "for sale by owner" (FSBO) mistakes you need to avoid.

Part 5

Beyond Basics: Advanced Strategies for Experienced Investors

You have some foreclosure investing experience under your belt, so you might feel the need to stretch your investment muscles a bit. In these chapters, we describe some advanced techniques that may help you greatly increase your foreclosure profits. We cover the more challenging foreclosure investment techniques, from subject to deals to lease option arrangements. In addition, we describe a few additional creative financing strategies that our most daring readers might want to consider.

Chapter 18

Buying "Subject To"

In This Chapter

- ◆ What's this thing called subject to?
- ◆ The pros, cons, and controversy
- ◆ What lenders think
- ◆ The details of a subject to deal
- ◆ Why the seller often agrees to the deal

Buying properties "subject to" has become one of the most popular—and, in some circles, controversial—creative financing techniques in real estate investing. In this chapter, we discuss exactly how this technique works, and show you how to determine if this might be profitable for you—and beneficial for the homeowner.

What Does "Subject To" Mean?

The term *subject to* is shorthand for buying a property subject to the existing loan or financing.

Basically, the existing mortgage agreement or other financing arrangement remains intact and unchanged, even though the deed—and physical possession of the property—is transferred to someone else. Essentially, the person who buys the house just takes over the mortgage, regardless of how much equity there is.

How Subject To Started

Not long ago, all FHA and VA mortgages were assumable—meaning, you could buy a property from someone with one of these mortgages and you'd simply take over the existing loan. You'd transfer it to your name, but you wouldn't need to go through the application/approval process that an original borrower would. Ah, those were the good ol' days. Many investors kept themselves pretty busy stockpiling homes with government mortgages without any of the hassles or red tape of securing their own financing.

This gravy train came to a screeching halt in the late 1980s, though, when the regulations were changed, making most government mortgages nonassumable.

Although the surplus of assumable mortgages had pretty much dried up, investors still loved the concept, so they soon discovered that buying a home using the subject to strategy was just as easy and attractive.

The Big Difference—Shhh! It's a Secret

Although the basic idea remains the same, there's one crucial difference between assuming a mortgage and buying a property using the subject to technique: the lender's awareness. With assumable mortgages, the lender would be fully aware that the property had changed hands. When a "subject to" sale occurs, the lender is clueless that anything has changed. In fact, this is very important, and investors who use this method go out of their way to ensure that the lender stays in the dark.

Investors try to make as few waves as possible, maintaining the status quo so that—from the lender's viewpoint—nothing stands out. The investor's primary goal is to avoid anything that sends up red flags that attract a lender's attention, and thereby possibly

> **Land Lingo**
>
> The **due-on-sale clause** is a provision found in many mortgages stating the entire balance of the loan may be considered due immediately if the owner transfers or sells the property.

trigger the *due-on-sale clause*. In other words, the lender could accelerate the loan. This is the absolute worst-case scenario for any "subject to" investor, and is something to avoid at all costs.

Why All the Controversy?

This secrecy from the lender is exactly what makes the subject to form of investing so controversial and—to some investors—unattractive. Some people see subject to investing as too risky, whereas others just don't "feel right" about what they believe is an ethical gray area. This is because although the technique may not technically be illegal, it does violate the borrower's contract. However, lenders are well aware that this happens and aren't bothered by it—as long as the payments are made on time and there are no problems with the property, most lenders really don't care who is writing out the check. On the other hand, many investors are huge fans of this strategy. Because we know numerous investors who have been successful with subject to properties, we want to tell you about it, so you can be fully informed before deciding whether this is something you want to pursue.

Is It Legal?

Although it may violate the terms of a mortgage contract, transferring a property to someone else before paying off the loan isn't a criminal act. You (or more accurately, the seller) can't go to jail for this. Worst-case scenario? The lender exercises its right to accelerate the loan, and then starts foreclosure proceedings because the seller, presumably, can't pay the entire balance of the loan.

Foreclosure Fact

How do lenders really feel about subject to deals? It's something most savvy bankers are well aware of, but generally don't spend a lot of time worrying about. Sources at several lenders told us that—even though mortgage contracts often prohibit the transfer of a title before the loan is paid off—they usually look the other way when they suspect this has happened. That is, as long as the status quo is maintained and payments arrive on time, they don't care.

Also you don't want to broadcast the subject to status to the world. If you flaunt this fact in front of the lender's face, it may feel forced to take action to save face. Bottom line: This is generally one of those "don't ask, don't tell" situations.

What Rights Come with a Subject To Deal?

Most people are pretty clear as to their rights as an original borrower. How does this change when you buy a subject to property? Vena Jones-Cox, who specializes in educating people on what she calls the Real-Life Real Estate approach, explains in this excerpt from her Real Estate 201 course. (See www.regoddess.com for more information.)

"When you have a mortgage on a property, even if you took over that mortgage from another person, you by definition have title," says Vena Jones-Cox. "Title is the purest form of interest, and includes the entire bundle of rights in real estate. However, terms of your mortgage may modify some of these rights in order to protect the lender. For instance:

♦ **Your right to control the property** within the framework of the law can be terminated via a foreclosure suit if you do not pay as agreed.

♦ **Your right to exclude others** from entering or using the property may be modified to read that the lender can enter the property to make periodic inspections.

♦ **The right to use the property in any legal manner** will be changed in two ways: You cannot do anything to the property that will decrease the value of the seller's security (including letting it run down, tearing it down, etc.); and you cannot change the use from owner-occupied to nonowner-occupied (although changing the other direction is usually okay with the lender).

♦ **The right to dispose of (sell)** all or part of the property unless you pay the lender off.

Note that the penalty for violating any of these provisions of the mortgage is simply that the lender can call the entire loan balance due, and foreclose if you don't pay. And also note that, when writing a mortgage with a seller, you can agree to these provisions or not."

Promissory Note

Vena Jones-Cox, known as the "real estate goddess," is the author of several courses on real estate and a frequent lecturer on real estate topics. She is offering a free three-month subscription to her newsletter to readers of this book. To take advantage of this offer, simply visit her website at www.regoddess.com and click on the bright yellow link in the lower-left corner.

Benefits of Buying Via Subject To Deals

The main benefit of the subject to technique is obvious: you get a property, complete with financing in place, without going through the usual hassles of applying for a loan or other financing. Presumably, you "inherit" financing terms that are more attractive than those you'd be able to get on your own.

But there are other benefits, as Vena Jones-Cox explains, depending on what you do with the property, you can get:

- **Cash flow,** in the form of the difference between the payments you pay to the owner and the rent your tenant/buyer pays to you.

- **Tax advantages,** both by deducting any interest, taxes, and insurance you pay *and* from depreciation. "That's right: If you pay the mortgage payment, you get to deduct the interest, taxes, and insurance even though the lender reports another payer's name to the IRS," Jones-Cox says.

- **Appreciation,** because your purchase price typically stays the same as the value of the property increases.

- **Equity through mortgage pay-down,** if you use the property as rental property. "You'll also get equity through appreciation (your purchase price is set no matter how valuable the property becomes) and, if you choose, through sweat equity (your purchase price is set no matter how much you increase the value of the property through repair and improvement)," says Jones-Cox.

- And, of course, **leverage.** The less money you pay upfront, the more leverage you are exercising.

Your Responsibilities

In a subject to deal, the property is transferred into your name as the buyer. You are now the legal owner of the property, and assume all the responsibilities and obligations that go along with that position. First and foremost, obviously, is the responsibility of making the mortgage payments in a timely manner. In addition, any other financial obligations—taxes, insurance, and so on—are also your problem. Plus, you're responsible for maintaining the property, keeping it safe, and taking care of any problems that may occur with the property.

The Mechanics of a Subject To Deal

How exactly do you conduct a subject to deal? It's actually not as complicated as most people might think. The most important thing is to make sure the seller is completely informed—and totally clear—about all the details and implications that this kind of deal entails. Mainly, that the loan will remain in their name and won't be paid off until whenever you sell the property (or, if you plan to hold on to the property as a rental, whenever you manage to pay off the loan).

Then you have the seller authorize transfer of the deed to your name. You pay the seller any money you've agreed to pay them (or fulfill any other promises you've made) and assemble the necessary paperwork that will allow you to manage, control, and pay for the property.

Vena Jones-Cox has compiled this list of documents that you need for this type of deal:

- A deed conveying the property from the seller to you (or your trustee)

- A letter signed by the seller notifying his lender that he has put his property in the hands of a management company (yours) and that all further correspondence should be forwarded to you

- An undated payoff request from the seller to an unnamed lender (because the loan could be sold between the time you buy the property and the time you're ready to pay it off)

- A letter from the seller—preferably in his own handwriting—stating that he understands that he has sold the house, that the loan will not be paid off, and that this could affect his ability to buy a home in the future

- A Limited Power of Attorney allowing you to deal with the seller's insurance and lender

With subject to deals—just as with any other investment deal—always consult your attorney and other advisors before signing on the dotted line. Also make sure to do a title search on the property.

Sample Letter to Lender

Following is an example (provided by Vena Jones-Cox) of a letter a seller would send to the lender informing them that you will be managing the property.

June 13, 2005

To whom it may concern:

This letter is to notify you that we have retained a real estate management company to rent and manage our property at___, Cincinnati, Ohio, your loan number:

All future correspondence, including payment books, tax forms, and other communications should be made directly to my agent at the following address:

Proffitt Real Estate Services

P.O. Box 58279

Cincinnati, Ohio 45258

Sincerely,

Julia Doe

Social Security #

Arnold Doe

Social Security #

cc: Proffitt Real Estate Services

Sample Agreement Document

Following is a sample document (also provided by Vena Jones-Cox) in which the seller spells out his agreement to the subject to deal.

June 13, 2005

We understand that we are selling our home at ___ to ___, an Ohio Limited Liability Company.

We understand that our mortgage is not being paid off now, and that, although the buyer will be responsible for the payments in the future, no promise has been made to us as to when the mortgage will be paid off.

We understand that the mortgage will remain in our names and that this could affect our ability to get a new mortgage as long as this mortgage has not been paid off.

We understand that, since someone else is making the payments on our mortgage, including taxes and insurance, that we will no longer be able to take the tax deduction for making the payments.

Seller   Date

Witness

Seller   Date

Witness

Sample Limited Power of Attorney

A document like this one (courtesy of Vena Jones-Cox) allows you to act on the seller's behalf on matters involving the property.

Limited Power of Attorney

This Limited Power of Attorney is given to ___ for the purpose of settling insurance claims, endorsing refund or settlement checks made payable to the undersigned, requesting payoffs of any kind, dealing with representatives of insurance and mortgage companies, and any and all other actions necessary to manage, maintain, refinance, sell, or otherwise encumber or convey the property commonly known as ___, Cincinnati, Hamilton County, Ohio.

This Limited Power of Attorney shall take effect on the date signed and shall remain in effect until the final sale of the property by ___.

Granted by:

Seller   Date:

Witness

Seller   Date:

Witness

STATE OF _____, County: _____,

On this ___ day of _____, 20___, before me, a Notary Public in and for said County and State, personally appeared _____, and _____ the individuals(s) who executed the foregoing instrument and acknowledged that he/she/they did examine and read the same and did sign the foregoing instrument, and the same is his/her/their free act and deed.

IN WITNESS WHEREOF, I have hereunto set my hand and official seal.

(Seal)

My commission expires:

What's in It for the Seller?

You might be trying to figure out what's in this for the seller. Why, you may wonder, would someone agree to transfer the title of a property to someone else, yet allow the loan to remain in his or her own name? Well, several reasons, actually.

Think back to earlier in this book when we described some of the reasons why people end up in foreclosure, and reasons why sellers are motivated to sell their homes. Often they simply want to be able to walk away from the property. Or they may not be willing or able to cover the monthly costs any longer.

Many times, people in these situations have no plans—or no hope—of buying another house anytime in the near future, so the fact that they are still (on paper) carrying this loan may not matter to them. Plus, by keeping the loan current and making timely payments—and most likely paying it off early—you would actually be *helping* their credit. Finally, keep in mind that the worst-case scenario for the seller is that the lender gets wind of the subject to deal and decides to accelerate the loan—and keep in mind that this almost never happens. At that point, the lender may initiate foreclosure proceedings, which the seller was already facing when you first entered the picture. So they simply end up back at the beginning, in the same spot they were at the start.

Getting the Seller On Board

How do you sell the homeowner on the idea of agreeing to a subject to deal? Matt Bowman of www.REItoolbox.com, offers this advice:

One of the most important aspects of a subject to deal is the initial negotiation. The vast majority of sellers will not have ever even heard of a deal like a subject to, so it is important that you know what to say, as well as how and when to say it when trying to negotiate a subject to deal with a seller. This is the most important first step.

When you get in front of sellers after having done your initial negotiations over the phone with them, it is rare that they will even really care about all the paperwork that they are signing. Why is this? Because all the negotiations that have been done have enlightened the seller that this is perhaps not the only option for them—although many times it is—but it is the best option for them at the time.

Believe it or not, as complicated as subject to deals might first appear, they are one of the easiest "creative" deals to negotiate. Why is that? Put simply, you are just offering to take over the seller's payments on the house. This is the best way to explain it to the seller. This makes the deal easy to understand and is the basic idea behind a subject to deal.

Sample Dialogue for Negotiating a Subject To Deal

Wondering what exactly to say to a homeowner when proposing a subject to deal? Matt Bowman of www.REItoolbox.com says your first step in negotiating this kind of deal is listening carefully. There are certain key phrases that sellers will say when talking to you on the phone that will let you know that you have a good subject to candidate. Bowman says you want to listen for things such as the following:

- I just want to dump the place.
- I just want to sell it for what I owe on it.
- If I can't get it sold, I'm just going to let the bank have it.
- I just want someone to take it over.

These kinds of comments are tip-offs that the seller may be receptive to the possibility of someone just coming along and offering to take over their payments.

"Very often, if they owe back payments and have been unable to sell the house, they are getting used to the idea of just letting the bank foreclose," Bowman says. "If you are able to come along and take over their problem, catching the payments up and keeping them current, saving the seller's credit, this is music to their ears!"

Bowman offers this suggestion as to actual dialogue:

> If I were able to take over the house and the payments for you, does that sound like something that might interest you?

If they answer yes, you can go on to tell them:

> Well, I may be able to take over the house by having you deed it to me and leave the existing mortgage in place. I can then take over the payments and get and keep them current, allowing you to move on and just be done with the house. Does that sound like something that would work for you?

At this point, you will know whether you have a subject to deal or not.

Promissory Note

Sometimes sellers will want some references or names of people you have done these types of deals with—which can be a problem, especially if you have never done a subject to deal before. If this concern comes up, here is how Matt Bowman of www.RFItoolbox.com suggests you handle it:

> Tell the sellers that you are often dealing with people who are going through bankruptcy, foreclosure, or some other financial difficulty. As part of your standard business practice, you keep all sellers' information confidential. Then ask the seller this question. "If you were going through a bankruptcy and couldn't make your house payment and we signed a deal on your house, would you want me to share that information with everyone I met? Would you be comfortable getting a call from a complete stranger who says, 'So I hear you're going through a bankruptcy. By the way, how did the deal with the house turn out?'"

You can offer professional references such as your attorney or banker to vouch for you if you have these available. This makes you appear more professional and can alleviate the seller's concern about you being legitimate.

The Dreaded Due-on-Sale Clause

We'll say it again—the odds of a lender exercising their right to accelerate the loan because of a subject to loan (unless one of the parties involved does something to provoke them) are very slim. None of the investors or lenders we've spoken to have ever seen it happen.

In fact, Ward Hanigan of ForeclosureForum.com says it's often just the opposite:

> It's quite common for lenders to waive their due-on-sale rights when a hard-pressed homeowner voluntarily sells their property to a third party during the foreclosure process, prior to the actual trustee's sale. Lenders are especially accommodating if such a waiver is a condition precedent for a new owner stepping in and curing the foreclosure.

Still, we never guarantee it couldn't occur. So what happens if it does? Well, the best strategy is to pay off the loan before the lender has a chance to take any action. Obviously, though, this means you need to be able to either find a buyer quickly or come up with enough money on your own to satisfy the loan.

Foreclosure Fact

What should you do if a lender does discover you've bought a subject to property and threatens to invoke the due-on-sale clause? Matt Bowman of www.REItoolbox.com offers this insight:

> Usually, before a lender does this, they will attempt to contact you to convince you to formally assume the loan. At this point, they may use strong legal language and make threats to foreclose immediately if you say that you do not intend to assume the loan.
>
> You can answer these threats by explaining something to the lender. You can tell the lender that if they intend to foreclose, you would obviously have no reason to maintain the property any more. You may let them know that you have a tenant living in the house who may be very upset that they have to move and may decide to vandalize the house before they leave.
>
> You can make the lender aware that as the house sits vacant while they go through the long process of foreclosure, people may break in and do damage to the property since you no longer have any reason to maintain or protect the property. While it is important to bring these points up to a lender, *never* make threats! Do not tell them that you intend to damage the property in any way!
>
> You can go on to tell the lender that you have the next payment in the envelope and are just about to send it out, but if they'd rather foreclose than make money, that is their option. After reminding the lender of these facts, if they continue to make threats and continue to insist that you assume the loan, ask for a supervisor. You can then explain the same thing to the supervisor. As you go up the chain of command, you will start dealing with more experienced people who know the true cost of calling a loan due.
>
> You will then most likely be asked to simply make the payment and not worry about assuming the loan. The higher management knows that it is far better to get payments made and kept current than to harass someone into assuming a loan.

The better option is to quickly find a buyer, but this may not always be possible. That's why we generally don't recommend that investors take the plunge into subject to deals until they've amassed enough capital—or become adept at obtaining quick financing—to solve this problem, in the unlikely event it ever happens. Besides, this is somewhat of an advanced technique that probably shouldn't be attempted by investors until they've successfully completed a few more simple deals.

Land Trusts

One common method of handling a subject to deal is by using a land trust. This is where the property is being held "in the trust" of another party. What other party? An entity that is, in essence, you yourself. The trust agreement establishes an entity—kind of like a corporation—that is given control of the property.

This technique is also often used by people who want to keep their ownership of a property confidential, either for privacy reasons or less-honorable motives (hiding assets from the government, former spouses, creditors, etc.)—although this would often be illegal, and something we definitely aren't encouraging. It is also frequently used by people doing estate planning.

Matt Bowman of www.REItoolbox.com explains the popularity of using a trust arrangement. "One major advantage is that when the seller of the property deeds the property into a trust for their own benefit, the lender on the mortgage cannot, under federal law, call the loan due simply because ownership has transferred. After ownership of the property has been transferred into the trust, the sellers can then assign their beneficial interest in the property to you, giving you control and ownership of the property."

Maintaining the Status Quo

We've already explained why it's vital in a subject to deal to maintain the status quo and not attract the lender's attention. How exactly do you stay under the radar? Vena Jones-Cox offers these tips in her Real Estate 201 course:

◆ **Don't tell the lender what you've done.** This may seem obvious; but when a lender finds out that a loan has been taken over, it's because someone—most often a conscience-stricken seller—tells them about it.

◆ **Don't take the seller's name off the insurance policy.** Although a lender will never, ever notice that the monthly payment is coming from someone other than the seller, it will absolutely notice when the policy converts from "Sally Seller" to "Irv Investor." Unfortunately, there's no really good way to make sure that a) the seller's name is still on the policy, b) you are fully covered in the case of a loss, and c) your ability to collect on the insurance is not hindered by the seller.

The Insurance Issue

Here are the common ways that investors try to circumvent the insurance issue, as provided by Vena Jones-Cox:

♦ **Have the seller's policy changed to nonowner-occupied and have your name added as co-insured.** This has two potential problems: first, some insurance companies are hesitant to make this kind of conversion, or simply don't insure nonowner-occupied properties. Second, in case of a loss, the check will be issued to you *and* the seller, meaning that both of you will need to sign for the proceeds to be deposited. This could prove too much temptation for a seller, so it's a good idea to have a Limited Power of Attorney from the seller that allows you to sign his name to any settlements and checks.

♦ **Leave the seller's policy intact (continuing to pay for it, of course) and get a second, nonowner-occupied policy in your own name.** This creates a possibility that *both* insurance companies will refuse to pay, since the property is "double insured."

♦ **Put the property in a land trust and insure the trust and the trustee.** Again, this creates a *major* question in the mind of a lender who sees that the seller's name is no longer on the policy.

♦ **Put the property in a land trust with the seller as trustee and insure the trust and the trustee.** Needless to say, this creates some complications when it comes time to sell, because the seller will have to be tracked down to sign the deed. The best way to avoid this problem is to also have the seller sign a Power of Attorney at the closing, allowing you to act on his behalf with regard to the property.

Of these options, the first is the quickest, easiest, and most foolproof.

Some Subject To Pitfalls

As previously mentioned, subject to deals can be a bit tricky and probably shouldn't be attempted by the novice investor. Even so, they're not totally without headaches.

Vena Jones-Cox offers these caveats regarding subject to deals:

◆ **As always, do your research and get your documentation.** "These deals are so easy that it's tempting to just get a deed and get on with making money. But as always, you need a title search, title insurance, and so on. And don't forget to get a balance on the mortgage from the lender! I recently agreed to take over a property subject to the existing mortgage with the understanding that the loan was completely current. Upon calling the bank, I discovered that the ex-wife was three months in *arrears*, much to my surprise *and* the ex-husband's."

◆ **Seller bankruptcy is still a danger.** "You might think that, once the deed is in your name, a seller bankruptcy would not affect the loan. *Wrong!* The lender still has the property as collateral against the note. The fact that the deed is in your name just means that you will also be named in the foreclosure," says Jones-Cox. "And yes, the bank can and will foreclose on a loan that is completely current."

> **Land Lingo**
>
> When mortgage payments or other debt obligations have not been paid on time, the borrower is said to be in **arrears**.

◆ **Your biggest problems will come from the seller himself.** "Invariably, every single time I've taken over a loan, the seller has been as pleased as punch to get rid of the property, get the back payments made up, and so on," says Jones-Cox "Invariably, from a few months to a few years later, I get a call from the seller (or from a mortgage broker) demanding that I pay off the mortgage because he wants to buy a house/get a car/qualify for government assistance. And no amount of reminding them that you never said you'd pay the loan off will do you a bit of good. In fact, at least two sellers have threatened me with legal action for saving their credit! That's why I get it in writing. And why I consider this short-term financing."

◆ **Don't ignore the terms of the underlying loan!** Not every subject to is automatically a good deal. Some loans have interest rates or payment terms that just don't allow the property to cash flow. So make sure that you evaluate these deals the same as you would any other.

The Least You Need to Know

◆ In a subject to deal, the buyer basically just "takes over" the homeowner's existing mortgage, leaving the loan in the owner's name even though the investor will make the payments.

◆ Although some investors consider subject to investing unethical, it's not illegal.

◆ When you've bought a subject to property, it's vital that you and the seller maintain the status quo and don't attract unnecessary attention from the lender.

◆ The seller benefits from a subject to deal by not having to make the payments on the property, and also gets an improved credit score resulting from the buyer's timely loan payments.

◆ The longer you hold a subject to property, the more likely the seller will do something to upset the status quo. Best bet: Sell subject to properties quickly.

Lease Option Sales

In This Chapter

- ◆ Understanding lease option deals
- ◆ The two-step sandwich deal
- ◆ Finding interested sellers and potential tenants/buyers
- ◆ The benefits of lease option deals

The lease option is another increasingly popular real estate investing strategy. Sometimes also called a "rent-to-own" deal, this is where you find a tenant/buyer immediately upon buying the property. In this chapter, we describe how a lease option deal works, and give tips on finding a good tenant/buyer.

Lease Option Basics

Here's a very basic outline of how a *lease option* works: You buy a property, possibly using a "subject to" deal. You then quickly find someone who wants to lease the property with the option to buy. This *tenant/buyer* gives you an upfront payment—called an option payment—upon signing the deal and moving in. A certain portion of his monthly rent is credited toward his purchase price. He must exercise his option to buy the property within the specified time limit. If he doesn't, you keep his option payment anyway.

> **Land Lingo**
>
> A **lease option** is an agreement in writing in which the owner of a property allows someone to rent the property with the option to buy the property at a specific price within a certain time period. The person who rents the property is called a **tenant/ buyer.**

Have a Sandwich

The most common—and profitable—method of lease option investing is to do what is sometimes called a "sandwich lease option deal." In this scenario, you buy the property from the seller through a subject to or lease option deal, and then turn right around and find a tenant/buyer of your own. Think of it as subletting the property.

The key here, of course, is to make sure the numbers fall into place. You need to pay as little as possible to the seller—and keep your monthly payments as low as possible—while collecting as much as you can from the tenant/buyer. If all goes well, you'll make a tidy sum simply for playing the role of middleman.

> **Watch Out!**
>
> When seeking lease option deals, look for property that is well maintained, in a nice neighborhood, and falls somewhere in the middle price range of houses in the area. Avoid fixer-uppers or homes in low-income neighborhoods, which can prove to be more trouble than they're worth in a lease option situation.

The Two-Step Sandwich Deal

Completing a successful sandwich deal is a two-part process:

1. Convince the seller to let you get the property as a subject to or lease option deal.

2. Find a tenant/buyer who is interested in becoming a homeowner through a lease option deal.

Finding Good Seller Candidates

During your initial contact with a seller—after you've learned a bit about the property and determined it meets your target criteria—try to find out why the person wants to get rid of the property. If they have already moved and are now making payments on two different homes, you could be in luck. "Debt relief is the biggest reason why people will do a lease option," says Matt Bowman of www.REItoolbox.com.

You should then ask whether the seller definitely needs to have all cash, or whether they'd be willing to accept payments. Obviously, you're hoping they don't insist that they need all cash. If this happens, Matt Bowman suggests this response:

> Okay, I just ask that question because we are investors and if we have to come up with an all cash offer, we have to get a *substantial* discount from the appraised value of the house. However, if you would be open to the idea of taking payments on the house, we can usually offer you a *lot* closer to the appraised value of the house.

At that point, if the seller shows even the slightest interest in considering payments, you can then proceed with details about the specific arrangements, advantages to the seller, and so on. If they won't budge and insist they need all cash, tell them you need to discuss it with your partners and will call back if they're interested.

Persuading the Seller

If the seller does express interest in a payment arrangement, you need to be ready with your best sales pitch as to the merits of a lease option. Matt Bowman offers this sample:

> Well, I may be able to offer you a lease option. Basically what we do is take over the house payments and make them directly to the bank for you. We also guarantee in writing that our company pays for all maintenance, repairs, taxes, insurance, basically every expense related to the house during the term of our agreement. Then what we do is put a tenant/buyer in the house. This is someone that our company has put through an intensive screening process to ensure that they are able to buy the house sometime in the near future. We work with this tenant/buyer to help them get qualified for a mortgage and cash you and us out in the near future. It's in our best interest to deal only with quality tenant/buyers because we make our money by actually selling the house, not by charging you any fees. Does that sound like something that might interest you?

This may provoke any one of a number of common reactions from the seller. Ideally, they'd say something like, "Sure! When can we sign on the dotted line?" More likely, they'll raise some kind of concern—the most common being, "How long will this be in my name before they pay it off?"

Be honest with the seller, explaining that you can't make any promises as to the exact time when this will happen. Stress, though, that you will agree in writing to keep the mortgage payments and all other financial obligations current until the buyer/tenant can purchase the property.

> **Watch Out!**
>
> With a lease option deal, you should agree only to make payments directly to the lender. Never send the payments to the seller!

Finding the Tenant/Buyer

Step two of the sandwich deal is generally much easier than step one. It's generally pretty easy to find aspiring homeowners who want a place of their own but can't go the traditional route, for whatever reason.

Classified Ad

You can start by placing a classified ad in the local paper's real estate section—either the "Rent to Own" section (if the paper has one) or the "Homes for Sale" listings. Avoid the "Homes for Rent" section—you'll get flooded with calls from people who can't afford an option payment.

> **Promissory Note**
>
> You may want to include figures in your ad, especially if the payment is reasonable. Just include the monthly payment. Most tenant/buyers aren't immediately concerned about the purchase price—they're more worried about the option payment they need upfront and the monthly payment. Matt Bowman advises against mentioning a specific option payment in your ad. "It is possible that the tenant/buyer may have more than you are looking for. If you mention a specific amount, it is highly unlikely that they will volunteer the fact that they have more than that to put down."

Here's a sample ad, courtesy of Matt Bowman:

> West Mifflin RENT TO OWN Home. Credit problems OK. 3 bedroom, 2 bathroom house with 2 car attached garage. Central A/C. You can OWN this home for only $900 a month! 555-555-5555

You'd be amazed at how many more responses you'll get simply by including that "credit problems okay" line.

Screening Tenant/Buyer Candidates

Most likely, you'll get lots of response just from the classified ad alone. (If not, you may want to refer to Chapter 16, in which we describe additional ways of attracting buyers.) Now you need to start screening your candidates. First, get some information about their credit history. Although some credit problems are okay, you want to be fairly certain that this person will be in a position to qualify for funding within the next few years to buy the property from you.

You also need to make sure they have money for the option payment. Remember, let the potential tenant/buyer be the first one to mention a specific figure—it's possible he's willing to pay more than you'd planned to ask for.

Naturally, also check his references, just as you would for a regular tenant.

After you've screened all the applicants, simply pick the one who offers the best total package—satisfactory option payment, good references, and good likelihood of getting financing in the near future. Keep the information on the other applicants in your files for future reference if you have another property available in the area.

Are We Clear?

When you meet the tenant/buyer, make sure he completely understands how the lease option process works. You need to especially make sure he knows that the option payment is nonrefundable, so he won't get it back if he doesn't end up buying the property.

How you handle some of the specific details of the agreement is up to you. For example, maintenance is one issue you need to address. Some investors prefer to make the tenant/buyer responsible for all repairs and maintenance, whereas others set a limit as to how much the tenant/buyer would have to pay out-of-pocket in a single month.

Either way, it's a good idea to hold the tenant/buyer responsible for at least a portion of the cost to maintain the house. If for no other reason, this gets him in "home-owner mode" right from the start.

Why Investors Like Lease Option Deals

There are many benefits to lease option deals. First and foremost, you generally need to invest very little of your own money in these deals. Also your credit history (or lack thereof) isn't a factor because—just as with "subject to" deals—you aren't taking on a loan in your own name. You never need to go to the bank, wait for approval, or any of that stuff.

Foreclosure Fact

Here's a major benefit to lease option deals, as explained by Michael Carbonare of www.naked-investor.com: "Who do you think is going to take better care of your property? The tenant who views you as the greedy SOB who is taking his money every month, or the tenant/buyer who is taking care of the property as if it's their own—because in a year it may very well be?" Indeed, one huge advantage of lease options as opposed to rental property is that tenant/buyers tend to be very conscientious about caring for the property.

A Triple Payday

The most attractive aspect of lease option deals is the profit potential. As Matt Bowman points out, one of the nicest features of a lease option is that you can make money with them in three different ways.

♦ First, you make money from the upfront option deposit that you collect from your tenant/buyer. This option deposit is non-refundable, so even if your buyers pull out of the deal or you have to evict them, you still get to keep the deposit. How much money are we talking about here? Bowman says you should be collecting 3 to 5 percent of the purchase price for your option deposits. This means that on a $100,000 house, you should be collecting between $3,000 and $5,000 upfront from your tenant/buyer.

When you sign a deal with a seller, you will not put up any money of your own. You will not give them an option deposit, security deposit, or any other type of deposit.

♦ The next way that you make money from a lease option is from the monthly rental payments. You should collect more from your tenant/buyer than what you are paying out. For the most part, you will only offer to pay a seller's monthly mortgage payment. You are not interested in renting the property out at market rent from the seller. You are interested in only making the mortgage payment to the bank for them. You aren't just renting the property from them, you are agreeing to maintain the property, and for that service to them, you are willing to only make the monthly payment.

You then charge your tenant/buyer the going market rate for rent, or just above it. So if you are paying a mortgage payment of $688 on a $100,000 property, you will charge the typical market rent of $900 a month, giving you a positive $212 a month cash flow! On some properties, you may be able to get more, and on some, you will get less. Your typical lease option deal should yield you around $100 to $200 a month positive cash flow.

♦ Your third profit center from a lease option comes when you sell the property. You will be buying these properties for a lower amount than what you are selling them for. When your tenant/buyer exercises their option to purchase, you can then walk away from the closing with an even larger lump of cash than you collected upfront. It is not unheard of to get from $10,000 to $20,000 at a closing, according to Bowman.

Show Me the Money

Exactly how much can you make from a lease option deal? Matt Bowman offers this example:

Your terms

$100,000 house

$85,000 owed (This is what you will purchase the house for.)

$800/month payment

Your buyer's terms

$103,000 purchase price

$4,000 down

$988/month payment

12-month term

Bottom line

$4,000 upfront +

$188/month positive cash flow × 12 months

= $2,256 + $14,000 back-end profit = $20,256 from one deal!

Note: Back-end profit = $103,000 purchase price minus $4,000 down minus your $85,000 purchase price

Should you have trouble getting the homeowner to vacate the property in a timely manner, you may need to become more assertive. We covered techniques for getting a homeowner out of the home in great detail in Chapter 14.

Promissory Note _____

Matt Bowman suggests you never mention rent credits to your tenant/buyers unless they bring it up. "In some cases, to help the buyer get financed, you can just give them rent credits from the start. However, usually, if they don't mention it upfront, you shouldn't either. If they do mention it, which most don't, you can ask them what they think is fair.

"On a $900 payment, tenant/buyers might say anywhere from $50 to 50 percent of the payment was what they thought would be fair as a rent credit. If you hear a response like 50 percent of the payment, you can say, 'Well, let me ask you a question. If you were to go get a mortgage today on this house and had a $900 a month payment, how much of that $900 do you think would go toward the principal in the first couple of years? I can tell you it would be a *lot* less than half of the payment! It would probably be only a couple of dollars a month. How about this? I'll give *a hundred* bucks a month toward your purchase price! Does that sound fair?

"Of course, after you have already established that they would only be reducing their principal by a couple of dollars if they got a mortgage, $100 a month sounds more than fair. Very few people will argue with you on that point after explaining it that way."

A Dual-Contract System

Matt Bowman advises writing up two separate agreements to use with your tenant/buyer—a lease agreement and a separate purchase agreement. "You will do this to make it easier for you if you need to evict the tenant/buyer. By having a separate lease agreement and a separate purchase agreement, you make it easier to simply evict the tenant if they violate the lease agreement or do not pay for any reason. If you were to only write a single agreement with the tenant/buyer as you do with the seller, it would be easy for them to argue that they had already established an equitable interest in the house. This means that they would have some legal right to some part of the equity in the house.

"Another reason why a single agreement may be bad is because it is possible that the tenant/buyer would be entitled to get some or all of their rent back, even if they were in default of the agreement. Since they would have established an equitable interest in the property, a judge may decide that they are entitled to get some, or all of that 'equity' back."

When the Tenant Is Ready to Buy

Hopefully, your tenants will soon find themselves in a position to exercise their option to buy the property. At that point, you should make sure your attorney is capable of doing a *simultaneous closing*. If not, look for another attorney who can. Consult with the sellers to make sure they're able to attend the closing, and do the same with the buyers.

At the proceedings, you will actually be doing one closing right after another. First, you buy the property from the seller, and then you turn around and sell it to your tenant/buyer.

You use the funds from your buyer to pay off the seller's mortgage, plus give them any extra amount you may have agreed to. You then get a check for the remainder—your profit.

Land Lingo

In a **simultaneous closing**—commonly used in deals involving flipping or sandwich lease options—the property changes hands twice in rapid succession, from the seller to the investor, and then to another buyer or investor.

If the Buyer Bows Out

When considering offering a lease option deal, most investors' biggest fear is that the tenant/buyer will change his mind and decide not to exercise his option to buy. In reality, though, this is one of the best things that can happen to you.

Why? First of all, the option money the tenant/buyer paid at the start of the deal is nonrefundable—meaning, you get to keep it whether or not he decides to buy. When he walks away from the property, you can now start the process all over again with a new tenant/buyer. Bottom line: You can collect option payments twice (or even more) on the same property.

An added bonus: Most likely, the tenant/buyer took good care of the property while he lived there, because he intended to eventually buy the place.

The Least You Need to Know

- ◆ Many sellers may know little or nothing about lease option deals. Be prepared for skepticism and possible rejection.

- ◆ There are two parts of a "sandwich deal": finding an agreeable seller, and finding a tenant/buyer.

- ◆ Be sure to run the numbers thoroughly before agreeing to a lease option deal to make sure it will be profitable for you.

- ◆ Screen your tenant/buyers carefully to make sure they'll take care of the property and will have a good chance of getting financing in the near future.

- ◆ There are three ways to profit from lease options: up-front money from the tenant/buyer; monthly rental payments; and profit at the time of sale.

Chapter 20

Other Creative Approaches

In This Chapter

- ◆ Flipping vs. wholesaling
- ◆ Understanding the wholesaling process
- ◆ Wraparound mortgages and other financing approaches
- ◆ Why a good exit strategy is important
- ◆ Types of exit strategies

It seems like savvy investors are continuously coming up with new creative ways to finance their deals or make more money in real estate. The possibilities are limited only by your imagination. In this chapter, we'll discuss a few other techniques we've seen investors use successfully, such as wholesaling, wraparound mortgages, and other creative techniques. We also explain why a good exit strategy is vital for any investor.

"Flipping" to Other Investors

A popular way to make money with real estate—especially foreclosures and other "bargain" properties—is to buy and resell the property quickly, commonly referred to as *flipping*.

Isn't Flipping Illegal?

"Flipping"—in its original, legal meaning—*is* illegal. Flipping originally referred to a form of bank fraud in which someone purchased a property for someone else as part of an illegal maneuver.

> **Land Lingo** _____
>
> **Flipping** is a term commonly used when referring to the real estate practice of buying a property—usually at a bargain or below-market price—and selling it very quickly for a profit.

> **Land Lingo** _____
>
> A **shill** is someone who poses as a buyer or seller in order to garner interest or competition from other sellers or drive up the price of a property. **Wholesaling** refers to the practice of arranging the purchase of the property and finding a buyer, but never actually possessing the property yourself.

In her book *Buy Low, Sell Low: Your Complete Guide to Profits in Wholesale Real Estate*, Vena Jones-Cox illustrates how this illegal exercise would work:

Fred Felon finds a rental property that he'd like to buy for $50,000. Fred knows that his friendly neighborhood S&L—which has great interest rates and low closing costs—will only give him a purchase money mortgage of 80 percent of his purchase price, no matter what the actual value of the property is worth. Fred doesn't want to spend any of his cash on a down payment, so he has his buddy Sam Shill purchase the property from the seller for $50,000 cash (which Fred provides). The next day, Sam sells the property to Fred for $65,000. Fred goes to the S&L with this contract in hand and gets a loan for $52,000. At the closing, Sam "receives" $52,000 from the S&L and a $13,000 second mortgage from Fred. Later, out in the parking lot, Sam gives Fred the $52,000 check from the bank and a release for the second mortgage. Fred effectively fooled the bank into giving him a $52,000 loan on a property that he really paid $50,000 for.

The scenario described here—or any of its dozens of variations—constitutes about seven different kinds of federal fraud, and is *not* what we do in wholesaling. Wholesalers are not *shills*: the difference between what we contract to buy for and what we contract to sell for is a real expense to the buyer, a real profit to us, and is in no way intended to deceive a federally insured institution. Thus, it is not fraud, and not illegal. Still, it's not a good idea to tell your real estate agent, lender, or local magistrate that you "flip" properties for a living. You are a wholesaler. A *wholesaler.* Got it?

Okay, we got it. And we do prefer the term *wholesaling*. However, because *flipping* is the most popular slang term—and one that most of the general public seems to easily understand—we use it here.

The Wholesaling Process Explained

A wholesaler basically makes his living by playing "matchmaker." He finds good deals, executes them, and then matches the property up with the perfect buyer—the quicker, the better. A successful wholesaler in a good market can make an incredible living.

Vena Jones-Cox explains the basic wholesaling process:

1. The wholesaler finds a property that, for whatever reason, the owner is prepared to sell at a below-market price.

2. The wholesaler evaluates the property by researching the fair market value of the property, inspecting to determine what repairs might need to be made, and estimating the cost of the repairs.

3. The wholesaler determines mathematically what his buyers will be willing to pay for the property, then makes an offer to the sellers that will allow the wholesaler to make a profit when he resells the property.

4. The wholesaler goes through a negotiation process with the seller which (if successful) ends in the seller agreeing to sell the property to the wholesaler.

5. The wholesaler identifies a likely buyer or buyers for the property, and goes through a negotiating process to determine what the buyer will pay.

6. The wholesaler prepares information and takes steps toward the closing, such as completing a title search and pest inspection. This step usually happens simultaneously with Step 5.

7. The wholesaler either buys the property and then sells it to his buyer, or sells his right to purchase the property to the buyer, who then buys the property directly from the seller.

Types of Flippers

Investors who "flip" properties generally fall into three categories (although some investors employ more than one of these approaches):

- ◆ **The scout.** Sometimes known as a "bird dog," this person basically just acts as the "eyes and ears" for a bigger investor. Familiar with the other investor's needs and goals, the scout watches for any properties that might be available and meet the investor's needs. The scout then gathers as much information as possible— and perhaps does some of the initial legwork—and passes this lead on to the other investor.

- ◆ **The middleman.** Also known as a "dealer," this investor fulfills the stereotypical role of a flipper. The middleman finds the deal, works out the arrangements, and either takes part in a simultaneous closing or simply facilitates the deal between buyer and seller.

- ◆ **The retailer.** Of all flippers, the retailer invests the most time, effort, and money into his investment properties. The retailer buys bargain properties that need work, fixes them up, and then sells them for a nice profit.

Who Should Get Involved with Wholesaling?

Although wholesaling is an attractive—and relatively easy—way for new investors to make some quick money, it can also be great for more experienced real estate veterans.

- ◆ **Beginners** can get their feet wet by breaking into investing by wholesaling a few deals first.

- ◆ **People with no cash/bad credit** often think they have no chance of getting involved with real estate. Wholesaling is perfect for people like this. Your credit isn't a factor, and you rarely need more than a few hundred dollars of your own money.

- ◆ **Experienced investors.** Most investors who actively seek out properties will come across many properties that don't fit their criteria, for whatever reason. Generally, they just pass these properties by. In doing so, however, they're missing out on a valuable source of income. Just because they're not interested in the property for themselves doesn't mean the investor can't make money from it. Savvy investors know there's profit in playing "matchmaker"—finding the perfect investor who'd love to snap up that particular property.

The Downsides

Relatively speaking, the money you can make from wholesaling is peanuts compared to the big bucks you could earn from other forms of investing. Your pay as a wholesaler is basically a "finder's fee"—a nice finder's fee, in many cases, but still not the windfall you might earn through other investment strategies. Your profit from the deal will seem tiny compared to what the other investor/buyer will probably make.

Wraparound Mortgages

Wraparound mortgages are a less common form of creative financing for real estate deals. They're also a bit tricky, and not something we recommend a new investor attempt. Basically, this is where you pay the seller a monthly payment that covers both his existing mortgage as well as an additional amount toward the purchase price of the home.

For example, suppose the house is worth $100,000. The seller has a current mortgage balance of $80,000. You give him a $10,000 deposit, leaving your balance at $90,000. You make payments on the $90,000 figure, the seller makes their original loan payment for their $80,000 and keeps the difference.

The advantage to the buyer is that they get to sell their house, and get a little bit of profit every month. The buyer gets to purchase a property they might not otherwise be able to buy. The disadvantages? This can be a pretty tricky transaction to arrange, and lenders often won't agree to it.

> **Land Lingo**
>
> A **wraparound mortgage** is a loan that includes the remaining balance of an existing first mortgage, along with an additional amount requested by the borrower.

> **Watch Out!**
>
> Wraparound mortgages are illegal in some states, and many lenders also insert clauses in their contracts prohibiting their loans from being "wrapped."

Buying the Note from the Lender

In another relatively uncommon investment strategy, the investor buys the note—not the property, but the mortgage note itself—from the bank. The investor then, in effect, becomes the lender. The investor can try to collect money from the delinquent borrower or begin foreclosure proceedings himself. In cases where the bank is pretty sure it would take a loss, even by foreclosing and selling the property at auction, the lender might be willing to offer an investor the chance to buy the note for much less than its face value.

This is a technique investors rarely use, though, mainly because it requires a lot of available cash. Also, by buying the note, the investor would find himself in the same spot as a lender—meaning, the investor would be forced to try and collect money from a defaulting homeowner. This isn't something most investors want to bother with.

IRA as Investment Capital

We've heard of some investors who use their IRAs to fund real estate deals. An advantage to this is that any profit you make from the real estate deal can go back into your IRA tax-free. However, we think having a solid, secure retirement fund is essential, so we're very hesitant to recommend this strategy to anyone, especially new investors.

> **Foreclosure Fact**
>
> You can use your IRA to fund investments only if you have a self-directed IRA fund, this is the term for a specific kind of IRA in which the account holder makes the decisions regarding investment options.

The financial website www.bankrate.com has done numerous stories about investing using your IRA as capital. Do a search on the site for more information, or simply do a Google search using the terms "IRA" and "real estate."

Exit Strategies

Many people think the toughest part of buying foreclosures and REO properties is finding a good property and getting everyone to sign on the dotted line. After you've got the keys to the property in your eager little hands, it's smooth sailing, right? Um, wrong. We hate to be the bearer of bad news, but often the toughest part of a real estate investment deal isn't getting into it—it's getting *out* of it.

> **Land Lingo**
>
> An **exit strategy** is an investor's plan for how he will resolve or complete an investment deal that he has started.

Sure, what you do at the start of a deal is important. However, what you do at the end of a deal is crucial, mainly because this is generally where you get most—possibly even all—of your profit. This is why it's so important to have your *exit strategy* completely thought out in advance.

It's important to know how you'll get out of an investment deal before you ever get into it. Remember, you often don't get any money in your pocket until the deal is complete and you've walked away from the property. So you'd better make sure you have an exit strategy—and that it's a good one.

The Importance of Exit Strategies

Again, we can't stress this enough: *do not* enter into any investment deal until you have a specific, well thought out plan of how you'll get out of it. We don't mean to be repetitious, but we feel we can't stress this enough because we've seen so many new investors make the crucial mistake of giving little or no thought to their exit strategy. You can find the most amazing property, and finagle a knockout deal with the seller and/or lender, but until you've successfully executed a good exit strategy, you're just passing the time.

Think about it: That dream home may be nice to look at, but what good is it doing just sitting there? In fact, it's doing you more harm than good, because now you've taken on the financial obligations the house brings with it. At this point, if you don't take any further action, you're actually much *worse* off than you were before you made the deal with the seller.

Promissory Note _____

Ideally, in addition to your primary exit strategy, you should also have at least one backup exit strategy, just in case something goes wrong and foils your original plan. For example, suppose your original plan was to resell the property quickly for a profit, but something unexpected happened (perhaps market values in the neighborhood dropped dramatically for some reason) and you're unable to sell. Your backup plan might be to rent the property until market values rise again.

Types of Exit Strategies

Okay, so we think we've made our point about the importance of exit strategies. Hopefully, you are now fully convinced that an exit strategy needs to be a major part of your pre-purchase planning.

So how exactly do you come up with a good exit strategy? First, you need to evaluate your goals and needs. Do you want to get some money in your pocket right away? Then you want a short-range exit strategy. Generally, we prefer investment deals with short-range exit strategies. The one exception would be if you can find a nice rental unit that provides you with a steady monthly income.

Short-Range Exit Strategies

With a short-range exit strategy, the goal is to wrap up the deal quickly. You don't want to wait forever to see your profit. The ultimate example of a short-range exit strategy is a sandwich lease option deal, where the exit strategy involves a simultaneous closing. You technically only own the property for about two minutes before selling it and making a profit. Now that's what we call making a fast buck!

Next on the spectrum of short-range strategies are wholesale deals, where you buy and resell properties as quickly as possible. If you're selling the property to another investor, you most likely had him already lined up before buying (or negotiating a deal for) the property. So you should be able to execute the deal pretty quickly. Your exit strategy would probably involve completing the deal within a few weeks.

Then we have retailing deals. These can be at the far end of the short-range spectrum. Depending on how much work you plan to do on the property, it could be several months before you can try to sell the property. This exit strategy would involve finding a buyer for the property, and making sure your asking price more than covers the cost of the repairs you've made.

Long-Range Exit Strategies

If you don't have a lot of patience, or a lot of working capital to tide you over until you see your profit, deals involving long-range exit strategies might not be your best bet. Lease options involve long-range strategies, although you can greatly cut down that time period if you play your cards right. The exit strategy here involves the tenant/buyer purchasing the property. If you screen your tenant/buyer candidates well and choose someone with a high likelihood of getting financing in the near future, you may be able to wrap up this deal fairly quickly. Rental properties probably have the longest life span of any investment deal. With a rental property, your exit strategy may be to sell the property only after you've decided to get out of the rental business—which could be far in the future.

The Least You Need to Know

◆ Flipping—in the true sense of the word—is illegal. Wholesaling is not.

◆ You can make money from wholesaling even if you don't have much money or have bad credit.

◆ With some imagination and effort, you can probably come up with several creative ways to finance or find lucrative real estate investment deals.

◆ It's imperative to come up with a good exit strategy *before* you obtain an investment property.

Part 6

Real-Life Lessons

Finally, we prove that you're never too old (or experienced) to learn some new tricks. Even if you've bought a few foreclosure properties, we think you'll still learn a few things from these experienced investors. Veteran investors share horror stories as well as success stories, to help you benefit from their experience and learn from their mistakes.

Advice from the Pros

In This Chapter

- Why you shouldn't let the seller remain in the house
- Protecting your personal assets
- Don't attempt your first deal before you're ready
- Little things can sometimes yield big profits

We've given you lots of advice about what you should do. Now we want to spend a few moments sharing advice on what you shouldn't do. There are some common mistakes that many new (and not-so-new) investors make. Hopefully, by describing them in this chapter, we can help you avoid these pitfalls.

Letting Sellers Stay in the House

It's easy to feel sorry for homeowners in dire straits. However, don't make the common mistake of agreeing to let the homeowners remain in the property while they get back on their feet.

Matt Bowman of www.REItoolbox.com offers this warning:

> If you decide to allow a seller to stay in the house for "just a little while longer" while they look for another place, you are asking for trouble! Make sure that these sellers know that the only way you can get involved in the deal is if they will deed the property to you, leave the loan in place, and they *must* be out of the house.

Leaving Your Personal Assets Vulnerable

Most experts and experienced investors agree: It's foolish to buy and sell properties as an individual in your own name. We live in a lawsuit-happy society, and a single lawsuit—even if it's totally baseless and frivolous and winds up getting thrown out of court—can devastate you financially. You could end up losing your own house in the process. By forming a corporation, you can help protect some of your personal assets in case of lawsuit or other unexpected crisis. Most investors favor the LLC (limited liability corporation). Talk to your attorney and financial advisor to see which option would best suit your needs.

Renting to a Friend or Relative

It's tough to say no to friends and family, especially if they're in a jam and need a place to live. However, we know of countless investors who have rented a property to friends or relatives—and virtually all of them ended up regretting it.

Jumping In Before You're Ready

Real estate investing can be tricky business. There are lots of legal loopholes and pit-falls, many of which can cost you big bucks if you're not careful. This isn't something you can jump into blindly. Be sure to do as much research as possible into real estate investing—and foreclosure and REO properties specifically—before you even think about attempting your first deal.

Getting Emotionally Involved

It's great to have compassion for unfortunate homeowners who are down on their luck. However, be careful not to take sympathy too far. You won't be able to help everyone or solve every homeowner's problems. You need to remain objective enough to recognize when a deal just wouldn't be practical—or profitable—for you. Don't go against your better judgment just because you feel sorry for the homeowner. You won't be able to help *any* family—including your own—if you wind up bankrupt after pursuing a deal based solely on sympathy.

Underestimating the Importance of Curb Appeal

Some prospective buyers decide whether they're interested in a home before ever getting out of their car. It may not be fair, but when it comes to homes, appearances count. Buying a home can be an emotional process, and if buyers don't get a good "vibe" when they look at the home, they may not even bother checking out the inside. Make sure your home makes the best first impression it possibly can.

Misjudging the Amount of Fixing a Fixer-Upper Needs

Repairs and maintenance can be costly—especially if labor-intensive projects are involved. Sometimes problems that look small can prove to be big budget-busting headaches. If you don't have construction or maintenance experience, enlist the help of a qualified professional who can inspect a property *before* you buy it.

Going It Alone

No matter how smart you are, no one person can know everything about real estate law, tax regulations, home repair, and all the other issues associated with foreclosure investing. You need to assemble a team of qualified professionals, and utilize their skills as often as possible.

Not Researching a Property Carefully

Overlooking just a single lien on a property you're about to buy can be a very costly mistake. You can inherit an endless number of problems—legal, financial, and otherwise—when you buy a house. Be very diligent about researching the property thoroughly before you ever make an offer or shell out one cent to the seller or lender.

Being Clueless About Local Laws

This is one case where ignorance isn't bliss. Laws vary from state to state and region to region. If you're unaware that you're in a nonjudicial foreclosure state, you may wait too long to pursue a property, letting it slip through your fingers. Do you know if your state has a redemption period? If not, you might find out the hard way.

Giving the Homeowner a Check Too Soon

One of your main priorities when taking over a foreclosure or REO property is making sure the property is vacant. If it isn't, you need to get the occupants and their belongings out—the sooner the better. The promise of a check is like a carrot you're dangling in front of them—it gives them incentive to move out quickly. If you give them any money while they're still in the property, you can be sure they'll be in no hurry to leave.

Going Overboard on a Home's Makeover

With a fixer-upper or property that needs some touching up, you should try to make it look nice but not *too* nice. The more you invest into the home's transformation, the higher an amount you have to ask when you rent or sell the place. Before long, you may find that you've overpriced yourself right out of the market and can't find a tenant or buyer.

Little Tips That Can Make a Big Difference

Remember the old saying "Little things mean a lot?" Well, this is true in real estate investing, where a seemingly little detail can sometimes result in a big increase in profit.

Negotiate with Lenders and Lien Holders

When considering buying a distressed property—especially in the pre-foreclosure stage, you can greatly improve the potential bottom line by negotiating with lenders and lien holders. Let's say there's a mechanic's lien for $10,000. This is an obligation you'd inherit if you buy the property. However, if you can get them to agree to take, say $5,000—or even less—in exchange for removing the lien, you've netted yourself another potential $5,000. And it probably took you less than an hour.

Do a Little Sprucing Up

Tenants and buyers sometimes make judgments based on appearances. Hey, they're only human. And, yes, sometimes they can be impressed (or repulsed) by superficial things. Your building is structurally solid, yet buyers are bored. Maybe you need to make a few quick cosmetic fixes that will make a world of difference. Picture this: you have a brand new, top-of-the-line high-efficiency gas furnace in the property. You also have hardwood floors—complete with scuff marks, scratches, and stains. Which do you think a prospective buyer will remember? Veteran investors know that buyers and tenants love shiny hardwood floors, pretty landscaping, bright kitchens, and big bathrooms. Paying a little extra attention to any of these details can really pay off.

For My Next Trick ... I'll Instantly Add a Bedroom!

During an episode on the second season of the hit reality show *The Apprentice*, contestants had to take a fixer-upper property and try to improve its appraised value on a tight budget. One contestant made the fatal mistake of removing a wall, thus changing the four-bedroom home into a three-bedroom. This was, to put it mildly, not a smart move. However, making a change in the reverse could be a stroke of genius. Many families have three or more kids, and demand is always high for nice homes with lots of bedrooms. It wouldn't be cost-efficient to start constructing a huge addition to the home, but maybe there are other options. Is there a den that could easily do double-duty as a bedroom? Would the finished basement make a cool kids' room? Be creative and see whether you can improve the home's appeal on paper without actually lifting a finger.

More Advice from the Pros

Jackie Lange of www.SellYourHouseIn7Days.com offers these additional tips:

> Every market is different so you need to do your research before you buy. Just because you can buy a house below market does not mean it's going to be a good deal. If it takes six or seven months to get it fixed up, and then another six or seven months to sell it, you could lose all your profit on holding costs.

Speaking of holding costs—the biggest pitfall in real estate investing is not factoring in holding costs. Holding costs are all the costs you have while the house is being rehabbed or while it's sitting there vacant, waiting for a buyer or a tenant. Besides the monthly mortgage payments, you need to consider taxes, insurance, utilities, weekly lawn work, and maintenance. It adds up faster than you can imagine.

Gurus and Infomercials

Have you noticed how many "get-rich-quick" infomercials are on TV nowadays? On one recent morning, co-author Bobbi spotted at least a dozen different real estate "gurus," each with their own infomercial on which they'd make grand promises about how they could show viewers the secret to making a fortune buying mansions for no money down. Oh yeah, and all we had to do was shell out, say, a few hundred bucks to learn these mysterious secrets.

Foreclosure Fact
One of the most well-known cases of a guru-gone-bad involved William McCorkle. A few years ago, McCorkle was a staple on the light-night infomercial circuit. He promised to show you how to get rich in real estate with no money down—after you shelled out around $80 to buy his video course. In 2003, the federal government arrested McCorkle and his wife, charging them both with fraud and money laundering. Prosecutors accused the couple of using deceptive business practices, lying in televised commercials, failing to provide refunds, and stashing money in the Cayman Islands to hide it from the government, among other things. They were both sentenced to 24 years in prison.

It's not easy deciding who is and who is not an expert in this industry. Actually, it used to be easier before the Internet. Back then, one had to have some type of presence, either through TV, radio, and print or as a recognized lecturer/speaker. Generally speaking, this meant that the person had some organization behind him and all the expenses that go along with that burden.

On the Internet, everyone is an expert. There has been an explosion in the number of online foreclosure gurus. Why? Easy. Just put up a web page, make any claim you want, and the world thinks you're an expert. There are way too many websites that could be operated by some unemployed guy sitting at his kitchen table with a laptop computer—not what we'd call a valid business operation.

That's the downside to seeking expert help on the Internet. You just don't know who is who. With all the moneymaking schemes and revenue-generated affiliate websites, it's really hard to tell whom you're dealing with. Is this person legitimate? Is this really original material or copied from another website? Is this their website or are they just pushing products as an affiliate to make money? How can you tell? Co-author Todd has found his company's logo on more than a dozen sites through the years. Most of his articles appear on hundreds of other websites without his permission. So if you read his article on someone else's site, how would you know who wrote it?

Research and Compare

So how do you figure out who is an expert and who is running a scam? Buying this book was your first smart move because of its comprehensive, authoritative, and accurate information. Researching in this case simply means comparing. Go to the foreclosure message boards listed in Appendix B and ask questions. See who responds. Many experts will share their advice on several message boards. Read the posts. See the common answers that appear over and over. Identifying patterns will give you insight as to what the collective experts thinks. Remember that some of these boards will be biased and tend to promote only products and services they can make money on, but it doesn't necessarily mean those are bad products.

Search Engines

Google is a popular search engine. Yahoo! is another popular online searching tool. Be careful when analyzing the results returned from your Internet searches. They used to provide the most "relevant" results from your search, but not anymore.

Today, all search engines need to make money. They do this by taking payments in the form of advertising dollars from website operators. If you do a search for "foreclosures," the results displayed on the page could include legitimate websites, websites that have tricked or fooled the search engine (usually through tricky coding techniques) to be ranked high on the page, or just those that have paid a lot of money to be highly ranked.

Not all these sites will be good, legitimate operators or even offer what you're looking for. A classic example is the "debt consolidation" sites. Type in "foreclosures" and you'll get a lot of sites in your search results that want to save you from foreclosure. Why? Because these operators make a lot of money selling your information to larger consolidation firms. Therefore, they can and do pay a lot of money to be listed on the top of search results, even though they are not really relevant to what you searched for.

Sites with Guru Ratings and Rankings

We know of several sites that rate the various gurus in our industry. The problem is that most are biased. They don't recommend a particular guru, and then recommend their own work instead. Most of these lists are far from complete. I have yet to see one that's really accurate or unbiased. Most are self-serving in one fashion or another. Co-author Todd even tried to assist one website operator by letting him know that two of his gurus were in jail, two others were dead, and three others were not gurus at all. The information was blatantly inaccurate, but the author refuses to change the site to this day. Stay tuned for an unbiased website called ForeclosureGurus.com to be launched mid-year 2005. Also think about why a website containing foreclosure articles or listings would contain a section attempting to demolish their competitors, if they didn't have something to hide themselves.

Single-Page Websites

A single-page website is usually a dead giveaway that the company has little depth, little expertise, and is only interested in promoting a singular product or service. The offering may indeed be okay, but without supporting information, it would be very hard to tell. Often these websites are merely affiliates of other companies. They may not even be the original publisher of the work they're selling.

Classic examples are websites with a home page that scrolls on forever. They are filled with all the reasons why you "need to buy today." Some even include special incentives or discounts offers if you buy by the date shown on the page. Ever notice though, that the expiration date of the special offer just happens to end today? And if you revisited the site tomorrow, the expiration date would be that day, too? Think about that before you buy.

> **Foreclosure Fact**
>
> Real gurus and website operators, those who have been in the business for some time, tend to shout less. They tend to be less about self-promotion and more about quality content. If a website contains many pages, that generally (but not always) means more content, more expertise, and a better handle on the industry.

Or how about those sites with offers and promotions highlighted in yellow text? They look very much like the junk mail you receive in your regular mailbox at home. And yes, most of them are just electronic versions of junk mail.

Whether buying from TV ads, newspaper, or through the Internet, common sense always applies. Inquire about the company, ask about the product, and check out the return policy. All legitimate operators know that they can't please everyone. Although the product may be good, someone somewhere will want to return it. Returns and refunds are simply a part of doing business. Any company that makes it difficult for you to return a product is not a company you want to do business with.

> **⚠ CAUTION   Watch Out!** _____
>
> On the Internet, make sure the order page of any website is "secure." That means you'll see the "https" part of the website address in your address bar. This means that the order page is encrypted and is secure for transmitting your credit card information. Look for a security seal or logo from a nationally recognized provider like VeriSign or eTrust. If you cannot click on that logo, you'll know it's a fake. Yes, some website operators put the logos on their sites, but really have no secure solution for you. That also holds true with the BBB Online insignias. If a merchant legitimately participates in these programs, you should be able to click on that logo. It will take you to a page that verifies that the website operator is who he says he is, and that his site is secure. Look for contact information and toll-free numbers. If they are hidden or nonexistent, be wary.

Red Flags

Many legitimate real estate investors would make wonderful mentors, though. So how do you separate the keepers from the con artists? A few clues should send off red flags:

- ◆ **They make grandiose promises.** It's fine for an investing expert to say you can make a nice income if you apply yourself and work hard. However, anyone who promises you can become wealthy overnight without investing any money and by only working two hours a week is definitely stretching the truth.

- ◆ **They have a mysterious background.** Most legitimate experts will gladly tell you where they came from, even if it was the wrong side of the tracks. They'll be happy to list their backgrounds and qualifications. Shady "gurus," on the other hand, are usually pretty vague about their past. They always seem to be hiding something—a criminal record, perhaps.

◆ **Their world is really rosy.** Most ethical teachers and mentors will warn you about problems and pitfalls you may encounter. They'll also tell you that nothing goes perfectly 100 percent of the time, and advise you to be prepared for the inevitable deal that goes sour. Scam artists want to paint a wonderfully rosy picture, getting you in such a good mood that you'll happily shell out money for whatever they're selling.

◆ **Excessive oomph.** Con artists pepper their sales pitches with lots of adjectives and exclamation points. This is incredible! You'll make a fortune! Buyers will flock to your door! And your skin will clear up overnight, too! This is a diversionary tactic to distract you from the fact that their presentation is all sizzle and no steak. There are lots of eye-catching graphics and colorful packaging, but no helpful information.

Gurus That Won't Go Away

One common complaint about real estate gurus is that they don't know when to take no for any answer. We've heard many horror stories of people who bought one book or attended one seminar and found themselves on the receiving end of a constant stream of telemarketing calls and junk mail. When ordering one of these products, try to avoid giving your home phone number if at all possible. And if you should get a telemarketing call, ask to be put on their "Do Not Call" list.

That Free Seminar Comes with Strings Attached

Jackie Lange of www.SellYourHouseIn7Days.com offers this warning:

> Beware of the late-night television or radio ad seminar promoters offering a free seminar. The free seminar is just to get you into an emotionally driven sales pitch by a professional sales person. After you're there, they are very convincing at why you need to pull out your credit card and charge $1500 for a course or $3,000 or more for a seminar. They'll promise the moon to get you to charge on the spot. Don't do it!

> If you do go to the $3,000 seminar, then they will try to up sell you into a $5,000 seminar. You'll get weekly calls to buy more and more and more from the gurus with the infomercials. Most of the people teaching these expensive seminars are not even in the real estate business or have not been in a long time. They are in the seminar selling business.

I've been to those $3,000 and $5,000 seminars. My logic was that because they cost so much they must be the best. However, nothing could be further from the truth. In fact, the majority of the seminar time was not to educate about buying houses, but to sell you into the next seminar."

The Least You Need to Know

- ◆ Spend some time trying to think of creative ways that you can make your property more appealing without investing too much time or money.

- ◆ Take everything you hear on late-night infomercials with a really big grain of salt. If it sounds too good to be true, it probably is.

- ◆ At the very least, do a quick online search to find out about a specific real estate guru or company before handing over any of your money.

- ◆ It's crucial to do your research, study as much as possible, seek advice from seasoned pros and make sure you're totally ready before attempting your first investment deal.

Case Studies from Real Foreclosure Investors

In This Chapter

- ◆ Auctions can provide profitable foreclosure opportunities
- ◆ You can find a great lead in foreclosure lists
- ◆ Subject to deals can be tricky but rewarding

We've told you all about foreclosure investing in great detail, but putting all this knowledge into practice is a different ball game. So we thought it might be helpful to share the first-hand stories of investors and their actual deals. In this chapter, we'll share detailed case studies of several different types of foreclosure investment deals.

An Auction Success

Allen Watkins of www.homebargains.com shares one of his own experiences:

I got a call from a man who said he had gotten my letter and was interested in selling his home. He owed around $30,000 and wanted an offer. I knew the location was good. Of course I made an appointment with him right away. When I arrived at the home, I got no answer. I waited 15 minutes and then left a note. Later I called; no answer. I stopped by the property again one day. A woman answered the door. She said, "My husband is not home. You will have to talk with him." She abruptly shut the door. I knocked again, and she would not answer.

I attempted a contact a couple of more times over the next several months. No response. The address appeared on the auction list. My desire was to make a deal with the owners prior to the auction to avoid competition. I knocked on the door again. The woman answered the door. I immediately explained that I was not trying to bother her, but the property was scheduled for auction. I would hate to see her get nothing when I could possibly get her some money if she would talk with me. She asked, "How much?" I told her it all depended on the condition of the property. I asked her, "Would you allow me to inspect the interior? It will only take a minute." She did allow me to walk through. I learned the reason I never saw her husband; they were separated and getting a divorce. She did verify for me that her ex-husband would be available for a signature.

> **Promissory Note**
>
> Foreclosure investors must have a thick skin and lots of determination. If you get discouraged the first time a homeowner acts hesitant or even shuts the door in your face, you might miss out on some great opportunities.

The home needed much work. There were only two bedrooms; the tiny kitchen needed to be gutted and a wall taken down to open it up to make it larger. I told her I would consult with my investor and get back with her. I figured about $15,000 was needed to fix the home up right. I would be borrowing the money from an armchair investor by paying a $1,000 origination fee and 20 percent interest per annum, due and payable upon my resell. The numbers were getting tight. I felt I could only offer her $1,000. She said she would talk with her ex-husband and get back to me. She would not return my calls.

Therefore, I went to the auction and won the bid for a dollar more at $34,026. I was delighted that there was no competition.

The ex-owner moved right away on her own, refusing to respond to my attempts to communicate with her. As the remodeling was nearing completion, I got a buyer for the full price at $69,900. After the real estate commission and expenses, I netted about $17,000.

Mining Foreclosure Lists for a Gem

Prior to starting in real estate investing, Jackie Lange was a stay-at-home mom for 12 years. She started buying and selling houses full time in 1996. The first few years, she focused on wholesale flips. She simply found the great deals and then sold her contract to an investor who would fix up the house. "With very little effort, I was able to find and flip 40 houses my first year."

In 1998, Jackie did her first rehab and started keeping some houses as rentals. "In 2000, I started the very first membership site for real estate investors called www. SellYourHouseIn7Days.com. It has grown to more than 100 offices nationwide in 4 short years. Members license the use of all seven real restate websites, marketing materials, and domain names plus learn my tips and tricks to being successful through weekly teleseminars and our private message board."

Promissory Note

Wholesaling can be a good way to break into investing if you have a good attitude, great people skills, and a knack for matchmaking—but lack money or the time to devote to a full-time investing career.

Jackie Lange shares one of her success stories:

> Every month I get the pre-foreclosure list. The houses on the list are homes "going" to the foreclosure auction. But for now, they are still owned by the homeowner.
>
> One listing really jumped out at me because the list showed the mortgage balance to be $7,500 and the value of the house to be $100,000. That's a lot of equity so I drove right over to the house. When I arrived, I noticed the house looked like it had not been lived in for a long time even though I could see through the windows the house was still full of furniture.
>
> I asked the neighbors where the owner was. She told me she was in a nursing home. I called every nursing home until I found her. But they told me she had been in a coma for many years. So I asked for her guardian or a family member's number. They would only give me a daughter's name—but no phone number.
>
> You have to be a good detective to get the really good deals in this business. I tracked down the daughter but the phone was disconnected so I searched the tax records until I found where she lived.

When I knocked on the door and told her I was interested in her mother's house to stop the foreclosure—she was shocked. She assured me her grand-daughter was making the payments and there had to be a mistake. I showed her the listing on the pre-foreclosure list. Then we called the attorney so he could verify that the payments had not been made for more than three months.

Come to find out, the granddaughter had been using the money for drug money. The daughter was just devastated when she found out the truth. She was certain her 93-year-old mother would get well and wanted to keep the house so she could come home.

I knew at that moment the best thing to do was *not* buy the house but help her stop the foreclosure. So I called the mortgage company and explained the situation. I asked if they could add the back payments to the loan balance and reinstate the loan. They said they would only consider it if they got a check for $500. So I paid the $500 and got an agreement from the daughter that she would call me first when she did get ready to sell.

I knew I had a chance of losing the $500, but it was the right thing to do. Just six months later, she called and said she was ready to sell the house. I asked her, "If I pay you all cash and close within a few weeks, what's the least you would consider?" I added, "take whatever you want from the house then leave every-thing else. I will take care of everything."

Promissory Note

With foreclosure buys, you often find that you've not only bought a house, you've also inherited a ton of stuff along with it. This can be a mixed bag. Often this will be a bunch of junk you have to discard. But sometimes you'll find yourself with some unex-pected treasures—antique furni-ture, collectibles, or other valuable items.

She said she would like to get $25,000 and would like to leave everything in the house. Remember, this house is worth $100,000.

I got some great antiques, including a piano and a complete set of Theodore Haviland china. Plus she left a 1988 Mercury with only 40,000 miles in the garage—my sister got the car. After spending $20,000 in repairs, I sold the house for $105,000. Honestly, all the great things I got out of the house were almost as exciting as the profit.

Where did the money come from to buy and fix up the house? I did not use a penny of my own money! I used a hard-money lender from www. EasyInvestorMoney.com.

Subject To Deal

This is an example of an actual subject to deal. Information is provided by Matt Bowman, founder of www.REItoolbox.com. All the information is real, although (and we hope this is blatantly obvious) the names have been changed:

Sally Seller called Bill Buyer after seeing his sign at the side of the road that said "WE BUY HOUSES, Fa$t Ca$h Paid!" Ms. Seller told Mr. Buyer that she had a 5-year-old 3-bedroom, 2-bathroom house in a fairly new subdivision. There was a broken window in the front and a warped base under the kitchen sink where there had been a leak that was fixed a while ago, but no major problems with the house.

Sally Seller told Bill that the house would appraise for $89,000. She owed about $76,000 on her mortgage. Sally said that she was 3 months behind on her payments of $678.45, which included taxes and insurance. She said that she just wanted to sell the house for what she owed on it and didn't care about trying to make a profit.

Sally had recently gone through a divorce and could no longer afford her house. She told Bill that she intended to just move in with her sister so she could save some money for a place of her own that she could afford. She was worried that if she listed the house with a realtor, it would take too long and the house may be foreclosed on in the meantime since she didn't have the money to make the payments.

Bill asked her if he were to come along and "take over the house" for her, and just let her move on, then would that help her? She asked what "taking over the house" meant. Bill went on to explain that she would just deed the house to him, and he would try to find a buyer for the house. He couldn't absolutely guarantee when he would find a buyer, but as soon as he did, he would make up the back payments, bringing the loan current, and then continue to keep them current. He explained that this would keep Sally from having a foreclosure recorded against her credit as long as he found a buyer in time.

Bill Buyer made sure to impress on Sally that this was his business, and he intended to market like crazy to find a buyer fast to fill the house and bring the payments current. Since Sally's only other option was foreclosure, she agreed and set up an appointment with Bill.

Bill Buyer called up his friend who was a notary and told him when the meeting was. He told his friend Nelly Notary to meet him at the house so he could get the deal signed up and have the appropriate documents notarized. Bill and his notary friend then went to the house.

After inspecting the house, Bill found Sally to be truthful about the condition of the home. There were no real problems with the property, and it was a good-looking house that was located in a very nice neighborhood. Bill then invited Sally to sit down at the kitchen table with him to "review the paperwork".

Bill first got out the Purchase Agreement and said to Sally, "This is the agreement that we use to lay out our agreement. As you can see, it is pretty easy and straightforward. There are no contingencies in this agreement. We are not asking you to fix the broken window or do anything else to the house."

Bill pointed out the little X at the bottom where Sally needed to sign. He told her to go ahead and read over the agreement and see if she had any questions. After quickly glancing through the agreement, Sally signed at the X.

Bill then got out the trust agreement. He explained to Sally that he was having her deed the property into a land trust so the transfer of the property was more protected against triggering the due on sale clause in her mortgage. He showed her where to sign the document, which she did. Nelly Notary then signed and stamped the document.

Bill got out the warranty deed to trustee and explained to Sally that this deed transferred ownership of the property into the trust that they had just created. Sally signed the deed. Nelly Notary then properly notarized the deed.

The next document that Bill got out was the assignment of beneficial interest in land trust. He explained to Sally that this simply transferred interest in the land trust that they had just created over to him. He explained that this was needed in order to give him control and ownership of the property. After Sally signed the document, Nelly Notary notarized it.

Bill then showed Sally the letter of agreement and addendum. He explained that this was just showing that Sally had been informed about her mortgage having a due on sale clause. Bill also pointed out that it was restating what he had said about making up the back payments as soon as he found a buyer for the house. Sally signed and dated the letter.

Bill then brought out the authorization to release loan information. He told Sally that this document allowed him to call up the lender and get any information he might need about the loan. Sally signed this document after filling in her lender's name and address, as well as her loan number.

The next piece of paperwork Bill Buyer brought out was the *limited power of attorney*. Bill told Sally that this document gave him the ability to deal with any insurance or tax matters related to the house as well as selling the property or any other business that might come up related to the house. Sally signed it and had two witnesses sign it.

Land Lingo

A limited power of **attorney** is a legal document authorizing a person to act on another person's behalf for a specific legal transaction.

Bill smiled and sighed deeply. "Almost there!", he said to Sally. He then handed her the letter to insurance company. He said that this letter was simply letting the insurance company know that the land trust that they created was to be named as additional insured on the policy. He said that this made sure that his ownership interest in the house was protected in case of any loss, such as fire or vandalism. Sally signed the letter and dated it.

After signing all the paperwork, Sally turned to Bill and asked, "So this is what you do for a living? You just help people with their problems?" That put a *big* smile on Bill's face because that is what he had been telling people for some time that he was doing when he did these deals!

After leaving the house, Bill called up his attorney. He gave them the property address and seller's name. He asked them to do a title search and fax him the results. Bill's attorney usually had a report for him within 24 hours and would bill him $75 for each title search he had done.

Bill then called up the lender. He told them who he was and that he had a loan information release signed by the seller that he could fax in order to get information on the loan. The operator gave Bill a fax number to fax the release to and told him to call back in about two hours, and they would have the release and would be able to answer his questions.

Bill called the lender back and confirmed the amount to bring the loan current was $2,095.35, which was three months' worth of payments and late charges. Bill got the address where he would need to send payment to get the loan caught up and asked the operator if they had the ability to do a payment by phone. The operator told Bill they could do this for an additional $19 fee. He also asked whether the taxes and insurance were escrowed and current, which they were. Bill said that he would be back in touch soon to take care of the arrearages.

Bill then called up his friend Randy Realtor. He asked Randy to pull some "comps" (comparable property sales data) on the house to let him know what it might be worth. Randy faxed a list to Bill about an hour later showing a number of properties that were similar to Sally's that had sold recently. Bill determined that Sally's property would probably sell for about $95,000 at full retail value based on similar sales in the neighborhood.

The next day, Bill's attorney faxed him a title search that showed that the only outstanding lien against the property was the mortgage that Sally had told him about. Bill decided it was time to get to work and try to get the house filled. He made up some directional signs that said "Rent To Own Home" and wrote on them "Bad Credit OK," along with the address of the house.

Bill also made a sign for the yard that said "Rent To Own, Bad Credit OK, $900 a month, 555-555-5555." Bill put this on the sign because he knew that $900 a month was just at or slightly under market rent for this particular area and type of house. Bill then went out and put up the directional signs starting at the major highway about a mile and a half from the house and pointing back to the house. He then put up the yard sign while he was out.

That evening, the phone began to ring with interested buyers. Bill asked each caller what their credit looked like and how much they had to put down. After asking the questions to make sure that he was dealing with someone who had enough to put down and halfway decent credit, he told them about the house and told them to drive by. He told them that if they were interested in looking inside after driving by to give him a call, and he would set up an appointment to see the inside.

Three days after signing the deal up, Sally Seller called Bill to tell him that she was completely moved out of the house and had it cleaned out and ready to show. Bill began to make appointments to show the house. Bill had a showing that evening with a couple who didn't seem too interested in the house and asked about how old the roof was and if Bill planned on fixing the broken window. Bill explained that he was offering the house on special terms and anyone who wanted it would be taking care of any maintenance or repairs, just like any homeowner would do. The couple left saying that they would "think about it."

The next day Bill got a call from a woman who said that she saw the directional signs and had driven by the house. She was very interested and said that she really liked the neighborhood and how the house looked. After finding out that she had $3,500 to put down on the house, could afford the $900 a month payment, and that her only credit issue was a bankruptcy that was filed 2 years ago, Bill made an appointment to show the house to her and her husband that evening.

The woman and her husband, a young couple in their 20s, were waiting at the house when Bill arrived. They went through the house, whispering to each other then talking loudly about how much they loved the high ceilings and large master bedroom. After walking through the house, they turned to Bill and said, "Okay, what do we need to do now to get in?"

Bill gave them an application to fill out, which they did on the spot. Bill told them that he had several other applicants and made his decision based on credit and amount that they had to put down. He told them that he would probably be making a decision in the next day or so. In the back of his mind, Bill knew that the next payment would be due on the house soon. He knew that he had to make up the back payments soon in order to keep additional late fees from being added as well as keep a foreclosure from being filed.

The couple said to Bill, "Well please let us know as soon as you can. We really love the house and want it!" Bill assured them he would call them as soon as he had made his decision. He then faxed their application to his mortgage broker and had their credit pulled. Bill's mortgage broker confirmed that the woman had been honest and the only thing on their credit was a 2-year-old bankruptcy. Bill's mortgage broker added that he could probably even get them financed immediately.

Bill called up the couple the next day and congratulated them on their new home. He told them to meet him there that evening with a certified check for $3,500 and their first month's rent of $900. They met Bill at the house with the certified check and a regular check for their first month's rent. Bill went over the agreements with them. He was selling the house to them for $97,000.

Bill told them that they were responsible for all maintenance and repairs on the house. The husband responded that this would not be a problem because he worked in construction. Bill then told them to make sure that they kept a copy of the certified check and a copy of all rent checks for their own records, which would help when they went to apply for a loan.

After signing the couple up on a lease purchase and collecting their checks, Bill handed them the keys and said, "Congratulations on your new home!" The woman began to cry and hugged Bill. She said that they had wanted to buy a home for a while now and had worked hard to save the $3,500 for a down payment.

The next day, Bill went to the deed recorder's office and paid $8 to record the deed to trustee that Sally Seller had signed. He then called up the lender and paid the $2,095.35 plus another $19 for a payment by phone. The next payment wasn't due for 2 more weeks. Bill then called up Sally Seller and told her the good news that the loan was now current and the house had been saved from foreclosure. Sally was very happy and repeatedly thanked Bill.

So what was Bill's profit on this deal? Well, he made $2,285.65 right up front. This is because he collected $3,500 plus $900 from the new buyer and paid out $2,114.35 for late payments, late charges, and a payment by phone charge. He will make $221.55 each month as well. This is the difference between his outgoing payment of $678.45 and the $900 a month that he is collecting. When he sells, he will make at least $21,000 from the difference between the mortgage payoff of $76,000 and his sale price to the buyers of $97,000. Not too bad from one deal!

There was an added bonus to this deal though. Two weeks later, Bill Buyer got a call from Sarah Seller, Sally Seller's friend at work. Sarah was moving and had a house with only $6,000 in equity and did not want to take the time to try to sell it herself. She realized that she really didn't have enough for a realtor's commission. She wanted to know if Bill Buyer would do the same deal for her house that he did with Sally's! Sarah was current on her payments, so Bill grabbed the deal immediately!

The Least You Need to Know

◆ If the homeowner won't cooperate with a pre-foreclosure sale, an auction may provide a bargain deal.

◆ By studying foreclosure listings and notices carefully, you may spot a real gem of an opportunity.

◆ Subject to deals involve the most profit (and least headaches) if you can resell the property quickly.

Glossary

acceleration clause   A loan provision giving the lender the right to declare the entire amount immediately due and payable upon violation of any part of the contract (also known as due-on-sale clause).

acre   A measure of land equal to 43,560 square feet.

agreement of sale   Contract signed by buyer and seller stating the terms and conditions under which a property will be sold.

appraisal   A written estimate of a property's current market value completed by an impartial party with knowledge of real estate markets.

arrears   Overdue mortgage payments including interest.

asking price   Also known as the list price, this is the price placed on property for sale.

assessed value   The value of a property as established for tax purposes.

assumable loan   A loan in which the buyer can take over the existing loan with the original borrower's terms, often without going through the approval process required for an original loan.

auction   The public sale of property to the highest bidder.

balloon payment   An installment payment that is larger (generally much larger) than the other scheduled payments and is usually the last payment of the loan.

bankruptcy A proceeding in a federal court to relieve certain debts of a person or a business unable to pay its debts.

blanket mortgage A single mortgage that covers more than one property.

broker An individual who acts as a middleman between buyers and sellers and negotiates deals involving the purchase of property.

clear title A title that has no liens, judgments, or other encumbrances.

closing The formal meeting where loan documents are signed and funds disbursed in order to complete the purchase of a property.

closing costs Costs that must be paid during the finalization of purchase of a property. Examples include title fees, recording fees, appraisal fee, credit report fee, pest inspection, attorney's fees, and surveying fees.

cloud Any condition revealed by a title search that negatively affects the property's value or salability.

collateral Something of value deposited with a lender as a pledge to secure repayment of a loan; for a mortgage, the home or property is the collateral.

commission Fees paid to a real estate agent or broker for negotiating a real estate or loan transaction.

comps or comparables The prices of recently sold properties that are used to determine the value of a similar property.

contingency A condition that must be met before a contract is legally binding.

credit report Report detailing the credit history of a prospective borrower; used to help determine borrower creditworthiness.

creditor Person or business (such as a lender) to whom a debt is owed.

curb appeal The first impression you get of a home when viewing it from the street.

debt-to-income ratio The ratio of the total of minimum monthly debt payments to gross monthly income.

deduction An amount that you can subtract from the total amount on which you owe tax.

deed A written document that conveys title to real property.

default The nonperformance of a contractual or other kind of obligation, such as not making payments on a note.

deficiency judgment   A court order requested by a lender when the foreclosure sale doesn't raise enough money to satisfy the mortgage debt. The lender would seek the difference between the amount owed and the amount received at auction.

delinquency   The failure to make payments as agreed in the loan agreement.

demographic information   Information that gives a profile or picture of what the area looks like in terms of population characteristics.

depreciation   The reduction of value over time of an item that is usually large or expensive, such as a house, car, appliance, etc.

distressed   A property that is in poor financial or physical condition.

down payment   The amount of money initially paid by the buyer toward purchase price of property; usually comes from the buyer's own funds or a source other than that providing financing for the purchase.

due-on-sale clause   A loan provision giving the lender the right to declare the entire amount immediately due and payable if the home is sold before the loan has been paid off.

earnest money   A deposit made by the buyer as evidence of good faith when submitting a formal offer on a property.

encumbrance   Any claim against property that affects its value, including mortgage loans, unpaid taxes, easements, junior liens, or deed restrictions.

equity   The difference between the market value of a property or home and the amount owed on that property.

escrow account   The money that is held by a third party—not the buyer or seller—during the real estate transaction.

exit strategy   An investor's plan for how he will resolve or complete an investment deal that he has started.

eviction   The legal process in which a landlord removes the tenant from the property.

Fannie Mae (FNMA)   Federal National Mortgage Association, a federally chartered corporation that purchases mortgages and packages them to sell as securities.

Federal Housing Administration (FHA)   An agency within HUD that administers many loan programs designed to make housing more available.

first mortgage   A mortgage that is recorded at the earliest time.

foreclosure   The process in which a lender terminates the borrower's rights to a property, primarily due to a default of the loan.

Freddie Mac (FHMLC)   Federal Home Loan Mortgage Corporation is a federally chartered corporation that purchases mortgages and packages them to sell as securities.

FSBO   Short for For Sale By Owner, it means the owner is selling the property personally, without the help of a broker or real estate agent.

grace period   A period of time during which a loan payment may be paid after its due date but not incur a late penalty.

hard-money lender   A firm or private investor who makes high-interest loans to people who can't borrow money elsewhere.

home-equity loan   A loan secured by the equity in your home; generally a second mortgage.

homeowner insurance   Insurance designed to protect homeowners from financial losses related to the ownership of property.

Housing and Urban Development (HUD)   A federal government agency established to run certain federal housing and community-development programs.

judicial foreclosure   Foreclosure proceedings that take place through one or more court hearings.

land trust   A revocable, living trust primarily used to hold title to real estate for privacy and anonymity; also commonly used in "subject to" deals so as not to trigger the due-on-sale clause.

landlord   Person or company that owns property that is rented out to tenants.

lease   A contract in which the owner of a property allows another person to occupy the property for a specified period of time in exchange for monthly rent.

lease option   An agreement in writing in which the owner of a property allows someone to rent the property with the option to buy the property at a specific price within a certain time period.

lender   A bank, mortgage company, broker, or other financial institution that offers the mortgage loan.

lien   A legal financial claim against a property that must be paid off when the property is sold.

line of credit   An established, pre-approved loan that is available whenever the borrower needs it. After the line of credit has been established, the borrower can withdraw any amount up to the pre-set limit without filing a new application.

Lis Pendens   Latin for "suit pending," this is a written notice that a lawsuit has been filed, which concerns the title to real property.

mechanic's lien   Claim out against a property by contractor or other party who performed work on the property and is owed an outstanding payment.

mortgage   A contract allowing a borrower to buy a property while using it as security for a loan.

mortgage insurance   Insurance to protect the lender in case the borrower defaults on the loan.

Multiple Listing Service (MLS)   The system by which a number of real estate firms share information about homes that are for sale.

nonperforming asset   An asset that does not produce any income, such as a loan in default, or a home that has been foreclosed.

note   A written agreement to repay a debt under certain terms and conditions.

notice of default   A written notice to a borrower that a default has occurred and that foreclosure proceedings may begin.

position   When referring to a lien, its rank among all the judgments against a property; first mortgages usually have the top position, with lesser liens falling below.

Power of Attorney   A legal document authorizing one person to act on behalf of another.

pre-approved   When a person is approved by a lender for financing up to a certain amount, he is pre-approved.

pre-qualify   The process that puts a buyer through some kind of basic initial screening process.

principal   The amount of money owed to the lender not including interest.

property disclosure   A statement to a prospective buyer listing information that relates to a piece of property, such as the presence of hazardous materials.

recapture   Including part or all of the depreciation you deducted in prior years in this year's taxable income.

reinstatement   The period after the foreclosure begins when the borrower still has the opportunity to avoid losing his home by paying overdue balances and other fees.

REO   Short for "real estate owned" property, a property that the lender acquired at auction if no one bid higher than the default amount.

second mortgage   A mortgage recorded after another preexisting mortgage is already in place.

Section 8   A government rental assistance program for low-income families.

simultaneous closing   An event in which the property changes hands twice in rapid succession, from the seller to the investor, and then to another buyer or investor.

subject to   Buying a property subject to existing financing and mortgage contracts.

tax lien   A claim against a property for unpaid taxes.

tax sale   The public sale of property by a government entity as a result of non-payment of taxes.

tenant   A person who occupies rental property in exchange for monthly rent.

title search   The examination of public records to ensure that the seller is the legal owner of a property and that there are no liens or other claims against the property.

upset price   Also known as a reserve price, the starting minimum bid for a property at foreclosure sale. This is generally the amount in default to the mortgage lender.

Recommended Resources

We've found many website and other foreclosure resources that we feel are useful to foreclosure investors of any experience level. In this section, we list many of the best of a varied range of resources.

Pre-Foreclosure Sites

Arizona

S.B.R.E.C.
Appears to have quality data. Prices range by county and state. Check price charts.
http://www.sb-rec.com

California

County Records Research
Pre-foreclosure data for Los Angeles, Orange, Riverside, San Bernardino, San Diego, and Ventura counties.
http://www.countyrecordsresearch.com

The Blue Sheet
Trustee sales information for Santa Clara County. Prices from $150 to $660 for an annual subscription.
http://www.thebluesheet.com

S.B.R.E.C.
Appears to have quality data. Prices range by county and state. Check price charts.
http://www.sb-rec.com

Colorado

Outhouse Foreclosures
Pre-foreclosure data for Adams, Arapahoe, Boulder, Broomfield, Denver, Douglas, Jefferson, and Weld counties.
http://www.outhouseforeclosures.com

Fast Property Data
Pre-foreclosure data for Adams, Arapahoe, Boulder, Broomfield, Denver, Douglas, El Paso, Jefferson, Larimer, and Weld counties.
http://www.expresspropertydata.com

Florida

Florida Foreclosure Report
Pre-foreclosure data for Palm Beach, Broward, Dade, Orange, and Seminole counties.
http://www.floridaforeclosurereport.com

Foreclosures Daily
Pre-foreclosure data for Pinellas, Hillsborough, Pasco, Polk, Sarasota, Manatee, Lee, Charlotte, Collier, Citrus, Hernando, Nassau, Flagler, St. John's, Duval, Clay, Orange, Seminole, Martin, Dade, Broward, and Palm Beach counties. From $129 per month. Updated monthly.
http://www.foreclosuresdaily.com/index.asp

S.B.R.E.C.
Appears to have quality data. Prices range by county and state. Check price charts.
http://www.sb-rec.com

Georgia

Atlanta Foreclosure Report
Pre-foreclosures in Fulton, DeKalb, Cobb, Gwinnett, Clayton, Cherokee, Douglas, Henry, Fayette, Forsyth, Hall, Bartow, and Rockdale counties and the metro Atlanta area. Includes residential and commercial properties.
http://www.equisystems.com

Illinois

Foreclosure Report
Pre-foreclosure data for Cook county.
http://www.chicagoforeclosurereport.com

Midwest Foreclosures
Pre-foreclosure data for Cook, DuPage, Grundy, Kane, Kendall, Lake, and Will counties. See price chart for fees.
http://www.midwestforeclosures.com

Massachusetts

Boston Real Estate
Pre-foreclosure data for Massachusetts.
http://www.bostonrealestate.com

ForeclosureMass.com
Seems like a good site for Massachusetts pre-foreclosures. E-mail address required to log in as guest. Cost ranges from $19.95 per month (auto recurring) for one county to more than $200.00 per month for the full state.
http://www.foreclosuresmass.com

Nevada

County Records Research
Pre-foreclosure data for Las Vegas and Clark counties.
http://www.countyrecordsresearch.com

S.B.R.E.C.
Appears to have quality data. Prices range by county and state. Check price charts.
http://www.sb-rec.com

New Hampshire

The Registry Review
New Hampshire's statewide real estate and financial newspaper. Reports information abstracted from the 10 New Hampshire county Registries of Deeds.
http://www.real-data.com

New Jersey

New Jersey Pre-Foreclosures
Pre-foreclosure listings for all 21 New Jersey counties. Includes archived database going back to 1994 and New Jersey pre-foreclosure articles and information.
http://www.njpforeclosures.com

New Mexico

S.B.R.E.C.
Appears to have quality data. Prices range by county and state. Check price charts.
http://www.sb-rec.com

New York

PropertyTrac
Pre-foreclosure data for New York county (Manhattan).
http://www.propertytrac.com

Profiles Publications, Inc.
Pre-foreclosure data for Manhattan, Brooklyn, Bronx, Queens, and Richmond counties.
http://www.nyforeclosures.com/cgi-bin/SoftCart.exe/?E+scstore

ForeclosureTrac
Pre-foreclosure data Bronx, Brooklyn, Manhattan, Nassau, Queens, Staten Island, Suffolk, Westchester, and Rockland counties.
http://www.foreclosuretrac.com

Foreclosure Update of New York
Pre-foreclosure data for Bronx, Brooklyn, Manhattan, Queens, and Richmond counties.
http://www.foreclosure-ny.com

North Carolina

Foreclosures Daily
Pre-foreclosure data for Guilford, Forsyth, Alamance, and Orange counties. From $129 per month. Updated monthly.
http://www.foreclosuresdaily.com/index.asp

Texas

The Real Estate Almanac, Inc.
Pre-foreclosure data for Harris county.
http://www.realdata.net

Vermont

Real Data
Lists recent real estate transfer records from the State of Vermont Department of Taxes.
http://www.real-data.com/VTPub.htm

Washington

S.B.R.E.C.
Appears to have quality data. Prices range by county and state. Check price charts.
http://www.sb-rec.com

Bank Foreclosure (REO) Sites

National

ForeclosureNet.net
National database of bank foreclosed and government-owned foreclosures.
Current listings. Free trial offer.
www.foreclosurenet.net

Florida

Florida Foreclosures
Statewide bank foreclosures and government-owned properties. Free trial offer.
www.fl-foreclosures.com

Texas

Foreclosure Listing Service, Inc.
REOs and auctions for the Dallas/Ft. Worth Metroplex and the Austin Metro area.
http://www.dfwforeclosures.com

Texas Foreclosures
Statewide bank foreclosures and government-owned properties. Free trial offer.
www.tx-foreclosures.com

Bank Sites

Bank of America
www.bankamerica.com/oreo

Bank One
http://www.bankone.com/answers/BolReoSearch.aspx

Buy Bank Homes
www.buybankhomes.com

Country Wide Bank
http://www.countrywide.com/purchase/f_reo.asp

Downey Savings Bank
http://www.downeysavings.com/property/index.asp

Freemont Investment and Loan
http://www.1800fremont.com/REO/ReoProperties_Available.asp

Greenpoint Savings Bank
http://www.greenpoint.com/Index.cfm?spPathName=static/prop-home.htm

IndyMac Bank
http://apps.indymacbank.com/individuals/realestate/search.asp

Lexington State Bank
http://www.lsbbancshares.com/page.cfm?id=2472

National Bank of Arizona
www.nbarizona.com/BusinessBanking/CommercialRealEstate/BankOwnedProp.htm

Ocwen Financial Corporation
http://www.ocwen.com/reo/reofindbystate.cfm

Peoples Bank
http://www.peoples.com/im/cda/multi_elements/0,,1355,00.html

Premiere Asset Services
Manages and lists properties owned by banks and other lenders.
http://www.premierereo.com

Unity Bank
http://www.unitybank.com/foreclosures/index.cfm

Wilshire Financial Services
http://www.wfsg.com/realestate/realestate.aspx

Government Foreclosure Listings

Home Sales
Features data from several government agencies, including U.S. Departments of Housing and Urban Development (HUD), Agriculture (USDA/Rural Development), and Veterans Affairs (VA).
http://www.homesales.gov/homesales/mainAction.do

Housing and Urban Development (HUD)
http://www.hud.gov/homes/index.cfm

HUDForeclosures.com
National database of HUD and other agency foreclosures.
www.hudforeclosures.com

Veterans Affairs (VA)
http://www.ocwen.com/reo/reofindbystate.cfm

Federal Deposit Insurance Corporation (FDIC)
http://www2.fdic.gov/drrore/

Small Business Administration (SBA)
http://app1.sba.gov/pfsales/dsp_search.html

Internal Revenue Service (IRS)
http://www.treas.gov/auctions/irs/real1.html

First Preston
A marketing and maintenance contractor for the Department of Housing and Urban Development. Markets HUD properties in Georgia, Kansas, Kentucky, Missouri, New Mexico, Oklahoma, Puerto Rico, Tennessee, Texas, Washington, D.C., and the Virgin Islands.
http://www.firstpreston.com/index.asp

Golden Feather Realty
A marketing and maintenance contractor for the Department of Housing and Urban Development. Markets HUD properties in California, Northern Nevada, Washington, Oregon, Idaho, Illinois, Indiana, Tennessee, Kentucky, and Pennsylvania.
http://www.goldenfeather.com

Fannie Mae (FNMA) Federal National Mortgage Association
http://www.mortgagecontent.net/reoSearchApplication/fanniemae/reoSearch.jsp

Freddie Mac (FHLMC) Federal Home Loan Mortgage Corporation (HomeSteps)
http://www.homesteps.com/hm01_1featuresearch.htm

Tax Foreclosures

Official County Sites

Arizona, Coconino County
http://co.coconino.az.us/treasurer/invest.asp

Arizona, Pima County
http://www.to.co.pima.az.us/tax_sale_info.html

Arizona, Pinal County
http://apps.co.pinal.az.us/Treasurer/Search/index.asp?T=TLSale

Arizona, Yavapai County
http://www.co.yavapai.az.us/events/TaxSales/Treasurer/TaxLiens.asp

California, Kern County
http://www.kcttc.co.kern.ca.us/taxsales.cfm

California, Yolo County
http://www.yolocounty.org/org/treasurer/sales.htm

Colorado, Boulder County
http://www.co.boulder.co.us/treas/tax_sale/tsq.htm

Colorado, Broomfield County
http://www.ci.broomfield.co.us/centralrecords/TaxSale.shtml

Colorado, Denver County
http://www.denvergov.org/Treasury/4109248template1jump.asp

Colorado, Eagle County
http://www.eagle-county.com/treasurer/taxSale.cfm

Colorado, El Paso County
http://trs.elpasoco.com/faqlien.asp

Colorado, Garfield County
http://www.garfield-county.com/home/index.asp?page=810

Colorado, Gilpin County
http://co.gilpin.co.us/Treasurer/TaxLienSale.htm

Colorado, Larimer County
http://www.co.larimer.co.us/treasurer/taxsale.htm

Colorado, Logan County
http://www.loganco.gov/treasurer/tax_sale.htm

Colorado, Mesa County
http://www.co.mesa.co.us/treasurer/taxlien.htm

Colorado, Pueblo County
http://www.co.pueblo.co.us/treasurer/

Florida, Alachua County
http://www.clerk-alachua-fl.org/clerk/taxdeed.html

Florida, Miami-Dade County
http://www.miamidade.gov/taxcollector/property_tax_certificate_sales.asp

Florida, Palm Beach County
http://www.pbcountyclerk.com/legalrecords/taxdeed.html

Florida, Pinellas County
http://pubtitlet.co.pinellas.fl.us/servlet/taxdeed.saledates.DM79

Georgia, DeKalb County
https://dklbweb.dekalbga.org/taxcommissioner/TaxSaleGeneralInformation.htm

Georgia, Gwinett County
http://www.co.gwinnett.ga.us/cgi-bin/bvgwin/egov/page.
jsp?pm=Departments%7CTax+Commissioner%7CProperty+Tax&sm=Tax+Sales

Idaho, Ada County
http://www.adaweb.net/adaweb.nsf/0/03c608a349aa43f6872567be00621e61?OpenDocument

Ohio, Butler County
http://www.butlercountyohio.org/treasurer/index.cfm?page=foreclosure

Ohio, Cuyahoga County
http://www.cuyahoga.oh.us/sheriff/foreclosures/default.asp

Ohio, Erie County
http://www.erie-county-ohio.net/sheriff/sales.htm

Ohio, Licking County
http://www.lcounty.com/treasurer/delinquent_tax_dept.php

Ohio, Stark County
http://www.sheriff.co.stark.oh.us/pr11.htm

Kansas, Johnson County
http://www.jocogov.org/countyclerk/taxsale/tax_sale.htm

New York, New York County
http://www.nyc.gov/html/dof/html/liensale2.html

North Carolina, Buncombe County
http://www.buncombecounty.org/business/countyBusiness/taxForeclosures.htm

North Carolina, Haywood County
http://www.gov.co.haywood.nc.us/foreclosure.html

North Carolina, Orange County
http://www.co.orange.nc.us/revenue/pending_foreclosure_sales.htm

North Carolina, Pitt County
http://www.co.pitt.nc.us/depts/legal/foreclosure

Oregon, Washington County
http://www.co.washington.or.us/deptmts/sup_serv/fac_mgt/forclos.htm

Pennsylvania, Bucks County
http://www.buckscounty.org/departments/tax_claim_bureau/

Tennessee, Nashville and Davidson County
http://www.nashville.gov/chancery/tax_sale_listings.htm

Texas, Dallas County
http://www.dallascounty.org/html/citizen-serv/pubwks/div-prop.html

Texas, Douglas County
http://www.douglas.co.us/Treasurer/TaxLienInfo.htm

Texas, Fort Bend County
http://www.co.fort-bend.tx.us/Admin_of_Justice/County_Clerk/freq_info/foreclosure.htm

Texas, Fort Worth
http://www.fortworthgov.org/engineering/pub_services/fore_surplus.htm

Texas, Montgomery County
http://www.co.montgomery.tx.us/taxf.shtml

Texas, Tarrant County
http://www.tad.org/WebPages/tax_lien_sales.htm

Texas, Travis County
http://www.co.travis.tx.us/tax_assessor/foreclosure/tax_sales.asp

Texas, Waco County
http://www.waco-texas.com/city_depts/planningservices/propertymanage.htm

Washington, Chelan County
http://www.co.chelan.wa.us/tr/tr5.htm

Washington, Clark County
http://www.co.clark.wa.us/treasurer/Foreclosures/Foreclosure.asp

Washington, Jefferson County
http://www.co.jefferson.wa.us/treasurer/pdf/ForeclosureInformation.pdf

Washington, King County
http://www.metrokc.gov/finance/treasury/foreclosure

Washington, Kitsap County
http://www.kitsapgov.com/treas/foreclosures/foreclosure.htm

Washington, Pierce County
http://www.co.pierce.wa.us/pc/abtus/ourorg/at/bulletin/foreclosure.htm

Washington, Snohomish County
http://www1.co.snohomish.wa.us/Departments/Treasurer/Services/forclosures.htm

Washington, Spokane County
http://www.spokanecounty.org/treasurer/foreclosure/default.asp

Washington, Thurston County
http://www.co.thurston.wa.us/treasurer/delinquent.htm

Washington, Whatcom County
http://www.co.whatcom.wa.us/treasurer/auctions/foreclosures.jsp

West Virginia, Berkeley County
http://www.berkeleycountycomm.org/treasurer.htm

Wisconsin, Racine County
http://www.racineco.com/treasurer/index.aspx

Wyoming, Sweetwater County
http://www.co.sweet.wy.us/treas/propertytaxes/page5.html

Other Sites

Tax Sale List.com
http://www.taxsalelists.com/index.php?page=home

Tax Lien Certificateshttp://
www.tax-lien-certificates.com

Foreclosure Statistics

Mortgage Bankers Association
Good site for mortgage foreclosure statistics.
http://www.mortgagebankers.org

Federal Deposit Insurance Corporation (FDIC)
Gathers statistics on mortgage foreclosures nationally.
http://www.fdic.gov

Foreclosure Information Sites

All Foreclosure Information
Good site for straight information on foreclosures.
http://www.all-foreclosure.com

Inno Vest Resources Management
Another good site specializing in California information.
http://www.foreclosureforum.com

The Real Estate Library
Solid resource for foreclosure articles and information.
www.trel.com

Financing

Plus Mortgage program offered by Market Street Mortgage Corp., Clearwater, Florida.
Under the Plus Mortgage Program, the mortgage amount is based on the current market
value of the house, plus the cost of the renovation work. As with the Section 203(k) mortgages, however, the portion of the loan that covers the renovation projects is disbursed in
installments as the work is done.
www.marketstreetmortgage.com

HomeLoanCenter
www.homeloancenter.com

For Sale by Owner Sites

www.Owners.com

www.ForSaleByOwner.com

www.4saleByOwner.com

www.AllTheListings.com

www.FSBO.com

Hard-Money Lenders

Easy Investor Money
Nationwide provider of short-term financing for the purchase and resale of residential properties.
www.ezinvestormoney.com

Equity Funding
Offers quick turnaround, mainly handles loans in the six-figure range.
www.equity-funding.com

Investing Info and Help

About.com's Home Buying/Selling Site
www.homebuying.about.com

Be Aware of Real Estate
www.beawareofrealestate.com

CreClub
www.CreClub.com

Cutaia Mortgage Group/Cutaia Realty Advisors
Phone: 561-416-5834

Matt Bowman's Real Estate Investor's Toolbox
www.reitoolbox.com

Home Bargains
www.HomeBargains.com

The Naked Investor
www.naked-investor.com

Sell Your House in 7 Days
www.sellyourhousein7days.com

Vena Jones-Cox (the Real Estate Goddess)
www.regoddess.com

Message Boards

ForeclosureTalk
Geared toward the new and intermediate foreclosure buyer. Co-hosted by several top industry leaders.
www.trel.com/wwwboard/wwwboard.html

ForeclosureForum
Great board by Innovest Resource Management. Lots of good information. Special expertise in California foreclosures.
http://www.foreclosureforum.com/mb/index.html

All-Foreclosure
Very good board for foreclosure questions and answers.
http://www.all-foreclosure.com/forum/index.html

Creative Real Estate Online (CREONLINE)
Solid board with lots of expertise.
http://www.creonline.com/wwwboard/index.html

Public Records Sites

National

NETR Real Estate and Research Information
Good site for researching real estate information and public records.
http://www.netronline.com

National County Recorders Directory
Good resource for locating Recorder's Offices nationally.
http://www.zanatec.com/home.html

BRB Publications, Inc.
Good resource for locating public records sites nationally.
http://www.brbpub.com/pubrecsites.asp

Illinois

Record Information Services
Online public records for Illinois.
http://www.public-record.com/

Texas

Texas Association of Counties
Links to all Texas courthouses.
http://www.county.org

International Foreclosures

Canadian Foreclosure Sales
Information on available properties in Canada
http://www.foreclosures.ca

Real Estate Forms

NUPP Legal
Good selection of real estate forms by state.
http://www.nupplegal.com/realestate.html

LegalDocs.com
This site allows you to prepare customized legal forms online.
www.legaldocs.com

Free Forms & Documents
Contains lots of real estate forms and documents that you can print out.
www.fidtitle.addr.com/forms.htm

Reinstatement Services

Reinstatement Services, Inc.
Provides default management and foreclosure relief services.
http://www.reinstate.com

Real Estate Directories

The Creative Investor
Offers free ads, forums and other services for real estate investors.
http://www.thecreativeinvestor.com/

REALS.com
Large real estate portal. Lots of sponsors and advertiser links.
http://www.reals.com

Investment

REI Depot, Inc.
Large directory of resources for real estate investors
http://www.reidopot.com

Real Estate Investing
Offers numerous investment courses and other products.
http://www.realestateinvesting.com

Commercial

ReBuz.com
Big directory of commercial real estate resources.
http://www.rebuz.com

Real Estate News Sources

Inman News Features
Subscription required. Contains residential, commercial, and consumer news feeds.
http://www.inman.com

Realty Times
http://www.realtytimes.com

RIS Media
http://www.rismedia.com

Real Estate Forum Online
Good site with lots of commercial real estate resources.
http://www.reforum.com

National Real Estate Investor
http://www.nreionline.com

REI Club
http://www.reiclub.com

Resources for Locating People

Addresses.com
www.Addresses.com

Einvestigator
www.Einvestigator.com

Free People Search
Freepeoplesearch-online.com

Intelius
www.Intelius.com

KnowX
www.KnowX.com

QueryData
www.Querydata.com

REO Brokers and Agents

REO Network
Directory of REO brokers and agents nationwide.
www.reonetwork.com

REO Service
Foreclosure and REO resource portal providing many resources.
www.reoservice.com

Software

Shark Bait
Foreclosure investing software that uncovers hidden equity and can help you to buy valuable properties at a significant discount. This program can sort through hundreds of records, based on any combination of complex variables, and quickly find just the deals that meet your specific investment parameters.
www.digitaldeal.com

The Complete Real Estate Software Catalog
Offers many different software programs for real estate investors and brokers.
www.z-law.com

Tax Info

Tax Mama
www.taxmama.com

About HomeBuying Guide's Tax Calculators
homebuying.about.com/od/taxcalculators/

Demographics

U.S. Census Department
Quick facts about state demographics.
http://quickfacts.census.gov/qfd/index.html

American Demographics
Website and magazine devoted entirely to U.S. demographics.
www.demographics.com

Worksheets and Forms

In this section, we include the worksheets and forms mentioned throughout this book. We think these tools will prove helpful to you in evaluating properties and calculating the profit potential of possible deals.

Monthly Payment Schedule

In Tables C.1 and C.2, you can easily find your estimated monthly mortgage payment by selecting a loan amount and scanning across to the applicable interest rate. This will tell you your approximate amortized monthly payment. Please note this does not include property taxes, insurance, or other fees.

Table C.1 15-Year Fixed-Rate Mortgage by Percentage Rate

Loan Amount	8%	8.5%	9%	9.5%	10%	10.5%	11%	11.5%
$5,000	48	49	51	52	54	55	57	58
$10.000	96	98	101	104	107	111	114	117
$15,000	143	148	152	157	161	166	170	175
$20,000	191	197	203	209	215	221	227	234
$25,000	239	246	254	257	269	276	284	292
$30,000	287	295	304	313	322	332	341	350
$35,000	334	345	355	365	376	387	398	409

continues

Table C.1 15-Year Fixed-Rate Mortgage by Percentage Rate (continued)

Loan Amount	8%	8.5%	9%	9.5%	10%	10.5%	11%	11.5%
$40,000	382	394	406	418	430	442	455	467
$45,000	430	443	457	470	484	497	511	526
$50,000	478	492	507	522	537	553	568	584
$55,000	526	548	558	574	591	608	625	643
$60,000	573	591	609	627	645	663	682	701
$65,000	621	640	659	679	698	719	739	759
$70,000	669	689	710	731	752	774	796	818
$75,000	717	739	761	783	806	829	852	876
$80,000	765	788	811	835	860	884	909	935
$85,000	812	837	862	888	913	940	966	993
$90,000	860	886	913	940	967	995	1023	1051
$95,000	908	936	964	992	1021	1050	1080	1110
$100,000	956	985	1014	1044	1075	1105	1137	1168

C.2 30-Year Fixed-Rate Mortgage by Percentage Rate

Loan Amount	8%	8.5%	9%	9.5%	10%	10.5%	11%
$5,000	37	38	40	42	44	46	48
$10.000	73	77	81	84	88	92	95
$15,000	110	115	121	126	132	137	143
$20,000	149	154	161	168	176	183	190
$25,000	183	192	201	210	220	229	238
$30,000	220	231	242	252	263	275	286
$35,000	257	269	282	294	307	320	333
$40,000	294	308	322	336	351	366	381
$45,000	330	346	362	378	395	412	428
$50,000	367	384	403	421	439	458	476
$55,000	404	423	443	463	483	503	524
$60,000	440	461	483	505	527	549	571
$65,000	447	500	523	547	571	595	619
$70,000	514	538	564	589	615	641	666

Loan Amount	8%	8.5%	9%	9.5%	10%	10.5%	11%
$75,000	550	577	604	631	659	686	714
$80,000	587	615	644	673	702	732	762
$85,000	624	654	684	715	746	778	809
$90,000	660	692	725	757	790	823	857
$95,000	697	732	765	799	834	869	904
$100,000	734	769	805	841	878	915	952

Equity/Profit Calculation Worksheet

This worksheet will help you determine the equity in a property—and, as a result, its profit potential.

Equity/Profit Calculation Worksheet

Subject Property: _____

Owner's Names: _____

Address: _____

City: _____ County: _____

Legal Description: _____

Your Projected Sale Price: _____

Less

1st Mortgage—late payments/interest: _____

2nd Mortgage—late payments/interest: _____

Other Past-Due Loans: _____

Total Past Due: _____

Remaining Principal—1st Mortgage: _____

Remaining Principal—2nd Mortgage: _____

Remaining Principal—Other Liens: _____

Total Remaining Due: _____

Total Other Late Fees and Foreclosure Costs: _____

Total Amount Due on Property: _____

As Of (Date): _____

Roof Inspection: _____

Termite Inspection: _____

Electrical/Plumbing Inspections: _____

Appraisal Fees: _____

Insurance Policies: _____

Loan Origination Fees: _____

Transfer Tax: _____

Title Expense: _____

Title Insurance: _____

Escrow Fees: _____

Misc. Fees: _____

Broker's Selling Commission: _____

Estimated Repair Costs: _____

Estimated Holding Costs: _____

Total Closing & Selling Costs: _____

Sum of Closing Costs and Amount Due on Property: _____

Your Selling Price: _____

Less: Total Costs: _____

Equals Remaining Equity: _____

Offer to Seller: _____

Net Profit: _____

Housing Cost Worksheet

This worksheet helps you determine your budget for housing costs.

Housing Cost Worksheet

How Much House Can I Afford?

Monthly Income:

    Take Home Pay: _____

    Other Income: _____

Total Monthly Income: _____

Monthly Expenses:

    Auto Loan: _____

    Auto Insurance: _____

    Clothing: _____

    Commuting: _____

    Credit Cards: _____

    Education: _____

    Entertainment: _____

    Food: _____

    Hobbies: _____

    Household Items: _____

    Insurance—Health: _____

    Insurance—Other: _____

    Medical Bills: _____

    Savings: _____

    Other: _____

Total Monthly Expenses: _____

Total Monthly Income: _____

    (subtract)

Total Monthly Expenses: _____

Total Monthly Income Available for Housing: _____

This worksheet takes your budget a step further, helping you determine the dollar amount you can afford.

Step-by-Step Worksheet

The Housing Cost Worksheet gives you a very rough idea of how much you would have available for housing expenses, after you've paid all of your other monthly expenses.

This Step-by-Step Worksheet will give you a rough estimate on your monthly mortgage payment, and the dollar amount of house you can afford.

For a conventional mortgage, lenders typically use a standard formula to qualify the prospective borrower. A lender will require that your monthly mortgage payment not exceed around 28 percent of your total monthly income, and that your total monthly obligations are less than 33 percent of your total monthly income.

> Step 1.   Annual Income (gross) _____
>
> Step 2.   Divide by 12 (monthly) _____
>
> Step 3.   Multiply Line 2 by 28% (.28) _____

Line 3 equals the approximate amount you can afford for monthly housing expenses, including principal, interest, taxes, and insurance.

> Step 4.   Multiply Line 3 by 80% _____

Line 4 equals the amount you can afford for principal and interest payments only.

Loan Analysis Worksheet

This worksheet helps you keep track and evaluate the loans against a specific property.

Loan Analysis Worksheet

Subject Property: _____

Owner's Names: _____

Address: _____

City: _____   County: _____

Legal Description: _____

1st Loan or Mortgage

Lender _____

Loan # _____

Address _____

City _____ State _____ Zip _____

Amount _____ Recording Date _____

Contact _____

Loan Type _____ Loan Balance _____

Monthly Payment _____ Interest Rate _____

2nd Loan or Mortgage Lender _____

Loan # _____

Address _____

City _____ State _____ Zip _____

Amount _____ Recording Date _____

Contact _____

Loan Type _____ Loan Balance _____

Monthly Payment _____ Interest Rate _____

Other Liens/Loans

Lender _____

Loan # _____

Address _____

City _____ State _____ Zip _____

Amount _____ Recording Date _____

Contact _____

Loan Type _____ Loan Balance _____

Monthly Payment _____ Interest Rate _____

Insurance Company

Name _____ Policy # _____

Address _____

City _____ State _____ Zip _____

Starting Date _____ Ending Date _____

Phone Number _____

Contact _____

Policy Type _____ Amount _____

Amount Due—1st loan or mortgage _____

       Will settle for _____

Amount Due—2nd loan   _____

       Will settle for _____

Amount Due—Other lien/loan _____

       Will settle for _____

Total Amount Owed   _____

Total Amount Lien Holders Will Settle For _____

Verified with Preliminary Title Report? _____

Date_____

Property Evaluation Worksheet

Property Evaluation Worksheet

Owner's Name _____ Date _____

Address _____ City _____

Community/Sub-Div _____ County _____

Daytime Phone _____ Evening _____

Legal Description _____

Property Type _____Size ____ Sq. Ft. Age _____

Construction _____ Bedrooms ____ Baths _____

Information Derived From:

__ Courthouse Records __ Reporting Service __ Newspaper

__ Advisors   __ Other

Loan Information From:

__ Lis Pendens   __ Notice of Default   __ Owner

__ Title Company   __ Advisor   __ Other

Case Number _____

Document Numbers _____

Loans	**Payment**	**Rate**	**Type**	**Lender**	**Balance**
#1					
#2					
#3					

Total Monthly Payments _____   Balance Due _____

                                            Estimated Value _____

                                            Profit Potential _____

Lease Agreement

This is a sample of a lease agreement, which is usually used in conjunction with the option to buy contract when you are the seller. Do not use this or any contract without consulting a competent real estate attorney. Contract and comments provided by Vena Jones-Cox, known as the real estate goddess. Visit her website at www. regoddess.com for a free three-month subscription to her newsletter.

AGREEMENT OF LEASE

THIS AGREEMENT is made by and between <u>Mr. Seller,</u> (hereinafter called "Owner"), and <u>Mr and Mrs Tenant,</u> (hereinafter called "Tenant").

WITNESSETH:

1. LEASED PREMISES. Owner, in consideration of the rents to be paid and covenants to be performed by Tenant hereunder, hereby leases to Tenant for the term and subject to the covenants and conditions hereinafter set forth, the following described premises, (hereinafter called "the premises"): 11454 Easy Street, Cincinnati, Hamilton County, Ohio.

2. TERM. The term of this lease will be <u>12</u> months, commencing on the <u>25th</u> day of <u>October 2004</u>. This term may be extended by the Tenant for one additional renewal period of <u>Twelve (12) Months</u>, following the expiration of the initial term, for consideration of <u>ONE HUNDRED DOLLARS ($100.00)</u>. The Tenant shall give notice to the Owner of his intent to extend the term of this lease by mailing a written notice of same and payment of the renewal consideration at least Sixty (60) days in advance of the expiration of the current term.

Promissory Note

The above clause includes a right for the tenant to renew for one 12-month period for a fee of $100.00.

Promissory Note

Note that in all of the leases, the rent is first calculated yearly, reinforcing the fact that this is a one-year lease, and that the rent is due through the ENTIRE lease period.

3. RENT. Tenant will pay Owner as rent for the premises during the term of this lease <u>ELEVEN THOUSAND FOUR HUNDRED</u> dollars <u>($11,400.00)</u> per year to be paid in installments of <u>NINE HUNDRED FIFTY</u> dollars <u>($950.00)</u> per month. Each payment shall be due on or before the TWENTY FIFTH day of each month during the term IN ADVANCE.

4. APPLIANCES. Any appliances provided by the Owner are the property of the Owner. However, replacement and repair of said appliances are the responsibility of the Tenant.

5. CONDITION OF PREMISES. All systems are believed to be operational, but are not warranted. Tenant has inspected the premises and agrees to lease said premises "as-is".

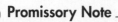

Watch Out!

The "as-is" wording in this clause does NOT relieve you of your responsibility to provide the Tenant with a Seller Disclosure of Property Condition, if required in your state, or with the HUD-approved lead-based paint disclosures.

6. USE OF THE PREMISES. Tenant will not commit or suffer any waste in the premises, use the premises or permit them to be used for any unlawful purpose or any dangerous, noxious or offensive activity or cause or maintain any nuisance in the premises. At the end of the term of this lease, Tenant will deliver up the premises in as good an order and condition as they now are, reasonable use and ordinary wear and tear thereof and damage by fire or other casualty excepted.

7. NONASSIGNMENT AGREEMENT. Tenant shall not assign this agreement, nor sublet the premises in part or in whole, without written permission from the Owner. Owner reserves the right to charge an additional fee in return for permitting assignment of this contract or sublet by the tenant.

8. UTILITIES. Tenant shall pay for all water, gas and electric current which may be assessed or charged against said premises. Tenant shall be responsible for having these utilities placed in the Tenant's name no later than one business day after the date of this lease.

9. REPAIRS AND MAINTENANCE. Tenant shall pay for all repairs and maintenance incurred in connection with premises and shall maintain the premises in good condition throughout the lease term, and upon termination of the lease, return the premises to Owner in the same or better condition as it exists at the time that this lease took effect.

Owner or Owner's agent shall have the right to inspect the premises at any time subject to rights of residential tenants. Should it be determined that any of the above conditions are not being met, written notice will be given to the Tenant to make the necessary changes. If the changes are not made within a reasonable time, Owner shall have the option of making the changes and/or canceling the lease. Should the Owner make the required changes, Tenant agrees to pay for the cost of the changes plus 10% for profit and overhead. Such payment shall be made to Owner within thirty (30) days after a bill is submitted to Tenant.

Promissory Note

The first paragraph of this Repairs and Maintenance clause is unenforceable in most localities, as it requires the tenant to maintain the property as part of the lease. However, it does serve to reinforce to the Tenant that repairs and maintenance are his responsibility.

10. INSURANCE. Tenant agrees to purchase insurance at Tenant's expense sufficient to protect Tenant and Tenant's property against fire, theft, burglary, breakage, and all other hazards. Tenant understands that any insurance policy carried by the Owner covers damage to the premises only, and acknowledges that neither Owner nor Owner's insurance provider is liable for any loss of Tenant's personal property.

11. DEFAULT. In the event that: (a) the rent or any part thereof remains unpaid for four (4) days after it becomes due, (b) Tenant's interest therein is sold under execution or other legal process; (c) Tenant makes an assignment for the benefit of creditors;

(d) any proceeding in bankruptcy or for a wage earner's plan, an arrangement or re-organization, or any other proceeding under any insolvency law is instituted by or against Tenant; (e) a receiver or trustee is appointed for the property of Tenant; or (f) Tenant fails to keep any of the other covenants of this lease, it will be lawful for Owner to re-enter and repossess the premises. Said repossession shall not release the Tenant from his obligation to make payments for the remaining term of this lease.

12. LATE CHARGES. Monthly rent installment is to be delivered to the Owner on or before the twenty fifth day of each month in advance. Should Tenant fail to deliver said rent by the first day of the month, Tenant shall pay an additional 10% of the rent installment as liquidated damages to compensate Owner for the added expense of processing such delinquent account. If the charge is not tendered with the monthly rent, Owner shall not be obligated to accept the rent. Payment will be considered late if the bank fails to honor your check. Tenant will pay the late charge plus a $25 service charge on each returned check. In addition, Tenant will pay all fees and costs associated with eviction proceedings against the Tenant or other legal actions necessary to enforce the terms of this lease.

Promissory Note _____

The maximum late fee may be set by law, statute, or custom in your area. You can usually charge late fees as a percentage of the total rent, or as a per diem, or both. If you set the late fees too low, you are not giving the Tenant any particular encouragement to pay on time. If you set them too high, you will put tenants on the position of not being able to catch up once they get behind on their rent.

13. QUIET ENJOYMENT. Owner agrees that if Tenant pays the rents and keeps and performs the covenants of this lease on the part of Tenant to be kept and performed, Tenant will peaceably and quietly hold the premises during the term hereof without any hindrance, ejection or molestation by Owner or any person lawfully claiming under Owner.

14. BINDING EFFECT. This lease and the agreements of Owner and Tenant contained herein shall be binding upon and inure to the benefit of heirs, executors, administrators, successors and assigns of the respective parties.

15. HOLD HARMLESS AGREEMENT. Tenant agrees to hold Owner and Owner's agents harmless and indemnify against all liability resulting from accident, injury, or property damage occurring on premises, whether said accident, injury, or damage occurs to the person or property of the Tenant, Tenant's guests, or other persons on

the premises. Work or repairs undertaken by the Tenant will be undertaken only if the Tenant is competent and qualified to perform said repairs. Tenant will be responsible to assure that all work is performed in a safe manner, whether by the Tenant or by persons hired by or otherwise authorized by the Tenant. Tenant further agrees that any person or persons performing work will be responsible for obtaining insurance. Tenant will hold the Owner and the Owner's agents free from harm, litigation, and/or claims from any and all persons arising from work or repairs performed on the premises.

16. LEAD WARNING STATEMENT. Housing built before 1978 may contain lead-based paint. Lead from paint, paint chips, and dust can pose health hazards if not taken care of properly. Lead exposure is especially harmful to young children and pregnant women. Before renting pre-1978 housing, landlords must disclose the presence of lead-based paint hazards in the dwelling. Tenants must also receive a federally approved pamphlet on lead poisoning prevention.

Promissory Note

This language regarding lead paint is now required in most residential leases.

IN WITNESS WHEREOF, Owner and Tenant have executed this agreement on this _____ day of _____, 20____.

Signed and acknowledged in the presence of:

_____

WITNESSES OWNER(S)

_____

WITNESSES Tenant(s)

Sample Option Contract

This contract—and accompanying comments are provided by Vena Jones-Cox. Visit her website at www.regoddess.com for a special free sample of her newsletter. Do not use this or any contract without consulting a competent real estate attorney.

Sample Option Contract

Option Purchase Terms

The undersigned Tenant/Buyer and Owner, having executed a lease dated

_____.

On the property commonly known as _____.

further agree as follows:

(1) PRICE AND TERMS: Tenant/buyer shall have the right to purchase the property at any time during the term of the attached lease as long as all terms and conditions of said lease have been met. Tenant/buyer agrees to pay for said property the sum of <u>EIGHTY FIVE THOUSAND</u> Dollars (<u>$85,000.00</u>), less the option fee paid, and less any payments credited to the Tenant/Buyer as per clause "3" of this agreement; the net sum to be paid in cash, certified check, cashier's check, or building and loan check at closing.

(2) OPTION FEE: Simultaneous with the execution of this Option to Purchase, Tenant/Buyer has paid the sum of <u>TWO THOUSAND</u> dollars (<u>$2,000</u>) as a non-refundable option fee. This option fee gives the Tenant/Buyer the right and option to purchase the property during the term of the attached Lease Agreement, in accordance with the provisions of this Option to Purchase. This amount shall be credited against the purchase price of the property if the Tenant/Buyer elects to exercise the option and purchase the property. This option fee shall be non-refundable in the event that the Tenant/Buyer elects not to exercise the Option to Purchase.

Promissory Note

Note that this rent credit is part of the rent already outlined in the attached lease and is not an additional payment. It is also not optional—the full rent must be paid every month whether or not the tenant/buyer intends to exercise the option to buy.

(3) RENT CREDIT: An amount equal to <u>ONE HUNDRED DOLLARS</u> (<u>$100.00</u>) for each month that the rent is paid on time and in full, shall be credited to the Tenant/Buyer and applied to the purchase price of the property in the event that the Tenant/Buyer exercises his option to purchase granted hereunder; otherwise, this credit shall be non-refundable and considered forfeited if the option is not exercised.

(4) INCLUDED IN THE PURCHASE: The property shall also include all land, together with all improvements thereon, all appurtenant rights, privileges, easements, buildings, fixtures, heating, electrical, air conditioning fixtures and facilities, window shades, Venetian blinds, awnings, curtain rods, screens, storm windows and doors, affixed mirrors, wall-to-wall carpeting, stair carpeting, built-in kitchen appliances, bathroom fixtures, radio and television aerials, landscaping and shrubbery, water softeners, garage door openers and operating devices, and all utility or storage buildings or sheds. The property shall also include the oven/range and refrigerator contained on the premises at the time of the execution of the attached lease; however, the condition of these appliances is not warranted.

(5) TITLE: The Owner shall convey marketable title to the property with the above-described inclusions, by good and sufficient General Warranty Deed in fee simple absolute, with release of dower, on or before closing; said title to be free, clear, and unencumbered, except for restrictions and easements of record. Title to be conveyed to the Tenant/Buyer and/or to his assigns or designees.

Watch Out!

The seller offers a General Warranty deed here—not always a good idea, since a General Warranty deed requires you to defend the title against all claims arising against the title since the first deed. A Limited Warranty deed only requires you to defend the title against claims arising from the period when you were title holder. In lieu of this clause, you could offer "General Warranty deed or other marketable title available to Seller" or simply "marketable title."

(6) CLOSING: The deed shall be delivered and the purchase money shall be paid at the lending institution or other location of the Tenant/Buyer's choice, no later than SIXTY (60) days after notification to the Owner of the Tenant/Buyer's exercise of the option.

(7) COSTS AND PRORATIONS: There shall be prorated between the Owner and the Tenant/Buyer, as of the date of closing, all real estate taxes and assessments, with Tenant/Buyer having responsibility for such items following closing. Tenant/Buyer shall be responsible for title search, deed preparation, loan costs, and all other costs associated with financing and closing.

Promissory Note

In this case, the owner has agreed to prorate the taxes at closing. In other words, the Seller will pay the real estate taxes due up until the day of closing: the Buyer will pay the taxes afterwards. Some investors do not prorate—the Buyer pays the taxes due from the day they moved in on the original lease.

You may also use this clause to assist the Buyer in financing the home by offering to pay limited closing costs and/or points. If you agree to do this, you can often increase the option price to cover these expenses.

(8)) LEAD WARNING STATEMENT AND WAIVER. Every purchaser of any interest in residential real property on which a residential dwelling was built prior to 1978 is notified that such property may present exposure to lead from lead-based

paint that may place young children at risk of developing lead poisoning. Lead poisoning in young children may produce permanent neurological damage, including learning disabilities, reduced intelligence quotient, behavioral problems, and impaired memory. Lead poisoning also presents a particular risk to pregnant women. The seller of any interest in residential real property is required to provide the buyer with any information on lead-based paint hazards from risk assessments or inspections in the seller's possession and notify the buyer of any known lead-based paint hazards. A risk assessment or inspection for possible lead-based paint hazards is recommended before purchase.

Tenant/Buyer hereby waives the opportunity to conduct a risk assessment or inspection for the presence of lead-based paint and/or lead-based paint hazards.

IN WITNESS WHEREOF, the parties hereto have set their hands to this Option To Purchase agreement on this _____ day of _____, 20____.

WITNESS:

_____

witness
Tenant/Buyer

_____

witness
Tenant/Buyer

_____

witness
Owner

Tips for Buying Real Estate Out of Probate

The material for this appendix was taken from Bruce K. Packard's article "Tips for Buying Real Estate Out of Probate." Bruce is a Litigation Shareholder at Davis Munck, P.C. in Dallas, Texas. You can find this article and other helpful resources on the Newswire section at www.legalpr.com.

Buying property in probate isn't difficult, but it does contain several "traps" for the unwary. Here are some tips to help guide the uninitiated:

1. Start by finding out why the property is being sold in probate. Is it pursuant to a will? Is it to satisfy a bequest? Is it to satisfy the debts of the estate? In any deal, you want to discover the motivating force behind the sale because it can often serve as an indicator of the strength of the bid you must submit. In probate, the reasons for the sale are often a matter of public record, or they can be easily gleaned from speaking with the executor or administrator of the estate.

2. Be sure you know what's being sold. Purchases in probate are usually without any warranty of title. You must know and understand the physical description of the land, as well as the contents and fixtures, if any, that are being sold.

3. Get a title examination. This isn't done often enough—and problems in the chain of title not only are obvious impediments that lower value, it may well be possible to clear them up in probate proceedings.

Land Lingo

Fiduciary obligation is the legal duty of one party to look after the well-being of another.

4. Don't anticipate any superb bargains. The sellers have *fiduciary obligations* to the estate—so they don't give the property away. There are deals to be had, relatively speaking, but don't expect to offer 50 percent of the property's value and win a bid.

5. Typically, any extra profit potential lies in recognizing a better use for the property. Most probate property is valued based on the use the last owner had for the property. Use your business acumen to determine a more lucrative use for the property and you may well find a winner.

6. Know what you want to do with the property. Don't just buy it because you think its "cheap" or "desirable." Are you planning on flipping it? Fixing it up? Tearing it down? Renting it? Don't buy first and decide second. Have a plan.

7. Ask the neighbors. After a death, neighbors like to talk. Find out all you can about the prior owners, what they did in the home, and what the neighbors' thoughts are. You're likely to be asking for building permits, variances, or even rezoning in the future and, at a minimum, you'll want to know where possible neighborhood opposition lies.

8. Meet the neighborhood's local councilman, particularly if you're an outsider to the neighborhood. It only takes a few minutes and it's time well spent. He or she will know a great deal about the area, and you get the added benefit of political connections that might be helpful down the road.

9. Know when the sale will occur—and when it's final. Probate proceedings can face many delays. You could well miss your opportunity to resell in a hot market, or your financing commitment could expire. Be sure to make your offer revocable to prevent being caught in an endless cycle of court delays. What's more, the "final sale" might not be final. Are other heirs in existence that could retain statutory rights to an object to the sale, or who might decide to purchase it themselves? A quick hour with a probate attorney should answer these questions.

10. Be familiar with your standard state real estate forms. Most courts will insist that the standard forms be used, or else a court hearing will be held to explain why

the standard forms are not being used. The more hearings that are held in the probate, the more likely it is that you won't get to buy your property. The probate system is made to process property, so don't make waves by using aberrational forms or riders.

Some disadvantages to buying in probate:

1. No flexibility in payment options. The estate needs to be closed and you are going to be paying cash. There are rarely, if ever, any payment terms other than cash. And there are often significant earnest money deposits required before you can bid on the property.

2. Time. Not only must you wait for the probate proceedings to occur, in almost every state there is the potential that unknown heirs might come forward and make a claim to the property. You can't do anything to prevent this; your purchase is never completed until the statutory time for unknown heirs to make claims has passed.

3. The death property. In cases of notorious deaths, or crimes causing death, the property will not be nearly as marketable. Other realtors in the area will discourage interest in the home by overstating the "horrors" that happened there. In one famous case, the buyers of the *Amityville Horror* home sued because the seller had failed to disclose that the house might be haunted!

4. Limited sources for purchase money. Many lenders are not comfortable with, and may even refuse, to lend money on a probate-purchased property. The lenders that do loan on such properties are often at higher rates, and you will need to refinance the property later if you hold on to it.

5. Tenants. Just because the property is sold to you doesn't mean you can immediately kick the tenants out. This is particularly true when the tenants are on federal assistance for the poor. You should consult your attorney or other advisors regarding how to handle tenants who are reluctant to leave.

6. Poor condition. Many probate properties were owned by elderly people for many years. Often as their health declined, they were moved to nursing homes, or they were unable to keep the homes properly maintained. Even a great home inspector can't find everything, but tough disclosure requirements in many states put the burden on the seller to disclose all substantial problems with the home.

7. Long time to payday. The lengthy time to probate a property, repair it, and resell it means your using borrowed money for a significant period of time. That

opportunity cost is real, and it cannot be shortened very easily. You can make money, but you rarely make it quickly. If your cash flow dries up, you'll soon become the distressed seller and take a financial hit.

Top 10 Financing Fumbles to Avoid

Don't get caught up in a financing rut and risk falling out of escrow. Realtor and national real estate columnist Phoebe Chongchua shows you the Top 10 financing fumbles to avoid before you make your next real estate purchase. For more real estate articles and advice from Phoebe, visit www.phoebechongchua.com.

1. **Not knowing your credit history.** Check your credit report yearly, because there are often errors that lower your score. Many of these errors can be fixed.

2. **Not shopping the market for different loans.** Remember that banks want to loan money, so there are numerous loans available. Check with lenders, local municipalities, real estate agents, and the newspaper.

3. **Settling for a 30-year fixed.** This is often the most expensive loan; if you're not going to stay in the home for decades, check out other loan programs; and if your credit is bad, a short-term loan may be better because in a couple of years your scores will be higher and then you'll qualify for a better interest rate.

4. **Not understanding closing costs or focusing only on fees.** Borrowers who are caught up on watching fees often take out a loan that trades lower fees for a higher monthly rate; it's not necessarily the smartest financing move for the long run.

5. **Not asking enough questions.** The more questions you ask, the more you'll learn!

6. **Not getting a written estimate.** Written loan estimates will help you compare exact loan programs; it's important to compare apples to apples.

7. **Not having a seasoned down payment.** Sixty days is the minimum amount of time that a down payment should be sitting in your bank account.

8. **Thinking that 100 percent financing means no out-of-pocket money.** There are always some costs associated with buying a home. Expect to have to pay interest, taxes, and insurance. Make sure you have a reserve.

9. **Fearing that bad credit will stop you from buying a home.** Here's where a creative lender can help. Co-signers and a substantial down payment can greatly improve your chance for getting a loan.

10. **Not using real estate professionals.** When you need a medical operation, you go to a doctor for the right care; when you're ready to make the biggest purchase of your life, seek professional Realtors, loan officers, escrow firms, and so on.

Index

J

Jones-Cox, Vena, 212
judgments, 54
    cloudy titles, 55
    deficiency, 13, 108
    summary, 29
judicial processes, 10, 27-28
    comparing to nonjudicial
        processes, 33
    Complaint of Foreclosure,
        28
    Lis Pendens, 28-29
    Notice of Sale, 30
    Notices of Intent, 28
    stopping, 32
    Summary Judgments, 29
    vacating the property, 30

K

kitchens problems, 168
KnowX.com, 91

L

land trusts, 221
landlords, 178
    advertising, 182-183
    defined, 48
    depreciation, 179
    determining rent, 181
    entering properties, 189
    insurance agents, 181

learning laws, 180
leases, 188-189
networking, 181
overwhelmed, 22
property improvements,
    180
record keeping, 192
renters insurance, 190
security deposits, 189
tax breaks, 180
tenants, 183
    advertising to, 182
    applications, 186-187
    disabled, 185
    evicting, 190-191
    finding, 162
    investigating, 187-188
    military, 184
    moving out, 191
    perfect, 185
    renters insurance, 190
    Section 8, 184
    security deposits, 189
landscaping, 172
late charges, 26
late payments, 25-26
lead paint disclosures, 205
lease option deals, 151,
    188-189
    benefits, 230
    dual-contracts, 232
    overview, 225
    profit potential, 230-232

sandwich, 226
    finding sellers, 227
    finding tenants/buyers,
        228
    persuading sellers,
        227-228
    screening tenants/
        buyers, 229-230
    tenants, 233
legal notices, 79
legal obligations, 35-36
legal proceedings, 27
legal vulnerabilities, 58
lenders
    buying notes from, 239
    contacting about REOs,
        125-126
    defined, 26
    hard-money, 147-148
    high-interest, 103
    influences, 36-38
    legal obligations, 35-36
    motivations, 39, 49
    negotiating, 101, 250
    possession costs, 38
    properties, 123-124
    REO profits, 120
    traditional, 67, 76-77
liens
    cloudy titles, 55
    defined, 54
    holders, 250
    involuntary, 53-54
    negotiating, 99-100
    positions, 98
    secondary, 54

Check Out These
Best-Selling
COMPLETE IDIOT'S GUIDES®

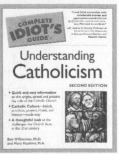

Understanding Catholicism
SECOND EDITION

- Quick and easy information on the origins, spread, and present-day role of the Catholic Church
- Catholic Culture—beliefs, practices, prayers, rituals, and history—made easy
- A thoughtful look at the challenges the Church faces in the 21st century

Bob O'Gorman, Ph.D. and Mary Faulkner, M.A.

1-59257-085-2
$18.95

Learning Spanish
THIRD EDITION

- Easy explanations of Spanish grammar and pronunciation
- Key phrases for travel, hotels, airports, shopping, business, and more
- New and expanded vocabulary lists with English/Spanish and Spanish/English translations

Gail Stein

0-02-864451-4
$18.95

The Bible
SECOND EDITION

- Fascinating explanations of the people, stories, and events of the Old and New Testaments
- Essential information on the Bible's culture and time
- Practical references to help you understand the Bible and make it a part of today's life.

James S. Bell Jr. and Stan Campbell

0-02-864382-8
$18.95

Being a Groom
SECOND EDITION

- Top 10 things to remember on the big day
- Brand-new ideas on key honeymoon destinations
- Idiot-proof advice on breaking the ice between the in-laws

Jennifer Lata Rung and Mark Rung

0-02-864456-5
$9.95

Grammar and Style
SECOND EDITION

- Easy-to-understand instructions on writing and speaking
- Perfect punctuation, from the apostrophe to the semi-colon
- Rights and wrongs of sentence structure, word usage, spelling, and much, much more

Laurie E. Rozakis, Ph.D.

1-59257-115-8
$16.95

Playing the Guitar
SECOND EDITION

- Tips and tricks to get you playing your own tunes in no time
- Easy-to-follow steps for learning to read music
- Words of wisdom from a professional musician and instructor

Frederick Noad

0-02-864244-9
$21.95 w/CD

Personal Finance in Your 20s & 30s
SECOND EDITION

- Savvy advice on getting and staying out of debt
- Idiot-proof tips on saving money for the future and still having money to spend
- Down-to-earth advice on making wise investments—especially when you're on a budget

Sarah Young Fisher and Susan Shelly

0-02-864374-7
$19.95

Knitting and Crocheting
SECOND EDITION
Illustrated

- An all-new selection of easy-to-follow patterns with step-by-step illustrated instructions
- Crafty tips on choosing the right yarns for your project
- Simple advice for going beyond the basics to create more advanced projects

Barbara Breiter and Gail Diven

1-59257-089-5
$16.95

The Perfect Resume
THIRD EDITION

- Winning resume techniques that will convince an employer to call you for an interview
- Expert advice on selling sticky resume issues such as layoffs, employment gaps, and career changes
- More than 100 up-to-date samples of successful resumes and cover letters

Susan Ireland

0-02-864440-9
$14.95

Buying and Selling a Home
FOURTH EDITION

- What to expect when you buy or sell a home—with or without a broker
- Updated coverage of financing options for buyers, including mortgages and refinancing
- Idiot-proof tips on getting the best possible price when you sell

Shelley O'Hara and Nancy D. Lewis

1-59257-120-4
$18.95

Low-Carb Meals

- Idiot-proof tips in planning great-tasting meals for the whole family
- More than 325 easy-to-prepare recipes for everything from main dishes to desserts—including bread
- A grocery list of foods every low-carb pantry should contain

Lucy Beale and Sandy G. Couvillon, M.S., L.D.N., R.D.

1-59257-180-8
$18.95

Calculus

- Descriptive concepts that simplify this most intimidating of math subjects
- Idiot-proof solutions to difficult, yet confusing equations
- Practice examples that will really help you understand the problems and their solutions

W. Michael Kelley

0-02-864365-8
$18.95

More than *450 titles* in *30 different categories*
Available at booksellers everywhere

ALPHA